Henry Parker

The Nature of the Fine Arts

Henry Parker

The Nature of the Fine Arts

ISBN/EAN: 9783337033903

Printed in Europe, USA, Canada, Australia, Japan

Cover: Foto ©Thomas Meinert / pixelio.de

More available books at **www.hansebooks.com**

THE
NATURE OF THE FINE ARTS

THE NATURE

OF

THE FINE ARTS

BY

H. PARKER

FELLOW OF ORIEL COLLEGE, OXFORD

London

MACMILLAN AND CO.

1885

Printed by R. & R. CLARK, *Edinburgh.*

CONTENTS.

CHAPTER VI.

CHAPTER VII.

CHAPTER VIII.

INTRODUCTION.

THE term Fine Art, with its equivalents in other languages, is used in a loose and uncertain manner. Generally, unless the context shows that it must have a wider meaning, it is taken to mean the arts of painting and sculpture alone. This use of the term, moreover, is found, not only in ordinary language, where words are employed carelessly, but even in formal definitions. There is, for instance, an essay by Guizot called "Les Limites qui séparent et les Liens qui unissent Les Beaux Arts," which treats exclusively of painting, drawing, and the kindred arts. The Slade Professor of Fine Art in our universities, in like manner, is a professor of painting. Nevertheless, this limited use of the term is not the definition given in dictionaries and encyclopædias. Littré's list is painting, sculpture, music, architecture, poetry, and eloquence, with dancing as a subsidiary art. This is the usual list, though many authorities omit dancing and eloquence, and some

B

add landscape-gardening, or acting, or some other minor art. We may for the present drop all question about the propriety of these additions, and consider only whether music and poetry should be included. They differ greatly in several respects from the other arts, and many propositions which are plausible about painting, sculpture, and architecture, are manifestly untrue of them. A brief history of the term Fine Art will best show that Littré was justified, and that neither poetry nor music can be excluded.

There were founded in Paris in the seventeenth century certain academies, one of which was a school of painting and sculpture. To this was afterwards added an academy of architecture. In the year 1793 an École des Beaux Arts took the place of these academies. This term was adopted when subsequently the Institut was established, and music was then formally recognised as one of the Fine Arts, being incorporated in the Académie des Beaux Arts. Poetry, however, does not belong to the Académie des Beaux Arts, and this seems to have perplexed some French authors. In the *Dictionnaire* of the Académie a doubt is expressed whether poetry ought to be called a Fine Art. The proof that it must be so called is to be found in the *Réflexions critiques sur la Poésie et sur la Peinture* of the Abbé Dubos, which were published early in the eighteenth century, for these show that the similarity which was seen to exist between poetry and painting had produced a feeling of respect for the latter, and that the term Fine Art, as well as the word artist in the modern sense, came into use owing to this feeling. Our word "artist," it may be observed, has had three meanings. First, it was a University technicality, applied to those who took a degree in the Faculty of Arts. Next, it was, as in the works of Johnson, an equivalent of artisan or artificer. Thirdly, it became, as it now is, the designation of an artisan of the Fine Arts. The terms Beaux Arts and Artiste had not come into fashion when Dubos composed his essays, and he explains to the reader that he is reluctant to call the poet and the painter artisans. He begs him therefore to understand that though they are so called, a complimentary epithet of some kind must be always understood in connexion with the term, which is omitted solely because an incessant repetition of it would be awkward and inconvenient. This was the sentiment which led to the introduction of the term · Beaux Arts. It is, therefore, incumbent on those who deny that the arts of poetry and painting resemble one another to show that they attach some meaning to the term Fine Art, if they employ it.

A writer may, if he pleases, ignore the term altogether, taking for granted that it has no meaning, as Johnson did, but, if used, it should either be allowed to retain its historical meaning, or be defined intelligibly in some other way. Johnson wrote essays on some of the arts, but did not class them together as having a common characteristic, and did not use the term Fine Art. A writer who takes up this position may be right or wrong, but cannot be convicted of inconsistency. It is different if the term is admitted. The reader is at the author's mercy if a term is used which may mean anything or nothing, and there are no means by which it can be ascertained whether his opinions hold together or not. The argument about the nature of the Fine Arts must be in part verbal, in order that it may not be purely dogmatical. It is easy, and it has been usual, to begin discussions of this kind with affirmations, more or less direct, about the proper functions of the Fine Arts. Some have said that they ought to refine, some that they ought to instruct, some that they ought to amuse. But it is useless to beg the question in this way. There is only one " ought " which should be allowed to find its way into such discussions : that is the " ought " which belongs to logic and common sense. Words ought not to be employed which mean nothing, or

employed in different senses in different places, and
propositions ought not to be laid down as certain
which many reasonable persons would deny to be
true. As, therefore, the term Fine Art comes from
France, and its history can be traced there, the first
point to be established is that French authority
justifies Littré, and that there is no significance in
the fact that the Académie des Beaux Arts does not
take in poetry. This was a natural result of the
fact that it is a part of literature, and, as such, had
found a place elsewhere when this Académie was
formed. There can be little doubt that Dubos was
the true author of the term, though he did not invent it. His essays were greatly admired, and
went through several editions. The fourth was
published in 1740, and about twenty years afterwards appeared the *Traité de Peinture* of Dandré
Bardon, in which the terms Beaux Arts and Artiste
are used as well-known words. But their full meaning, as now understood, was not established so long
as it was doubtful whether music is a Fine Art.
This was not admitted when Dubos wrote. He
added an essay on music, but did not treat it as an
art which has a *locus standi* apart from other things.
It was regarded at that time in France, as elsewhere,
as an art which is valuable in conjunction with religious ceremonies and dramatic performances, but

was not supposed to be able to stand alone. Lulli was, in the eyes of Dubos, the prince of musical composers, and the popular estimate of music was still in France that which Lulli's compositions had determined. Dubos, ignorant that a star of the first magnitude, John Sebastian Bach, in whose presence Lulli was destined to pale his ineffectual fires, had appeared, declares that Frenchmen and Italians alone have a taste for music, and that the colder races of the north are for ever disqualified to enjoy it. This error had been dispelled at the end of the century, and it was understood that the kingdom of music is a wider one and her dignity higher than was sup-posed. When this secret was disclosed she became a Fine Art, and was admitted to a place in the Académie des Beaux Arts. French authority, there-fore, fully supports the view that poetry stands at the head of the list, and that music cannot be ex-cluded. The name was invented because poetry and painting were admitted to be sisters, and music was added when it was found that she belonged to the family. We can, therefore, trace the history of the Fine Arts to a remoter origin. The essays of Dubos were suggested by the metrical treatise on the art of painting of Dufresnoy. This treatise, which was celebrated throughout Europe, was itself a new ver-sion of the *Ars Poetica* of Horace, and Horace is the

first author of the classification of the Fine Arts.
Lessing, trusting, I suppose, to a statement which
Plutarch makes, affirmed that Simonides first called
poetry "vocal painting," and painting "silent poetry," ✓
but did not explain who this Simonides was, and,
indeed, apparently thought that only one writer of
this name was known. Plutarch, having said elsewhere that it was a popular formula, is not trustworthy, and, so far as is known, Horace has the best
claim to be considered the inventor of the now celebrated and familiar parallel between these two arts.
But the three essays of Horace, Dufresnoy, and
Dubos are very different. The first assigned the
prior place to poetry, and illustrated his argument
by a reference to painting ; the second wrote on
painting and scarcely touched on literature ; the
third balanced the two arts and treated them as
equals. Hence arose the need of the term Fine
Art, which admitted painting to be a kind of silent
poetry. But music had not then asserted her rights,
and musicians alone knew that she was the equal of
poetry and painting.

The ancient Greeks did not speculate about the
nature of the Fine Arts, and had no name for them.
The notion or conception of Fine Art is derived
from Roman, not Greek, civilisation. This will,
perhaps, seem a paradox. Lessing has had great

influence on opinion, and is supposed to have greatly improved on Winckelman, not only by correcting him as to some of his facts, but by cleverly advocating with a great display of learning a view which better pleases modern writers on art. There are, however, two things which Lessing should have explained, and which those who believe in him should explain. It should be explained why he, and writers like him, constantly require the term Fine Art, though no Greek author experienced this necessity, and why it never occurred to any Greek author to institute a comparison between poetry and painting and statuary like that which is the theme of the Laocoon. It will be allowed that if there is anywhere in ancient Greek literature a speculation about the Fine Arts, this exception is Aristotle's *Poetic*. In this fragment, for it is unfortunately only a fragment, something is said about music, and there is even a brief notice of the art of painting ; but these additions to the discussion of the drama, which is the chief topic, only serve to make more striking the total omission of statuary, the great art of ancient Greece. The faith of Lessing's disciples must be indeed robust if they venture to say that he was a greater philosopher than Aristotle, or knew more about the sentiments and opinions of the citizens of Athens. Though the Poetic Art is not complete, the plan seems to have been matured, but not a hint is to be found in it that Aristotle proposed to investigate the nature of statuary. Either he was unintelligent and inobservant, or Lessing's insight was not so perfect as he and his admirers have supposed. Plato, however, rather than Aristotle, is thought to be the great authority in matters of this kind ; and it is true that if the reader chooses to put on modern spectacles when he explores his dialogues, some passages may be found which seem to support the view that the Greeks admitted a distinction between the Fine Arts and the Useful Arts. Such a distinction was arising undoubtedly, but it had not reached, as Lessing assumed, the stage in which it becomes formal and explicit. There was a difference of opinion, but the two factions were imperfectly conscious of the difference, about the nature of all the arts except poetry. Plato's opinion may, perhaps, not have been quite fixed, but he certainly did not recognise a distinct class of arts, such as are now called Fine Arts. The following words, which are taken from Professor Jowett's edition, occur in the *Laws :*—" And that art sprang up after these and out of these (*i.e.* Nature and Chance), mortal and of mortal birth, and produced in play certain images and very partial imitations of the truth, having an affinity to one another, such as music and painting

create, and their companion arts. And there are
other arts which have a serious purpose, and these
co-operate with nature, such, for example, as medicine
and husbandry and gymnastic." Undoubtedly, if
there were no other passages which clear up Plato's
meaning, these words might be understood as a
division of the arts into Useful and Fine Arts ; but
there are other passages which show that this was
not his meaning. The following is an extract from
the *Republic :*—" Then will the city have to fill and
swell with a multitude of callings which go beyond
what is required by any natural want, such as the
whole tribe of hunters and actors, of which one large
class have to do with figures and colours, another
are musicians, and there will be poets and their
attendant train of rhapsodists, players, dancers, con-
tractors, also makers of divers kinds of utensils, not
forgetting women's ornaments." This shows that
Plato was not setting aside certain arts as " fine "
or admirable arts, but as trivial and comparatively
worthless arts. The distinction is such as Johnson
would have recognised, but is not such as constitutes
a peculiar class requiring a peculiar epithet. The
reason why the Greeks did not regard the Fine Arts
as a special class, about which it was necessary to
form a theory, was that on the one hand music had
not attained to such a stage of development as to

reveal its full character, and on the other, statuary, which was the chief art, was regarded as a part of the religion of the country. There is some doubt about the nature of ancient music, but the most competent judges agree in thinking that it could not have made great progress before keyed instruments were invented. It is at any rate certain that when Plato wrote it was in an elementary stage, and was still regarded as a novelty. The habit of taking for granted that modern sentiment about the Fine Arts was anticipated in ancient Greece, and the desire of glorifying music by classical testimony, has induced some modern writers to cite Plato's theories as if these proved that he attached extraordinary value to it. He is supposed to have thought that it was at once a Fine Art and something more than a Fine Art. The truth is that he perceived that many of his contemporaries were beginning to esteem it as such, that is, as an art which deserved to be cultivated for its own sake, without any question of utility, and was perplexed and angered at this strange phenomenon. He knew that in the early history of his country there had only been two forms of music ; the lyre which served as an accompaniment to the recitations of the bard, and the pipe which marked the time of the rustic dance, and he thought that the growing tendency to allow greater

importance to music was a sign and would be a
cause of mischief.   Experience has now completely
proved that no poison lurks hidden in a concord of
sweet sounds.   The modern writer has before him
Jewish as well as European history, and it is,
perhaps, not easy to imagine the feelings of a philosopher to whom the power of music revealed itself
for the first time.   But this was the case with Plato,
and it is not strange that his suspicions should have
been excited, and that he should have wished to
check a taste which seemed to him unnatural and
odious.   But his mistake was that he underrated,
not that he overrated, the power of sound.   He saw
that it had a mysterious influence, but was ignorant
that this influence was too potent for his purpose,
and that music would not condescend to be an im-
plement in the hands of a pedagogue or temperance-
lecturer.   The argument is singularly perverted when
Plato is cited in honour of music, for he strenuously
denied its legitimacy as a Fine Art, or as an art
cultivated for its own sake.   Three different opinions
may be found in ancient Greek literature about the
advance of this art.   Plato fought against it.   Aristotle in the last book of the *Politics* brings the dry
light of a scientific inquirer, who allows no prejudice
to interfere, to bear on it.   He observes that *now*
many persons regard music as an art of which the

end is to give pleasure, but that this was not the view which prevailed when it was admitted to a place in a scheme of education. He discusses it at some length, and allowing that it may be useful in education, in deference, apparently, rather to Plato's authority, than because he was convinced, winds up by saying that it has a cathartic quality. He promises a fuller explanation of this *catharsis* in the Poetic Art, but though the word reappears there, the full explanation is not given. Both in this phrase of Aristotle's, and in Plato's words about a playful imitation, there seems to be a kind of anticipation of the theory which Mr. Herbert Spencer has put at greater length and connected with physiology. The sentiments of Euripides contrast signally with Plato's about this change, which had been gradually taking place since the severance of music and poetry from each other. Euripides had the feelings of an artist, and was delighted with the innovation which shocked Plato. The following lines in the *Medea* show how he regarded it :—

σκαιοὺς δὲ λέγων κόυδέν τι σοφοὺς
τοὺς πρόσθε βροτοὺς οὐκ ἂν ἁμάρτοις,
οἵτινες ὕμνους ἐπὶ μὲν θαλίαις
ἐπί τ᾽ εἰλαπίναις καὶ παρὰ δείπνοις
εὕροντο βίου τερπνὰς ἀκοάς,
στυγίους δὲ βροτῶν οὐδεὶς λύπας
εὕρετο μούσῃ καὶ πολυκόρδοις

ᾠδαῖς παύειν, ἐξ ὧν θάνατοι
δειναί τ᾽ τύχαι σφάλλουσι δόμους.
καίτοι τάδε μὲν κέρδος ἀκεῖσθαι
μολπαῖσι βροτούς. Ἵνα δ᾽ εὔδειπνοι
δαῖτες τί μάτην τείνουσι βοάν ;
τὸ παρὸν γὰρ ἔχει τέρψιν ἀφ᾽ αὐτοῦ
δαιτὸς πλήρωμα βροτοῖσιν.

(Medea, L. 190, etc.)

"Truly, you may say that mankind were formerly obtuse and unintelligent. For they introduced songs at their feasts and banquets, to add to the delights of life ; but it occurred to no one to assuage with melody and the sound of stringed instruments the troubles and miseries of existence, whence death and ruin proceed. Yet, if music can heal these, it is indeed a gain. What needs the luxurious banquet such superfluous aid ? Its own appropriate pleasures are sufficient for the feast." Even Euripides treats music as a kind of mental medicine to be applied in certain cases, resembling Plato in this, and does not write of it quite in the modern vein.

Plato's objection to music was not simply caused by reluctance to admit a novelty. It was part of a sentiment which may be observed in different forms in all civilised races, and his protest was repeated, though with a difference, in the early ages of modern Europe. Music was a part of the religious ceremonial of the Christian Church, and was assiduously cultivated. The ecclesiastics were startled after a time at finding that it was ceasing to be a useful art, and was asserting its prerogative as an independent art. They saw that a carnal delight was felt, where, in their opinion, such delight was improper, and they attempted, as Plato had done, to check this insidious advance, and to confine it to its proper sphere. A comparison of a passage in Burney's *History of Music* with one in the *Republic* of Plato will show how exactly history was repeating itself. " These (essays of simultaneous harmony) were censured at first as innovations, and while the new art of counterpoint was extending its limits and forming its code from new combinations of sounds, great scandal was given to piety, simplicity, and ancient usage, and complaints having been made to Pope John XXII. that, etc. etc., a bull was issued at Avignon by the advice of the conclave about the year 1322 to suppress these licenses under severe penalties." (Burney, *Hist. of Music*, vol. ii., p. 149, ed. 1783.) The following extract from Plato's *Republic* will show that he had seen, as the ecclesiastics saw, that the line must be drawn and the battle fought where melody becomes harmony :—

" Then we shall not maintain the artificers of lyres with three corners and complex scales, or of any other many - stringed curiously - harmonised instruments ? Certainly not.

" But what do you say to flute-makers and flute-players ?   Would you admit them when you reflect that in this composite use of harmony the flute is worse than all the stringed instruments put together, for even the pan-harmonic music is only an imitation of the flute ?   Clearly not.

" There remain then only the lyre and the harp for use in the city, and you may have a pipe in the country." (*Republic.   Dialogues of Plato,* Jowett, vol. ii., p. 225.)

The art of music continued to advance in spite of the obstacles which prejudice interposed, and a national school might have been formed in this country if the puritanical cataclysm of the seventeenth century had not swept away all traditional knowledge when the goal was almost reached.   But a void was then created in which only an occasional amateur like Pepys can be discerned, and the history of music would be, during the latter part of the century almost a blank, in spite of Charles the Second's patronage, were it not for the great name of Purcell.   The genius of Purcell, however, perhaps because he was in advance of the age, did not create a national taste, and music ultimately reappeared as an exotic.   When this happened, once more, and for the last time, a cry was raised that the art of music ought not to be tolerated.   Superficially, the attack took the shape of a protest against foreigners; but there was a profounder prejudice in the background, as will be seen in the following passages :—" Letters from the Haymarket inform us that on Saturday night last the opera of *Pyrrhus and Demetrius* was performed with great applause. This intelligence is not very acceptable to us friends of the theatre; for the stage being an entertainment of the reason and all the faculties, this way of being pleased with the suspense of them for hours together, and being given up to the shallow satisfaction of the eyes and ears only, seems to arise rather from the degeneracy of our understanding than an improvement of our diversions. That the understanding has no part in the pleasure is evident from what these letters very positively assert : to wit, that a great part of the performance was done in Italian." (*Tatler*, No. 4.) Here the objection to music appears in its modern shape. It is unintellectual, and therefore despicable. Some letters were published in the *Spectator* which show how great a change of opinion has taken place since the beginning of the eighteenth century. Certain musicians who were trying to arrange some concerts made the following appeal to Addison :— " We whose names are subscribed think you the properest person to signify what we have to offer the town in behalf of ourselves, and the art we profess—

music.   We conceive hopes of your favour from the
speculations on the mistakes which the town run into
with regard to their pleasure of this kind, and believ-
ing your method of judging is that you consider
music only valuable as it is agreeable to, and
heightens the purpose of poetry, we consent that
that is not only the true way of relishing that pleasure, but also that without it a composure of music
is the same thing as a poem, when all the rules of
poetical numbers are observed, but the words have
no sense or meaning ; to say it shorter, mere musical
sounds are in our art no other than nonsense verses
are in poetry.   Music, therefore, is to aggravate
what is intended by poetry.   It must always have
some passion or sentiment to express, or else violins,
voices, or any other organs of sound, afford an entertainment very little above the rattles of children."
(*Spectator*, No. 258.)

It must have been greatly against their will that
these unfortunate musicians signed this confession
of faith, and it appears from another letter that they
did not well understand why it was required of
them.   But they submitted in order to obtain
Addison's patronage.   There was soon to appear a
mighty champion whose genius would make such
tyranny impossible.   Handel did for this country
what Bach did for continental Europe.   He estab-

lished for ever the right of instrumental music to rank as a Fine Art, and silenced unmusical critics who held that music is only "to aggravate what is intended by poetry." Handel's compositions—those at least which made his reputation—were, it is true, accompanied by words ; but no one who had heard them could continue to assert that the musical element is subordinate to the literary. No one—least of all, musicians—said at the end of the century that "violins, voices, or any other organs of sound afford an entertainment very little above the rattles of children." The concertos of Haydn completed the work which Handel's compositions had begun ; but these would not have obtained a hearing if the arbiters of taste had not been put to silence by Handel's success. There is abundant evidence in the literature of the last century of the effect produced on popular opinion by the latter. An anecdote which is recorded of Pope is one of the most curious. Having attended a performance of some music by Handel, and having been struck by the enthusiastic admiration which it seemed to excite in the audience, he asked Arbuthnot whether he thought that this apparent admiration was genuine, or whether it was not a piece of affectation. It is remarkable that a scholar like Pope, who knew what Shakespeare had said of music, should have seriously suggested this, but it illustrates a universal tendency.   Mankind will generally fall back on the most far-fetched explanations, rather than admit that there can be in others tastes and perceptions which they do not find in themselves.   Others besides Pope have propounded this ridiculous theory, though no one has ever attempted to show how such a gigantic conspiracy could be first organised, or why composers should first invent, executants practise, and auditors applaud, combinations of sound which really charmed none of them.

The dispute about the nature and legitimacy of music has now been practically settled.   There are many who are insensible to its charms, but they do not any longer dare openly to protest.   They are content to turn aside and, repeating in a whisper Byrom's famous sneer that it is strange such difference can be twixt tweedledum and tweedledee, allow that the difference exists.   But a similar dispute still exists about the nature of painting, and the point has never been decided because it has been concealed under a cloud of words, and the battle has not been fought openly.   It is admitted now that the pleasure which the lover of music feels is not a purely intellectual pleasure, and it is admitted that it is not necessarily for that reason a contemptible pleasure.   But innumerable essayists have endeavoured to demonstrate that the pleasure which the art of painting affords is of a purely intellectual kind, or would be, if the art were rightly understood and practised. When in the middle of last century the practice of collecting and exhibiting pictures first called the attention of those who take no real interest in this art to the fact that the taste exists, a protest of an exactly similar kind was made. Goldsmith wrote as follows: " It is true, painting should have due encouragement, as the painter can undoubtedly fit up our apartments in a much more elegant manner than the upholsterer. But I should think a man of fashion makes but an indifferent exchange who lays out all that time in furnishing his house which he should have employed in the furniture of his head. A person who shows no other symptoms of his taste than his cabinet or gallery, might as well boast to one of the furniture of his kitchen. I know no other motive but vanity that induces the great to testify such an inordinate passion for pictures. After the piece is bought and gazed at eight or ten days successively, the purchaser's pleasure must surely be over." (*Letters of a Citizen of the World*, xxxiv. " The present ridiculous passion of the Nobility for Painting.") If all mankind spoke as honestly as Goldsmith, some such sentiments as these would be often heard, but

" Fine Art " is now fashionable, and it is understood
that they must be suppressed.   An escape from the
necessity of a frank avowal of indifference is possible in the case of pictorial art, though impossible
in the case of music, because the former is, though
the latter is not, an art of representation.   There
are some few instances in musical compositions, in
which sounds are imitated.   There is a piece by
Handel in which the rhythm is supposed to represent the sound of a hail-storm.   In some operas
there are more less direct imitations of the roar of
the wind and the rattle of thunder.   It has been
said that the sounds of a farmyard are imitated by
Beethoven in the " Pastoral Symphony."   These few
and partial exceptions prove that music is not an
art of representation in the sense in which painting
is.   No one could say of these instances that the
music is bad because the similarity is not great,
though it might be said that it is bad because the
similarity is excessive.   But in painting the case is
reversed.   It is always possible to point to a tree,
an animal, or a group of objects, and say that the
picture is bad because the imitation is imperfect,
and it is impossible to contend that the picture is
bad because the resemblance is too perfect.   It is
owing to this fact that the Fine Arts are some of
them arts of representation, while some are non-

representant arts, that painting monopolises so frequently the term Fine Art. Statuary and poetry
are also arts of representation ; but the former of
these attracts comparatively little attention at the
present day, while the latter, as a part of literature,
and the common property of all educated men,
stands apart. Any grossly false statement about
the nature of poetry would be immediately detected,
and essayists on Fine Art, who propound untenable
theories, are obliged to avoid it. Thus practically
they confine their arguments to painting alone, and
disguise in rhetorical phraseology inconsistent positions. The non-representant arts are music and
architecture. All authority is in favour of the
admission of these to the list of Fine Arts. But if
they are admitted, the presumption is that the perfection of representation cannot be the test of
excellence in any of the arts. It is, moreover,
obvious that this test would not be admitted in
poetry. The representation which Thucydides gives
of a part of the history of Greece is more exact
and more complete than the representations which
Æschylus gives of another part. If such a test were
valid in Fine Art, Thucydides should be the greater
poet of the two.

The Fine Arts have everywhere been developed
in subservience to the three chief interests of primi-

tive races—religion, war, and festivity. Statuary is
the art whose history can be most clearly traced,
and its development is most closely connected with
the religious sentiment. The author of the *Wisdom
of Solomon*, wishing to maintain the view that the
true faith was once universal, offered a theory of the
growth of superstition which later theologians accepted and expanded. Statues or images, he said,
first suggested the notion of false gods. " The
devising of idols was the beginning of spiritual
fornication, and the invention of them the corruption of life. . . . For by the vain glory of men they
entered into the world, and therefore shall they
shortly come to an end. For a father afflicted with
untimely mourning, when he hath made an image
of his child, soon taken away, now honoured him as
a god, which was then a dead man, and delivered to
those that were under him ceremonies and sacrifices.
Thus in process of time an ungodly custom grown
strong was kept as a law, and graven images were
worshipped by the commandments of kings. Whom
men could not honour in presence, because they
dwelt far off, they took the counterfeit of his visage
from far, and made an express image of a king
whom they honoured, to the end that by this their
forwardness they might flatter him that was absent
as if he were present. Also the singular diligence

of the artificer did help to set forward the ignorant to more superstition. For he, peradventure, willing to please one in authority, forced all his skill to make the resemblance of the best fashion. And so the multitude, allured by the grace of the work, took him now for a god which a little before was but honoured as a man." Enough is known of the archæology of Greece and other countries to make it certain that this account of the connexion between images and religion is unhistorical. The earliest representations of the Deities were shapeless blocks and masses of stone or other material, and Greek mythology was the parent, not the offspring, of Greek statuary. The statues were, as is said in the passage quoted, made in honour of absent potentates; but these potentates were dwellers in Olympus, and not human beings. It is untrue of all the Fine Arts that "by the vain glory of men they entered into the world," though, as will be subsequently shown, Alison adopted this theory, and ingeniously twisted the facts to make them suit his argument. They all of them, after the most rudimentary stage was passed, were fashioned and developed as aids to war, religion, and festivity, and religion has been in every case the chief motive influence. The earliest buildings of architectural value are in all countries the temples. The early pictures of the Renaissance

were of a devotional kind.   The music of the Jewish
race was part of their religion, and musical recitations
were instituted in Greece in honour of the gods.
But the art of making statues retained longer than
any of the other arts this close alliance with religion,
and religious sentiment was in ancient Greece never
completely lost in the art of statuary.   Lessing
shut his eyes to this truth, and his misrepresentation
of Greek feeling has misled innumerable subsequent
writers.   The reason why Aristotle did not regard
the art of statuary as a Fine Art was that it seemed
to him a part of religion.   It was only when the
Romans invaded Greece and found these works,
which had no religious significance for them, that
the unaccountable beauty of the Greek statues gave
the formal and explicit conception of art for the
sake of art.   It is a most remarkable fact that even
the spoliations of the Romans did not fully reveal
this to the inhabitants of Greece.   The proof of
this is to be found in the narrative of Pausanias.
Pausanias, it has been said, was exceedingly prosaic,
and it has been thought that a writer of a different
temperament might, if he had undertaken the task
which Pausanias undertook, have left a description
of Greek art more in accordance with modern views.
The fact is that the modern art-sentiment cannot be
discovered in any Greek writer.   Lucian was in

most respects the very antithesis of Pausanias. He
was as irreligious and incredulous as Pausanias was
credulous and devout; but though he writes from an
exactly opposite point of view, and though he has
described some of the celebrated statues, he is, like
Pausanias, not an art-critic. Whatever may be said
of the prosaic character of the latter, it must be
allowed that he was observant of facts which came
before him. It is certain that if he had found that
anywhere in Greece weight was allowed to the
artistic question, as it would now be called : that
some statues were held in honour on account of
their superior beauty, and others neglected on the
ground that they were inartistic ; he would have
been horrified at what would have seemed to him a
profane tendency which might have disastrous results
on the fortunes of Greece. But it does not appear
that he anywhere found this tendency. It does not
seem that any of the Greeks with whom he con-
versed looked at the statues in any light except as a
part of the history and religion of the country. His
sentiments are clearly shown in his account of the
statues of the victors in athletic contests, where, if
anywhere, we might expect to find the artistic
question. He says that there is reason to think
that the prizes were not always fairly awarded. He
therefore intentionally omits all notice of those with

regard to which such a suspicion was possible. How trivial and inadequate such a reason as this would seem to a modern art-critic ! Yet there is no reason to think that any Greek would have regarded it as unsatisfactory. But to the Roman invaders the splendid display of Greek art—the temples, the poems and plays, the pictures and statues—was a novel and inexplicable phenomenon, which captivated the attention and suggested the notion of art for the sake of art. The Roman did not trouble himself to ask whether the victor in the games had or not won his prize fairly, or whether the god whose image was carried away would or not be angered. Pausanias comforts himself with thinking that the disease of which Sulla died was a sign of divine vengeance ; but Roman scepticism was proof against such super- stition. To the Roman the Greek statue was a statue, and it was nothing more.

There are other subdivisions of the Fine Arts besides the subdivision into representant and non- representant art. There is one which is in truth a superficial division which vanishes when the nature of these arts is fully explored, but which, as it is the most popular, cannot be ignored. Three of the arts, viz., painting, statuary, and architecture, are arts which belong to the sense of sight. It is rather a defect in language that there is no name for these three to distinguish them from poetry and music. A great many attempts have been made, both in this and in other countries, to utilise the word " plastic " as a name for this class. But these attempts have failed and are doomed to fail. The word " plastic " suggests forms without colour, and is thus an inappropriate name for painting, and is hardly suitable even for architecture and statuary, inasmuch as it is frequently used in the still more limited sense of modelling in a soft material. French writers at present seem to have agreed to use the term *Arts du Dessin* for these three; but it is only a technical expression, and many Frenchmen would be as much puzzled if told that architecture is an *art du dessin* as an Englishman would be if told that it is an art of drawing. They may, perhaps, be called the visual arts. Otherwise we must fall back on Virgil's classification of the mute and the vocal arts. Virgil, however, it must be remembered, was not discussing the Fine Arts, and his *mutæ artes* included many besides painting, statuary, and architecture. In the next place, there is the distinction between poetry on the one hand, the Fine Art of the understanding, and the other four, which have a special connexion with the senses. Lastly, there is a distinction which is not at first obvious, but which is not unimportant, between architecture and the

other Fine Arts. Alone of these arts, architecture
is primarily a physically-useful art. The poet, the
painter, the sculptor, and the musician, address themselves in the first instance directly to the mental
feelings. The first poems, pictures, statues, and
musical compositions were not intended to produce
any physical satisfaction. But the first and immediate end of a building is always to shelter the
occupant from the physical discomfort of cold and
heat and wet. The art is then developed in three
directions, and buildings may be roughly classified
under the three heads of castles or fortified structures,
representing war; temples or churches, representing
religion; and mansions or palaces, representing
festivity. But fundamentally, architecture is a useful art in the strict sense of the term, differing in
this respect from its sister arts. There is, therefore, a reason why, in the controversy about the
nature of the Fine Arts, this art as well as poetry
should have escaped. The questions whether a
particular building is beautiful, and whether it is
convenient, are so plainly distinct that they cannot
be confounded. On the one hand it is immediately
condemned if obviously unsuitable or insecure; on
the other, it clearly may be quite suitable and secure,
and yet not be a great work of art. Consequently
all architectural controversies turn on questions of

style and details about modes of construction or ornamentation, but are not about the general nature of architecture. The brief sketch of the history of music which has been given above shows what has happened with regard to this art. Prejudice has opposed its progress, but music has triumphed over its adversaries. There are left the two representant arts of sculpture and painting, whose nature has never been satisfactorily ascertained.

As both those who write, and those who talk about art, are for the most part content to deal with generalities, and do not carefully examine the import of art-criticism, all these introductory observations will possibly seem to be pointless. I will, therefore, in the hope of making the argument which follows intelligible, explain their bearing. Every one who has paid any attention to art-criticism must know that, when this criticism deals with painting, it is usual to introduce eulogistic terms about the honesty, the conscientiousness, and the industry of the artist. Now it is obvious that, at least in the case of poetry and music, this kind of eulogy is not admitted. A poet would think that a poor compliment had been paid him if his critic, by way of exalting him, were to point out that he had evidently taken great pains, and was very honest. In like manner, either a composer or an executant of a piece of music would be ill satisfied if no higher praise were awarded than honesty or painstaking. It is, therefore, worth while to ask whether, when such praise is accorded to the painter, he is in truth dealt with as one who practises a Fine Art, or whether he is not regarded rather as an artisan or artificer who practises a mechanical art. Aristotle in the Poetic Art points out that in the drama, which he takes as representing poetry, the actions which are introduced with the plot are a necessary condition, but are not, taken by themselves, enough to constitute a work of art. They are only the machinery which enables the poet to create character, and the test of excellence is the effect which the play as a whole produces on the feelings of the spectator. If painting is a Fine Art because it resembles poetry, the presumption is that a similar test should be applied to it. The presumption is that the critic who points out that this or that object is not faithfully imitated is dealing with a point of minor importance which cannot decide the artistic value of the work. If any one were to argue that the *Iliad* is not a poem because its historical value is doubtful, he would be laughed at. The question is, can criticism of a parallel kind be valuable in paint-ing? This kind of criticism was in this country supreme, chiefly with regard to landscape-painting, about twenty years ago. The celebrity which certain French landscape painters—chiefly Daubigny, Corot, Troyon, and T. Rousseau—have since obtained gave it a severe blow from which it has not entirely recovered. But it is now making itself heard in France, and is affecting the style of French painters. It has one invariable characteristic. It is always accompanied by an ostentatious attack on Academic authority. In the *Esthétique* of M. Eugène Véron, a violent onslaught is made on the Académie des Beaux Arts, and he makes two curiously inconsistent accusations against the professors. He declares that the Académie is the enemy of the arts; firstly, because the teachers in the École study with an excessive zeal the work of their predecessors; secondly, because they are profoundly ignorant of all technical questions. "Parmi ces ennemis, le plus puissant sans contredit est l'Académie des Beaux Arts. Les hommes de talent et de mérite qui constituent ce corps sont d'autant plus dangereux pour le progrès de l'art, qu'ils sont plus sincèrement convaincus des services qu'ils lui rendent. C'est cette sincerité qui fait leur force. S'ils se posaient en ennemis du progrès, ils seraient bien vite réduits à l'impuissance. Mais non, ce qu'ils veulent, ce qu'ils poursuivent avec ardeur, c'est le développement de l'art. Seulement ils sont persuadés que ce

D

développement n'est possible que par l'étude assidue des arts d'autrefois." (*Introduction,* xvii.)

"Le malheur, c'est que nos professeurs ne connaissent guère plus que leurs élèves les procédés des grands exécutants.   Ils ne les ont pas étudiés de près ou se croient plus forts qu'eux, mais en revanche ils sont plus ou moins complétement imprégnés de l'esprit rétrograde des Académies aux-quelles ils appartiennent.   Ils sont académiques de nature, d'éducation, d'habitude et de profession, et naturellement ils enseignent les principes de l'Académie, c'est-à-dire l'imitation, l'obéissance, l'étroitesse d'esprit, les théories toutes faites, les admirations et les haines préconçues, les dangers de la spontanéité.   Le reste leur importe peu.   C'est-à-dire qu'ils renversent précisément les termes, éliminant tout l'enseignment pratique qui peut se donner utilement sans porter atteinte à ce qu'il faut respecter dans l'artiste, puisque c'est le germ même de l'art, la personnalité, et réservant toute leur éloquence pour l'exposition de ce qu'ils appellent les règles immuables du beau, les principes éternels de l'idéal académique." (*Peinture,* p. 328.)

This fancy picture of the professors of the École, as a class of men who sedulously eliminate practical study, and waste the time of their pupils with rodomontade about the eternal principles of beauty, must,

I should think, have amused any French artist who may have read it. But such talk is now very fashionable in France, and many French writers seem to think that a knowledge of the art of painting comes as Dogberry thought reading and writing do. M. Eugène Véron states his opinion with unusual force and clearness, but it is one which universally prevails. Everywhere it is thought that if all academic authority could be swept away, some very perfect kind of painting might appear which the world has not yet seen. This essay is an attempt to examine this view.

CHAPTER I.

ART AND SCIENCE.

THE term Liberal Art is more venerable and famous than the term Fine Art. The former meant originally a pursuit which one of free birth and cultivated tastes might follow without impropriety, but accidentally acquired in early European history a narrower meaning. It became a name for science. This meaning it retained in the language of accurate writers down to a very recent period, though many . allowed it to revert to the wider etymological meaning. Its meaning at the present day is not well established, but apparently the received opinion is that the Fine Arts are Liberal Arts, though some Liberal Arts are not Fine Arts. Though this is in part a verbal question, it is not simply a verbal question. Real questions are often hidden in verbal disputes, and one lies hidden here. A Liberal Art is still a science rather than a Fine Art or a Useful Art, and when the terms are confounded the question about the nature of the Fine Arts is begged. It is taken for granted that they are of the nature of sciences. A history of the term Liberal Art will best establish the facts.

It is evident that there is a difference between science and knowledge, for, were it not so, the term "scientific knowledge," which is in common use, would be tautological and meaningless. It is at the same time certain that the sciences include all knowledge of every kind. This contradiction compels us to assume that a given proposition may belong to science in one place, and may be unscientific in another. This is found to be the case when instances are examined. The savage knows that by rubbing together two pieces of wood heat can be obtained, but his knowledge is not scientific. The same fact belongs to science when put in connexion with the general facts that heat is a mode of motion, and that force is imperishable. A science may, accordingly, be defined as a body of propositions between which there is a logical connexion. They are usually subdivided into the inductive and deductive sciences ; but induction is in truth deduction aided by experiment and observation. In both kinds there is a union of more extensive with less extensive propositions. Cicero's name for a classification of this kind was *ars*. In that part or

edition of the Academics which has been called
Lucullus, *ars* is defined as a generic term which
includes art and science. "Cumque artium aliud
ejusmodi sit ut tantummodo animo cernat, aliud ut
moliatur aliquid et faciat." It is said in this passage
that one kind of art discerns with the mind, another
makes and fashions things. The former is science ;
the latter art. Though all will allow that *ars* was
Latin for art, perhaps some will deny that it was
also a name for science. There are, however, other
passages in the Academics, of which the following is
one, which prove this to have been the case :—" Quid
fiet artibus ? Quibus ? iisne quæ ipsæ fatentur con-
jecturâ se plus uti quam scientiâ, an iis quæ tantum
id quod videtur sequuntur, nec habent istam artem
vestram quæ vera et falsa dijudicet ? " This is part
of an argument about the certainty of knowledge
and the relative advantages of inductive and deductive science. No sense can be made of it unless
artibus is translated sciences. It is "What will
become of the sciences ? Which ? Do you mean
those which avowedly rely on conjecture rather than
knowledge, or those which pursue that which is evident
to sense, and have not your boasted faculty of discern-
ing between truth and falsehood ? " There is a play
upon words in the use of *conjectura*. The sciences
in question trust to *conjectura* in the original sense

of the word, that is, a casting together or synthesis.
It suits the supposed disputant to pretend that this
is equivalent to an admission that synthetical science
is mere guess-work.   But in any case, however this
word *conjectura* may be interpreted, it is indisputable
that the sciences, not the arts, are in question.   But
there was also the word *disciplina*, which is in
Cicero's writings usually, if not always, a school of
philosophy, but which, it seems, sometimes meant a
science.   Varro, apparently, so used it.   He composed a treatise called the *Nine Disciplines*, which
seems to have been an encyclopædia of science, as
science was then understood.   This treatise has
perished, but its effects remain, and it determined
the meaning of the term Liberal Art in the following
manner :—Some time in the fourth century, for there
is a doubt about the date, Martianus Capella composed a kind of philosophical romance, which was in
its day very celebrated.   This still exists, and is
written in so tedious and affected a style that it is
hard to understand the taste which admired it.   It
is called the *Nuptials of Mercury with Philology the
daughter of Phronesis*.   The wedding is a pretext
for the introduction of essays on seven arts which
appear as attendants or bridesmaids.   These seven
arts are the following:—Grammar, Dialectic, Rhetoric,
Geometry, Arithmetic, Astronomy, Music.   It is

almost certain, though Martianus Capella does not
avow this in so many words, that these seven arts
were taken from Varro's *Nine Disciplines*, and it is
obvious that the word discipline would be less suitable for a figurative bridesmaid than the word art.
It may be gathered from Book IX., which treats of
music, that the omitted disciplines were architecture
and medicine.   It is said in this Book that Apollo
advanced and proposed that these should also be
invited to attend ; but after the question had been
discussed it was decided that they would be out of
place in a celestial assembly, as being arts which
minister to the bodily wants of the human race, and
therefore base and ignoble.   It must here be observed that the modern distinction between the fine
art of architecture and the useful art of building did
not occur.   They are identified and dismissed as
useful.   Nevertheless, it is possible that if the author
had not been fettered by the necessity of an odd
number he might have included architecture.   The
introductory part of the narrative contains a disserta-
tion on the value of odd numbers, and is apparently
meant as an apology for reducing the nine disciplines
to seven arts.   He could not omit medicine without
omitting one of the others ; otherwise eight would
have been left.   The profane narrative of Martianus
Capella, who seems to have been a pagan, would

have been soon forgotten, if it had not caught the
eye of Cassiodorus ; but he rewrote these essays from
an orthodox point of view, and thus a list of studies
was provided when the universities of Europe were
founded. Cassiodorus is, indeed, not quite ingenu-
ous. He refers to Varro, but says nothing about
Martianus Capella. It is, however, as certain that
he borrowed from the latter, as that the latter was
indebted to Varro. The similarity is too great for
the possibility of a coincidence, and it is not surprising that he should have wished to suppress the fact
that he found his seven arts in the disreputable
society of the heathen deities. Cassiodorus gave
these seven arts the name of the Liberal Arts, which
they have retained down to the present day, and
thus attached to the term the meaning of a science.
I will recur presently to the nature of music, but all
these studies, with that exception, would now be
called sciences. The introduction which Cassiodorus
prefixed to his essays is devoted to make it clear
that they are sciences, and he insists on the importance of science from a theological point of view,
identifying, in the spirit of Plato, the good and the
harmonious. In support of this he gives a false
derivation for the word Liberal, declaring that the
Liberal Arts are those which are contained in books.
The meaning thus given has remained unchanged

almost down to our own time. Johnson uses the
term Liberal Art as another name for science in the
following passage as elsewhere :—" There is, I think,
not one of the Liberal Arts which may not be com-
petently learned in the English language. He that
searches after mathematical knowledge may busy
himself among his own countrymen, and will find
one or other able to instruct him in every part of
those abstruse sciences." (*Idler*, No. 91.) This term,
accordingly, as thus introduced into modern Europe
is not the exact equivalent of the *ingenuæ artes*.
The latter were any pursuits which one of free birth
might take up. The Liberal Arts are more strictly
defined. They are not simply the non-servile
pursuits, but are studies which need no technical or
manual instruction, being of a purely intellectual
kind. Hence was formed the idea of a university
which Newman has described as a centre of intellectual activity. It does not appear that these seven
arts, which are now known as the seven University
Arts, were, when the Faculty of Arts was established,
rigorously necessary. They were a type, and as
occasion required one might be omitted, or others
added ; but they gave the Faculty of Arts its character, and by means of it decided the general
character of the universities of Europe. At the
present day a complication has resulted. There is on

the one hand a desire, almost universal, to support
the view that the Fine Arts can be taught, as the
Liberal Arts are taught, theoretically. On the other,
the University of Oxford has for the first time in its
history, with one doubtful exception, departed from
the traditional ideal and included practical instruction.

The word science when first introduced did not
mean what it now means. Theology was called
scientia, not because it contained deductions or in-
ductions, but because it dealt with a higher, surer,
and more venerable kind of knowledge than the
Liberal Arts. It has now abated its pretensions.
Its warmest advocates only claim for it that it is
knowledge, and it is no longer *scientia scientiarum*.
But the sentiment that some of the sciences ought
not to be called sciences, and that this term should
be reserved for the more important, which thus
arose, may still be traced. Professor Max Müller
was once attacked for a too lavish use, as his critic
thought, of this word, and made the following
reply:—" Whatever artificial restrictions may have
been forced on the term science in English and
American, the corresponding term in German, *Wissenschaft*, has as yet resisted all such violence."
(*Chips from a German Workshop*, vol. iv., p. 499.)
It is implied here that the restriction is a recent one,
but it is more probably a remnant of the academical

prejudice derived from the consecration of the word
scientia to theology, and it seems to be dying out.
The word *Wissenschaft* did not apparently obtain in
Germany the meaning of science as distinguished
from knowledge until a comparatively recent period.
It seems from the article on the word *Kunst* in the
new edition of Grimm's *Wörterbuch* that the earlier
writers used *Kunst* for science.   It is therefore intelligible that the word *Wissenschaft*, not having
been prematurely forced into circulation in an untenable sense, should have at once occupied its
rightful position.   The distinction between art and
science is hardly required until civilisation has made
great progress.   Ancient Greece had, indeed, this
distinction ; but the philosophy of Greece was far in
advance of the speculation of mediæval Europe.   It
is not at first understood that knowledge can be
sought for its own sake, nor that mechanical appli-
ances and manual dexterity are less important than
intelligence.   The astronomer is confounded with
the astrologer ; the mathematician with the diviner ;
the chemist with the transmuter of metals.   A skilful
use of globes, retorts, and measuring implements is
thought to be more effectual than the right use of
the mental faculties.   Art and science are barely
distinguishable in this stage of opinion.   They become distinct when it allowed that knowledge is

desirable for its own sake, and that he is the greatest astronomer, mathematician, and chemist, who knows most, not he who is most dexterous in manipulating mysterious implements. This was not clearly understood when the Faculty of Arts was established. There has been some dispute about the origin of this Faculty or Department ; but there is an extract from the Statutes of the University of Vienna in the *Glossary* of Ducange, under the word *Ars*, which doubtless contains the truth. The pith of it is comprised in the following words :—" Filii namque Facultatis Artium aptiores sunt ad quævis studia altiora, dummodo tamen non duxerint se emancipandos ante tempora a providâ matre, Facultate, scilicet, Artium." The sciences were studied in this spirit. They were the subjects of an elementary school, and theology was chief among the *studia altiora* to which they were subservient. This notion that there is only one kind of knowledge desirable for its own sake, viz., theological knowledge, gradually died out. The Faculties of Law and Medicine became more scientific, and the various Arts which compose the Faculty of Arts acquired a value of their own. But the original view, supported by academical authority, that there is only one true science, remained, and a Liberal Art had thus a variable signification. It was according to the

opinion of those who used the term, either a true
science, *i.e.*, a kind of knowledge sought for its own
sake, or a semi-science, valuable only as an aid to
some end.   Then came in the formula Science and
Art, in which the question is evaded.   Art might
be taken to mean useful art, or science.   Every one
knew that there was some difference between science
and art: no one knew what the difference was, or how
to reconcile the different opinions.   This indiscrimin-
ate use of the words produced comparatively little
inconvenience so long as no one discussed the Fine
Arts.   But when this new term was added, and these
were called shortly the Arts, just as the Liberal Arts
had been frequently called, for the sake of convenience, and as they are still called in university
formulas, confusion arose.   Some authors, chiefly
French authors, of whom Diderot is one, confidently
assumed that Fine Art is another name for painting
and sculpture, and is, at the same time, a name for
Liberal Art.   Others, while deterred by the academical usage from entirely repudiating the word
art as a name for science, began to manifest a
reluctance to use it in this sense, seeing intuitively
that the Fine Arts. differ from the sciences as well
as from the useful arts, and that the term is not
required, except for the purpose of marking this
difference.   Hallam in his *Literature of Europe* has

occasion in various places to name the Academical or Liberal Arts; but when he discusses them evidently prefers the word science.

There is at Oxford a Faculty of Music, the origin of which Antony à Wood apparently does not know, and which, I infer, is lost in obscurity. There is also at Cambridge a Faculty of Music. I do not know whether anything is more certainly known about this. There is a probability, so great as to be almost a certainty, that this Faculty was established in these universities when all academical interests were subordinate to theology, and a knowledge of music was wanted for the celebration of religious services. A satirical poem of the seventeenth century is extant, in which the author laments that the puritanical rage destroyed the most agreeable element of Oxford life when it expelled the musicians. It is therefore probable that at one time the art of music was taught at these universities. But however flourishing the faculty or department may once have been, it has never recovered from the effects of the puritanical attack, and students do not now go up to the universities with any expectation of finding a staff of music-masters or singing-masters. The music which figures in the list of Liberal Arts is the science, not the art, of music. The essay of Cassiodorus would prove this, if a proof were wanted.

It is true that the science was studied formerly, and is studied now, with a view to the art, but this does not affect the fact that it is distinct. Geometry may be studied for the purpose of mensuration, but it is not the less a science. In France the science and the art are placed apart. The former belongs to the Académie des Beaux Arts ; the latter to the Conservatoire. This is not the strictly logical arrangement, for the school of music should in theory belong to the Académie like the school of painting ; but strictly logical arrangements are some-times inconvenient. Now, though it is quite certain that there is a science of music, and that music is consequently one of the Liberal Arts, there is no such certainty as regards painting. It is on the contrary quite certain that there is not, and never can be, a science of painting, in the sense in which there is a science of music. It remains to be seen whether there is one in any other sense. The fol-lowing are the reasons why there can be a true, or exact, science of music, though there can be no corresponding science in the art of painting :—Sounds can be divided under two heads—noises and musical sounds ; the latter of which alone belong to music. There is an ill-defined territory between the two classes, and noises may be more or less musical, while musical sounds may be partly unmusical ; but

the distinction is valid notwithstanding, and musical
sounds alone belong to music. No such subdivision
of colours is possible. All colours are the property
of the painter. This is a necessary result of the
fact that painting is an art of representation, for the
artist who represents must use all the colours which
he sees. In the next place, musical sounds can be
reduced to language or signs. Music can be written.
Colours can be stated in language only in an exceedingly imperfect way which is quite inadequate
for scientific purposes. Colour is continuous, sound
is discrete. A strip of paper may be produced which
is crimson at one end and orange at the other, and
these two colours may so intermingle and pass into
each other that the smallest fragment which can be
detached will be heterogeneous in kind, inclining to
orange on one side and to crimson on the other. In
addition to this, colour varies in accordance with its
relation to other colour. If a scrap of gray paper
which is lying on a sheet of white paper is cut into
two halves, and one of these halves is laid on a sheet
of red, the other on a sheet of blue paper, the
original colour will entirely cease to exist, and will
be replaced by two new colours. One of these
· portions—that lying on the red—will be bluer than
the original gray, the other—that lying on the blue
—will be redder. The nature of sound is different.

E

A given musical sound is not raised or lowered in the scale by the addition of other sounds, either simultaneous or in succession. It may be concordant or discordant, but it remains a fixed quality, and is not changed as colour is changed by circumstances. Again colours combine to form new units. Purple is a compound colour with regard to its genesis, but is a simple colour for sensation. Sounds do not unite to form new units. When a chord is struck each note retains its individuality, and the practised ear of the musician can analyse it, and detect the various elements. Lastly, the vibrations which cause visual sensations have only a hypothetical existence. The phenomena can be explained on the assumption that there are such vibrations, but they cannot be seen or felt. The vibrations, on the contrary, which cause sound sensations, have their being in ordinary matter, and are known by observation as well as inferentially.

A comparison of these differences will show that there is a possibility of a scientific treatment of musical sound, which does not exist for colour. The condition of a true science is that it should contain propositions, the terms of which have a definite meaning. We find this condition fulfilled in music. As musical sounds are produced by the vibrations of known material substances, a wire or string of such

length and tension as to produce a musical sound
can be divided into two exact halves, and thus can
be ascertained the sound which the half produces as
well as the sound which the whole produces. Both
these sensations are fixed qualities. They can
accordingly be represented by signs which have a
definite signification. The sign represents on the
one hand the sensation, on the other the string or
wire of a certain length and tension. But an induction which is valid, because no instance has ever
been discovered to contradict it, proves that the
sensation of concordance or harmony is determined
by the mathematical concordance or harmony of the
vibrations. In the instance given here we have the
most perfect mathematical concordance, viz., the ratio
of 2 to 1 ; the vibrations are as nearly synchronous
as they can be without being identical ; and we have
at the same time the most perfect sensational harmony, viz., the extreme notes of an octave. It is
perfectly well-known that this parallel between the
mathematical harmonies and the sensational harmonies can be traced farther, and that the musical
quality diminishes as the mathematical coincidence
diminishes, until at last we quit music for noise.
Cassiodorus, accordingly, was quite right when he
affirmed in the introduction to the *Liberalium Litter-
arum* that music belongs to *mathematica.* Colours,

however, cannot be so treated. The proposition
" this is brown " is indeterminate. It may have one
of an interminable series of meanings. There is no
possibility of fixing exactly the meaning of any
colour-name. If it were proposed to determine the
meaning of a colour-name by its relation to white,
there would occur the prior difficulty of determining
what is white. Here, as everywhere, an endless series
of different tones is summed up under one name,
and white represents all the cold as well as all the
warm whites. Further, there is not the slightest
reason for supposing that colour harmony is determined, like sound harmony, by mathematical or
numerical harmony. The popular theory about
colour harmony is that the ingredients of the composite ray of light determine it ; that those arrangements of colour which most nearly resemble the
proportions of colour found in the rainbow are most
harmonious. Professor Bain in the chapter on Sight
(*Senses and Intellect*) speaks of this principle as if it
had a scientific certainty. I do not, for my part,
know whence this certainty arises. It is, assuredly,
not a self-evident truth, like the axioms of Euclid,
and is doubtfully supported by evidence. But, true
or false, it is not the same as the theory of sound
harmony. It must, with reference to this principle,
be observed that some essayists, assuming it to be

certain, have sought to persuade their readers that there is a science of painting. If, however, the arguments and examples are examined it will be found that they deal exclusively with decorative colouring, and do not touch the nature of painting proper, which is an art of representation. If the principle is granted, and though its value may be overstated, there is possibly some truth in it, a quasi-scientific treatment of decorative colouring is possible. Though colour-names are indefinite, there is a partial exception. When the ray of light is broken up by the prism, all the colours of which it is composed appear together in fixed order and proportions. The names of colours, therefore, when understood of the prismatic colours, have a more definite meaning than elsewhere. Thus the decorator who is not bound by the necessity of imitation, can at least in some measure rely on science. He can bear in mind the ingredients of the composite ray, and add such colours as make up the sum total. But the painter, in the proper sense of the word, cannot do this. He cannot put patches of red and green in his sky, because the blue is in excess of the quantity which the rainbow recommends. There are, therefore, two reasons why there cannot be a true or mathematical science of painting, though there is such a science of music. There is no cor-

respondence between numerical and sensational harmony in colour, and propositions about colour have
not an exact meaning.   The most definite names
of colours are the names of the primaries.   The
secondaries—those which are formed by the mixture
of two primaries—are less definite.   The tertiaries
—those which are formed by the mixture of two
secondaries—are still more indefinite.   There are
left an infinite series which are comprised under
brown and gray, and one or two other names.   The
primary colours are, in the language of artists, red,
yellow, and blue, and these are the primaries intended
in this arrangement.   In science the primaries are
red, green, and a third colour, which is either blue or
violet.   But a primary colour, however the word is
understood, is not a pure colour.   Professor Helmholtz points out that the purest colour which can be
found in nature, or produced by art, becomes more
intense when the eye has been previously fixed on
the complementary colour.   This in the received
theory implies that some of the complementary colour
is present.   It is supposed that fatigue makes certain
nerves less sensitive, and that this is the explanation
of the law of successive contrast.   As all colour is
thus complex, composed of elements the quantities
of which cannot be ascertained, there is an *a priori*
impossibility of an exact nomenclature.   One colour

passes into another without the possibility of distinction, and each colour changes when adjacent colours are changed. I am greatly indebted to Professor Helmholtz's *Popular Lectures* for what I have written on this subject ; but I have recast what he has said with a view to the argument. It is impossible for me to disentangle my own additions from the matter which his *Essays* have furnished, but if errors are detected, the reader may assume that I am original at least in these.

The science of music is a part of Acoustic, and was developed before the latter and wider science, with a view to the art. It would, perhaps, be more accurate and convenient if it were called Harmonic to distinguish it from the art. Tradition formerly ascribed to Guido of Arezzo the more important of the discoveries ; but Burney affirms, and later writers support him in this, that Guido cannot claim all which tradition formerly assigned to him. It is a science which is interposed between Acoustic and the Fine Art of music. No corresponding science can stand between Optic and Painting for the reasons given above. Colours cannot be subdivided as sounds are subdivided, nor can the harmonic effect be calculated as in music. Nevertheless there is a true science which is related to painting, as harmonic to music, though in a less degree. This is Perspective.

Perspective is a part of *mathematica*, like harmonic
science.   Colours exist in space and consequently in
forms.   Within certain limits scientific calculation
can determine these forms.   But as the condition of
science is terms which have a definite meaning, and
scientific treatment ends where the possibility of
language ends, those forms alone can be calculated
which can be stated in geometrical terms.   The
perspective of the circle, and of all curves which can
be described in scientific language, can be calculated,
because they can be inscribed in a rectilinear figure,
the perspective of which can be first calculated.
Even curves, the nature of which is not known, can
be calculated in architectural drawing, if an initial
assumption is made.   The artist who draws a series
of arches, the curves of which he does not know,
must trust to his eye for the curve of the first ; but,
this being assumed, can calculate the others, because
he can assume that the others are exact repetitions
of the first, and that they are equi-distant.   Even
with regard to the first he need only trust to his eye
for one half, for he can assume that the two sides
correspond.   Scientific drawing is thus practically
confined to architectural drawing, for the forms
which are known and can be stated in the language
of geometry are in natural objects exceedingly rare.
The sun is round : the outline of the sea is horizontal

and straight : perhaps some other instances may be found, but practically the artist wants the data for a scientific calculation.   Mr. Hay, in his ingenious *Essay*, in which he endeavours to demonstrate that the arts of painting and statuary are as scientific as music, though mankind have shut their eyes to the truth, omits all notice of the fact that the forms of the human body are composed of curves which cannot be mathematically described, and cannot be given by any calculation.   He keeps solely to the more general proportions, and contends that science can determine these, forgetting that the artist, whether sculptor or draughtsman, who has determined the general proportions alone, has hardly begun his task. The truth of all which Mr. Hay says is, I imagine, very doubtful ; but if every word is granted his case is not proved.

Supposing that what is here said is granted, it is plain that Fine Art begins where science ends. Scientific drawing of architecture is mechanical drawing, and is, as such, contrasted with artistic drawing. How then, it may be asked, can there be a Fine Art of music ?   Harmonic effect can be calculated and stated in language.   Why, then, is not music a mechanical art, like scientific drawing ?   The answer is that although music can be written or reduced to language, it cannot be adequately written ;   and though effects can be calculated, they cannot be entirely calculated. The extent to which calculation can go in the present stage of the arts is illustrated in the barrel-organs which we know so well and love so little. There is much with regard to which the composer can give hints, but nothing more. He can mark the *forte* and *piano* passages, the *rallentando* and *accelerando ;* he can indicate the notes which are to be sounded abruptly, and those which are to be connected, those which are to be emphatic, and those which are to be sounded faintly ; but the signs thus given can be interpreted in a thousand ways, and the executant may obey them literally, and yet shock the musician's ear. But there is another way in which musical signs are, as all language is, more or less imperfect. A written musical note does not represent the whole result. It represents only the set of vibrations, with the corresponding sensation, which is directly caused. Musical quality is, how-ever, given by the self-engendered harmonics which accompany this set of primary vibrations. Different instruments give these self-created companion notes in different degrees, and apparently the skill of one executant can call them forth more perfectly than another. It has often been observed that some performers seem to make the violin and the piano " sing," though others have not this mysterious gift.

This is pure art beyond the region of science. It
cannot be written and it cannot be calculated.
Lastly, though mathematical science can determine
harmonic effect, it cannot furnish the melody which
must underlie the harmonic quality.   The executant
alone is called an artist ; but the Fine Art of music
must be held to include the composer's part as well
as the executant's.   The science and the art can be
distinguished.   The science can be studied apart
from the art, but it exists for the sake of the art,
and is subordinate to it.   A perfect knowledge of
the theory is compatible with an absolute sterility
of invention.   The composer practises an art, though
he is also master of a science.

The Slade Professor of Fine Art in the Universities
of Oxford and Cambridge is bound by the terms of
his office to give theoretical lectures, as well as
historical and practical instruction.   The belief thus
implied that it is possible in some way to teach
painting theoretically is, I believe, almost universal.
It is, as I have endeavoured to show, the same as
the belief that the art of painting is a Liberal Art.
Theoretical discussion is only another name for
scientific discussion.   A theory must contain a
general proposition, and the proposition must be
certainly true if the theory is sound.   There is
such a proposition in musical science.   It is cer-

tainly true that there is a correspondence between the rates of vibrations which produce the feeling of harmony and this feeling itself. It is certainly known that a given combination of certain sets of vibrations will produce the effect known as a major key; that another combination will produce the effect of a minor key; that a third will produce discord. No general proposition of this kind can be discovered in the art of painting. What, then, can the theory be which is unfolded in theoretical lectures on painting? Widely held as the doctrine is that theoretical instruction is possible, it is accompanied by the suspicious doctrine that in the art of painting the proverb *cuique in arte suâ credendum* does not hold good. It was observed in the last chapter that critics who praise painters for their honesty, attack academic authority as the root of evil. The same peculiarity marks the belief that theoretical instruction is possible and desirable. It is accompanied by the doctrine that painters cannot be trusted in the criticism of pictures. It will not be disputed that even as a purely speculative question the nature and origin of this belief deserves investigation; but it has a practical importance—for those, at least, who are interested in the art—besides the speculative interest. The founder of the Slade Professorship undoubtedly intended to promote and do

honour to Fine Art, as it is called. But benefactions
have not always borne the fruit which they were
intended to bear, and things as well as men are
made ridiculous when put in false positions. Pre-
tended theoretical lectures—if they are only a false
pretence—can but bring into contempt the subject
which they are meant to encourage. They can be
nothing more than a few confident expressions of
opinion distended with more or less irrelevant digres-
sions. Historical lectures, of course, are possible.
There is a history of painting, as of all other things,
and lectures on it, whether ancient or modern, find
a natural place in a scheme of intellectual education.
But it was a hazardous step to authorise theoretical
lectures without some inquiry whether these are in
any way possible. Yet it may be doubted whether
the practical instruction would have been readily
admitted except in connexion with such lectures.
It must not be taken for granted that because Sir
Joshua Reynolds lectured on painting he held that
theoretical instruction is possible. The real nature
of his opinion on this matter will be shown in a
subsequent chapter. But if his lectures are set
aside, who will contend that any profit has been
derived from the successive courses of the Royal
Academy? The answer, I presume, will be that
to which I have referred. Painters of all men are

most ignorant of the principles of painting. The
prevalence of this opinion makes it difficult to frame
an argument. Sir Joshua Reynolds was the friend
and intellectual equal of Johnson and Burke. He
wrote, when his opinions were matured and his
reputation established, on the art to which he had
devoted his life. Yet when a graduate of Oxford,
wholly unknown to fame, announced that Sir Joshua
Reynolds was inaccurate in his facts and false in his
principles, not one educated Englishman in twenty
felt any surprise or incredulity. These words are in
the Preface to the second edition of *Modern Painters.*
It would make no difference if they were expunged.
It would still be certain that they must be applied
either to Mr. Ruskin or to Sir Joshua Reynolds.
As a recourse cannot be had to the usual kind of
authority the only method is a *reductio ad absurdum*
of the doctrine that theoretical or non-practical
teaching can do anything for painting. But lest it
should be supposed that no authority can be cited
for this view, I will quote a passage which even
historically is interesting. De Piles, a French author,
published some observations on the treatise of Dufresnoy, of which there is a translation in the works
of Dryden. He says, "I have learned from the
mouth of Monsieur Du Fresnoy that he had often-
times heard Guido say that no man could give a

rule of the greatest beauties, and that the knowledge of them was so abstruse that there was no manner of speaking which could express them." (*Dryden*, vol. xvii., p. 408, ed. 1821.)

If this is the true theory, that there are no rules, the materials for a course of theoretical lectures must be somewhat scanty, and the discussion of qualities, so abstruse that no manner of speaking can express them, cannot be very valuable. If all artists had understood this as well as Guido understood it—if they had always replied to the *littérateur* that his arguments and criticisms touched only points of minor importance, and that the essential qualities of their art are outside the sphere of language, and thereby of logic, their case would be stronger than it is. But they have shrunk from this, and by attempting to argue where argument is impossible, have put a weapon into the hands of their adversaries. The race of artists is proverbially irritable. Their critics have thought, not unnaturally, that this irritability is a sign of inordinate vanity, and springs from an excessive desire of commendation. It is in truth the sign in many cases of a feeling that they are judged on what seems to them a side-issue, and an inability to argue the point. They pass over the prior question, whether argument is possible, and are embarrassed at the results of their concession. In an old

Greek epigram, of which Porson made a famous parody, it is said that All Lerians are bad—not this one or that one—all except Proclees, and Proclees is a Lerian. This, *mutatis mutandis*, may be said of Sir Joshua Reynolds. His true opinion was the same as Guido's, and he was in a false position when he lectured. It is exceedingly improbable that he can have been wholly wrong where his statements are definite, and are about a tangible question ; but it is no disparagement to him to think that he may in some places have endeavoured to argue where the nature of the case made it impossible. Constable, who was too intelligent, and knew too much of art to speak with arrogance and disrespect of so great a man, thought this. In one of his letters he wrote as follows :—" C. has been drivelling a parcel of sad stuff in the Worcester paper in the name of Lorenzo. God knows not Lorenzo di Medici, but it is all about ideal art, which in landscape is sheer nonsense, as they put it. Even Sir Joshua is not quite clear about this." (Leslie's *Life of Constable*, ch. xv. p. 269).

CHAPTER II.

THEORY AND PRACTICE.

IT was very commonly thought, not many years ago, that theoretical teaching of some kind could be advantageous to the useful arts. This notion has now been in some degree dispelled by experience and competition with other countries. It has been found that lectures on taste lead only to feeble imitations of foreign styles and incongruous mixtures, and that the true way to improve the manufacture of carpets, porcelain, and furniture, is to provide a sound practical or technical system. But it is thought that the Fine Arts are altogether different in their nature. Theory, it is supposed, is all-important for them, and an indefinite belief prevails that there are some principles from which the true practice may be deduced. A revolution in the system of teaching drawing, which has recently taken place in this country, shows how rash it is to rely on such an assumption. Less than twenty years ago a

F

student of our Royal Academy would have hardly
found words strong enough to express the contempt
which he would have felt for a crayon study shaded
with a stump ; but at the present day a visitor to the
British Museum may see students copying the antique
statues, and shading them with paper stumps, ignorant, apparently, that they can be accused of an
artistic crime.   This change of method has been the
result of an experience which some English artists
have had of the superiority of the French method,
and theory must always have remained, as it always
had been, impotent to touch the question.   It will
seem to many that whether drawing is taught in
one way or another must be a trivial matter.   This
is part of the doctrine that theories and principles
are all-important.   But artists know that a faculty
of drawing is the foundation of excellence in painting, and that the correct draughtsman has more time
at his command, and paints in a better style than
others.   The half-taught artist who finds out too
late that his outline is faulty is condemned to a
long and laborious process if he would fain make
good his initial error, and sometimes, after days of
wasted labour, is obliged to reject the canvas on
which he has been at work, and begin his task afresh.
Even if the first mistake can be corrected, the result
is rarely as satisfactory as it would have been if no

mistake had been committed. French artists, however, have always maintained that France produces better draughtsmen than England, and that their superiority can be traced to the employment of a true system of shading. Perhaps some Englishmen will be found to deny the excellence which Frenchmen claim for themselves; but no Frenchman, and, indeed, no foreign artist of any kind, will be found to defend the old English method of shading with the point of the crayon. This is, however, a purely technical question which experience alone can decide. There are others of a more general description which can be discussed without technical words or technical knowledge by an appeal to common sense. Such a discussion is, indeed, superfluous for artists; but as it is a part of the doctrine of the day that artists cannot be trusted in their own profession, an attempt to put the question in its true light may be forgiven. Art, as it is called, is now very fashionable. Institutions are founded on all sides to promote it, and orations are delivered in its honour, and it behoves those who take an interest in it to look whither they are going. The practice of academies is the fruit of a long experience, and it is unwise to take for granted that traditions are always the offspring of prejudice. It should be remembered that theoretical writers have long proclaimed their

intention and capacity to do great things for the art
of painting.   Lessing announced that he had come
to reform the arts.   The modern artist had, he declared, sunk to a deplorable baseness of temper, and
he undertook to cure him.   Other writers have given
a diagnosis of artistic maladies, and have propounded
their various remedies.   It is time that the tree
should have borne some fruit, or that its sterility
should be explained.   We should be told why
Phidias or Titian, who owed nothing to theoretical
instruction, have not been eclipsed, and how their
styles were formed, if theories are a *sine quâ non.*
The art teacher, in truth, bears testimony against
himself.   Though he cries aloud that his mission is
to refine the arts and restore the glories of Greek
sculpture and mediæval architecture or painting, he
admits that he is a Cassandra, and that a stubborn
generation turns a deaf ear to his exhortations.   A
dry and minute investigation of such points as admit
such treatment may be tedious ; but some, perhaps,
may be willing to consider what can be said in behalf
of the academic system of teaching drawing, and
this discussion will form a convenient introduction
to the more general question.

The practice in academies is to teach drawing,
both by the aid of casts and statues of the human
body, or parts of the human body, and also from

"the life," as it is technically called, *i.e.* the natural
or living body. In this country a long course of
study of casts or statues has usually preceded the
study of the natural body ; but in all academies both
methods are adopted, and special studies of the extremities—the head, the hands, and the feet—are
made by means of casts. It is unnecessary to quote
evidence about this, for no one, I imagine, will dispute the facts. There is another system, which may
be called the anti-academical method, different in
two respects. The peculiarity of the academical
system is, that in it drawing is taught by means of
solid objects or things in three dimensions, and that
these solid things are the human body, or parts of it.
In the anti-academical system drawing is taught first
by setting the pupil to copy drawings, photographs,
and engravings, and the course is completed by studies
of stones, plants, trees, branches of trees, and other
objects of this kind. Mr. Ruskin has advocated the
latter system in his *Elements of Drawing.* There are,
therefore, two questions. If the academical method
can be justified, it must be shown that solid things are,
as models, more instructive than things in two dimensions ; and it must also be shown that of things in
three dimensions the forms of the human body are
preferable to all others. Both these questions can
be examined without any intrusion of technicalities.

It is very commonly supposed that a kind of instruction is requisite for landscape distinct from that which is needed for portrait and figure-painting, and that Academicians limit their course of teaching to the human body because they despise landscape, or, at any rate, think it a lower kind of art than figure-painting. There may be Academicians who think this. Every one is naturally disposed to rate his own vocation highly, and perhaps portrait or figure painters do think that their department is the higher. It is, however, quite unnecessary to investigate this point. A knowledge of drawing is in the art of painting what a knowledge of grammar and syntax is in literature. It is as superfluous to ask whether the pupil in the one case proposes to paint landscapes or figures, as it is in the other to inquire whether he intends to write on history or science. The only question is which is the more efficient system. But this popular error is connected with, and is, indeed, almost identical with, another. It is thought that the practice of copying pictures and of copying statues or casts rests on the same ground : that professors who advocate the one advocate the other, and that the object is to form what is called a classical style. The fact is, that all recommend studies of casts and statues, but that opinions differ greatly about the necessity of copying pictures.

The former practice is everywhere a part of the necessary course, while authorities differ about the latter, and all agree that it may be abused. Leonardo da Vinci wrote as follows :—" The Adversary says that to acquire practice and do a great deal of work it is better that the first period of study should be employed in drawing various compositions done on paper or on walls by divers masters, and that in this way practice is rapidly gained and good methods. To which I reply that the method will be good if it is based on the works of good composition and by skilled masters. But, since such masters are so rare that there are but few of them to be found, it is a surer way to go to natural objects than to those which are imitated from nature with great deterioration and so form bad methods." (*Leonardo da Vinci*, Richter, p. 246, ed. 1883.) There is, I believe, a further reason why it must be held that such advice comes from the mouth of " The Adversary." Although it is indisputable that the practice of drawing forms a manual dexterity, and that the finished artist has a touch and quality of line which is all his own, the end of the drawing school is to cultivate the eye, not the hand, and the style of drawing is only an incidental result. The necessity of a special cultivation of the eye is a result of the peculiar connexion between the sense of sight and the sense of touch

which Berkeley made the basis of his celebrated
metaphysical and theological speculation.   Sight
alone, if it had never been exercised in co-operation
with the sense of touch, would know nothing of distance or the third dimension.   But a long experience
of visual sensations in conjunction with tactual sensations has so trained and educated the visual faculty
that it instinctively recognises distance.   The purely
metaphysical question whether there must be an *a
priori* intuition and Berkeley's theological inference
are distinct from the certain fact that visual sensations alone cannot contain an indication of distance.
The draughtsman must, however, forget the third
dimension.   His task is to project in a plane the
lines which, in natural objects, are not in a plane.
In order to do this he must mentally project them,
or imagine them, in a plane which would be cut at
right angles by a line drawn from a point between
his two eyes to the point on which the eyes are
fixed.   Strictly speaking, the eyes are not fixed on
one point, but it is assumed in the projection that
they are.   But the processes of nature are as sure as
they are slow.   Nature has taught the eye to see
objects such as tactual experience proves them to be,
and it is not easy to imagine that lines are in one
plane when it is certain that they are not.   A simple
experiment will prove how much more accurately

the eye can judge of the relations of lines to each
other when they are not seen in perspective than
when they are. Let any one draw on the wall, in
front of which he is standing, an angle of no matter
what dimensions, or let him fasten on the wall a
piece of paper on which there is such an angle, and
he will find that he can easily form a rough estimate
of its magnitude and copy it with tolerable accuracy.
If, however, he will then turn his eyes to the apparent
angle, which the walls make at the corner of the
room where they join the floor or the ceiling, and
attempt to determine the magnitude of this angle in
a similar manner, he will find that the problem is
not so easy. It is hard to determine the magnitude
in the latter instance, and even practised artists go
wrong who trust to their eyes for their perspective,
and refuse to call in a calculation to assist them.
But the *data* for calculation do not exist in artistic
drawing, and for this reason a special training is required in order to give, so far as is possible, the
power of imagining, or mentally projecting, forms in
a plane. Apparent forms and real forms would be
all one for sight if it had not acquired a kind of
intuition foreign to its own nature ; but its education
has been too perfect, and it cannot forget the lessons
which it has received. The complete conviction
that the perspective relations of lines to each other

will change if the point of view is changed, and the
certitude that touch or measurement will prove that
the apparent angle is not the real angle, perplex the
judgment and make it difficult to see truly the
apparent (*i.e.* which is seen) relation.   When, therefore, forms which are already projected in a plane
are copied, the chief lesson of the drawing school is
not given, and such studies are a waste of time.
Life is short and art is long, as the physician of Cos
said, and drawings are not copied in well-ordered
systems of instruction.

We may now pass to the second question, why
drawing can be thoroughly learned by a study of the
forms of the human body alone?   This is a deduction from the simple and obvious principle which
pervades all education that those exercises are most
valuable in which error can be most certainly detected.   A language cannot be thoroughly learned
without written exercises, because in these alone
faults of grammar and construction are certainly discovered.   False concords and wrong moods slip in
and pass undiscovered in speech, which attract attention when put into writing.   In the same way no
great proficiency can be obtained in musical execution without the practice of unmelodious exercises.
Melody distracts the ear, and little irregularities of
time and force escape notice which are observed

when melody is excluded. The sole question for the drawing school is what class of studies most certainly secures the detection of inaccuracy, and to this question there is only one answer. The human body is unique for this purpose. There is in animal organism a bilateral symmetry, perfect as all the works of nature are, which is found in no other objects. The growth of trees and plants is determined in part, like the growth of animals, by organic laws; but the difference is that the tree, the bush, the plant, is not an individual, but a group of individuals united together, and, this being the case, mechanical laws rather than organic laws determine the relations of one side of the composite individual to the other. There does not exist in the vegetable world a perfect bilateral symmetry such as found in the animal world. The forms of almost all animals, however, except man, are disguised by a coating of fur or hair or feathers. In man alone can all the various curves which the muscles form as they overlap each other be plainly seen. These curves change as the position changes, but the correlation of parts to each other remains. A change in the form of one curve implies a change both in the adjacent curves and in those which correspond on the opposite side of the body or limb. When, therefore, the human body is drawn there is a certainty

that false drawing will be discovered because it produces a manifest deformity.   The fatal objection to
Mr. Ruskin's system is that it enables the student to
persuade himself and his friends that he is an artist,
when he may, in truth, be ignorant of the A B C of
art.   The difference is that the more nicely and
neatly studies of non-animal nature are finished, the
more readily they pass muster ; the more perfectly
the human body is shaded and moulded, the more
inevitable the requisite criticism is.   This is the real
end of shading.   It is not to make the drawing look
pretty, but to give the form more perfectly, and the
importance of a right method of shading is the result
of this.   It is easy to illustrate the point.   There
are, for example, some heads by Greuze, in which an
ordinary observer, who has never studied drawing,
immediately perceives that the eyes do not correspond.   If these heads are closely examined it will
be seen that the error is infinitely small, and it is
not always easy to say whether the outline or the
modelling is in fault.   Such trifling inaccuracy could
not possibly be detected in a study of leaves, stones,
and objects of this kind.   In the natural face the
smallest displacement of the eyes is observed : an
exceedingly minute swelling on the face or hands is
observed.   Equally minute departures from the
normal forms catch the eye in a finished study.

Lastly, a lesson is taught when the living body is substituted for the statue or cast, which cannot be taught in any other way. This is that attention must be paid to the remoter relations of lines to each other as well as to the immediate relations. The statue or cast is immovable. The forms remain unchanged during the hours of study and from day to day. The living model is not so inflexible. Fatigue tells on him or her, and the pose, once quitted, cannot be re-discovered with precision. It is no longer sufficient to observe only the immediate relations of form. These are in the statue or cast trustworthy, and, if given correctly in each part, the whole which results must be true. But a slight change of attitude, whether caused by muscular fatigue or a difference of position, alters every part of the frame. A kind of computation is needed to correct the temporary fluctuations. This is a new difficulty, and the draughtsman who has not mastered it has no right to the name of artist. It is something like the difficulty which beginners find in reading music when they are required to see not only the passage which is at each moment in execution, but also the passages which are to follow, so as to be ready for the transition. It is proverbially difficult to attend to two things at once. Strictly speaking, it is impossible, and the so-called double attention is an incessant alternation of the attention. Practice alone can form the habit or faculty in drawing and in music.

The academic system is the product of an accumulated experience, and we find in this question how foolish the cry is that academies ought to be abolished, and that painters know less about their own art than any one else.   Theories about such matters are worthless.   They are superfluous if they confirm experience, and almost certainly wrong if they contradict it.   But the quarrel between theory and academical authority is not usually of this definite kind.   It springs out of a hasty assumption on the side of theoretical writers that the requisite technical instruction is not, and cannot be, difficult.   This notion is a tacit inference from the character of poetical literature, for it is forgotten that in this art, of which language is the instrument, the strict technical education is given in infancy, and that a knowledge of language, both spoken and written, is obtained by a long and laborious process.   It is, accordingly, taken for granted, without any exact inquiry, that theoretical teaching does, as a matter of fact, occupy the attention of pupils in drawing schools.   In other words, it is supposed that the main object of such schools is to form the style, and not simply to cultivate the perceptions of the eye.

Cousin is reported to have spoken as follows in his course of lectures on the Good, the True, and the Beautiful :—" D'après cette théorie, quelle méthode doit—on suivre dans l'enseignment des Beaux Arts ? Les élèves doivent—ils commencer par l'idéal ou par le réel ? Par l'unité ou par la variété ? M. Quatremère se déclare en faveur de l'idéal. Pour moi, je pense que les Grecs n'ont debuté ni par le réel ni par l'idéal tout seul, mais l'un et l'autre à la fois. La nature ne commence ni par l'un ni par l'autre, c'est-à-dire, qu'elle n'offre jamais le général sans l'individuel, ni l'individuel sans le général. Pourquoi ne mettrait—on pas les élèves aux prises avec la variété et avec l'unité en même temps, et ne les ferait—on pas marcher comme les Grecs et comme la nature ? " (P. 209, Hachette, 1836.) There is no more sense in this problem which Cousin propounds so gravely than there would be in a dispute whether the texts with which the first copy-book of an infant is furnished ought to be taken from Milton or from Addison. Comte took up the question of artistic education, and though for a moment he seemed to see the truth, immediately betrayed his belief that the technical instruction must be brief and easy. " Par cela même qu'elle (education) est profondément esthétique, elle leur rend superflue toute éducation spéciale, sauf celle qui résulte spontanément de l'exercice préparatoire. Aucune autre profession n'est autant dispensée d'un enseignment particulier, qui ne tend qu'à y éteindre une indispensable originalité en étouffant l'élan esthétique sous le travail technique." (*Politique Positive, Discours Préliminaire*, Vme. Partie, vol. i., p. 307.) The first part of this is consistent and intelligible. Comte says that if the technical instruction is given, the *élan esthétique* forms itself. But he then adds that there is a danger lest this *élan* should be ultimately stifled by the *travail technique*. This can only be thought by one who supposes that there is no real progress in the technical course, and that it is made up, after the first elements, of a monotonous and weariful repetition by which nothing is gained. In that case, doubtless, all *élan*, the æsthetic among the rest, might be stifled. But an increase of technical facility is created if there is an advance, and this increased facility cannot in any way suppress qualities which might without it be displayed. True, an increased facility does not necessarily of itself produce poetic or artistic quality. There have been poets whose mastery of language is perfect, but who have been only skilful versifiers. There have been artists whose technical powers have been admirable, but who have not been great artists. Still it is incredible that there can have been in these poets and artists impulses which would have been revealed under more adverse circumstances, and which did not find an outlet because the path was made too smooth. The mute inglorious : Miltons have lacked the requisite *travail technique*, have not been extinguished by an excessive amount of it. The opinion that the practical difficulties in the arts of painting and sculpture are very slight, and that any one who has a turn for such pursuits can in a month or two learn all which is desirable with very little exertion, is betrayed in various ways by those who discuss questions of this kind. The Pre-Raphaelite sect was partly made in this way. A number of young artists who had imperfectly mastered the technical difficulties were pleased to find that critics saw in their imperfections the signs of a deep theory, and were too wise to protest against so flattering a view. Novel writers betray the same conviction. The hero or heroine, who has been reduced to poverty by some accident, after looking about for some resource, decides to paint a picture. A subject is selected which would have baffled Titian and Michael Angelo combined, and a masterpiece is immediately produced. This error falsifies criticism. Artists seem to be perverse in their selection of subjects. The critic shows that it would have been easy to find a more interesting

G

theme, ignorant, or forgetful, that other considerations must be taken into account. Thus is formed
the doctrine which so widely prevails that Academicians, as representing artists generally, are the slaves
of prejudice.

There is a minor point which must be cleared up
previously to an investigation of the general question. An habitual concentration of the attention in
one direction invariably affects taste. The florist,
the pigeon-fancier, the breeder of horses and cattle,
learns to detect little differences, which escape the
observation of those who have less closely attended
to the peculiarities of flowers, pigeons, cattle, and
horses, and learns to think these minute differences
important. The constant and prolonged attempt
of the artist to render forms and colours, affects his
taste in a similar manner. Not only does he come
to attach greater importance than others do to
colour and form in the abstract, but he notes and
thinks important the particular mode of execution
which each artist may adopt. These peculiarities of
execution are known as touch and handling. The
practised eye discerns style, where others see no
style, and can distinguish between the laborious
manner of the tyro and the facile hand of the
accomplished artist, where the unpractised eye cannot detect a difference. This point, as many will

remember, occurred in the celebrated trial of Belt
versus Lawes. A number of Academicians were
summoned as witnesses to decide the authorship of
a bust which was produced, and every one was struck,
while many were perplexed, by the singular unanim-
ity of their testimony. It was, perhaps, faintly
hinted, but was not seriously asserted, that their
evidence was preconcerted. The judge who presided
over the first trial spoke as follows, with reference to
them :—" It is said that artists are better judges than
amateurs. This has been contradicted elsewhere.
It was the opinion of Sir Joshua Reynolds. I do
not cite my own opinion on such a subject as of any
weight, for I well know that in certain quarters anything I may say will be disputed, and perhaps naturally ; but I find on a recent reference that there is
authority for this position more venerable even than
Sir Joshua—to wit, Aristotle himself, according to Mr.
Froude, who gave it as his opinion that artists are
not so reliable judges of artistic merit as the public
who give usually a broader, juster, and safer judgment than those engaged in the pursuit themselves.
I must confront the *dicta* of Reynolds and Aristotle,
as reported by Froude, with that of the great
moderns, and leave you to choose which you prefer
to adopt in the decision of this portion of this case."
(*Times*, December 29, 1882.) I do not think that

the judge, or any one who took this view, attempted
to explain how the consensus of opinion, which was
found among the different members of the Royal
Academy, was formed. ⸱ The presumption is that
where a unanimous opinion is held, it must be broad
and safe and just. But there can be little doubt
that the words of the judge were in harmony with
common opinion. Innumerable comments, which
appeared afterwards in the newspapers, showed that,
in spite of many protests, the accepted view was that
the proverb *cuique in suâ arte credendum* does not
hold good in the arts of painting and statuary, and
the supposed opinion of Sir Joshua Reynolds was
thought to prove that he was a wiser man than his
successors in the Academy. I do not propose to
investigate Aristotle's opinion, for I do not think
that those who know the general tenor of his writings will be easily persuaded that he held skilled
opinions to be less valuable than unskilled. But as
literary reporters are less accurate than legal reporters, and the *dicta* of Sir Joshua Reynolds go to
the root of the matter, I will quote the words of the
latter. The following essay on criticism, which was
published in the *Idler* (No. 76), was his composition :—" I was much pleased with your ridicule of
those shallow criticks, whose judgment, though often
right as far as it goes, yet reaches only to inferior

beauties, and who, unable to comprehend the whole,
judge only by parts, and thence determine the merits
of extensive works.   But there is another kind of
critick still worse, who judges by narrow rules, and
those too often false, and which, though they should
be true, and founded on nature, will lead him but a
little way toward the just estimation of the sublime
beauties in a work of genius : for whatever part of
art can be executed or criticised by rules, that part
is no longer the work of genius, which implies excellence out of the reach of rules.   For my own part,
I profess myself an Idler, and love to give my judgment, such as it is, from my immediate perceptions,
without much fatigue of thinking, and I am of
opinion that if a man has not those perceptions
right, it will be vain for him to endeavour to supply
their place by rules, which may enable him to talk
more learnedly, but not to distinguish more acutely.
Another reason which has lessened my affection for
the study of criticism is that criticks, so far as I
have observed, debar themselves from receiving any
pleasure from the polite arts, at the same time that
they profess to love and admire them, for these
rules being always uppermost give them such a
propensity to criticise that instead of giving up the
reins of their imagination into their author's hands,
their frigid minds are employed in examining

whether the performance be according to the rules
of art.

" To those who are resolved to be criticks in spite
of nature, and at the same time have no great disposition to much reading and study, I would recommend them to assume the character of connoisseur,
which may be purchased at a much cheaper rate
than that of a critick in poetry. The remembrance
of a few names of painters, with their general characters, with a few rules of the academy, which they
may pick up among the painters, will go a great
way towards making a very notable connoisseur.

" With a gentleman of this cast I visited last week
the Cartoons at Hampton Court. He was just returned from Italy, a connoisseur of course, and of
course his mouth was full of nothing but the grace
of Raffaelle, the purity of Domenichino, the learning
of Poussin, the air of Guido, the greatness of the
taste of the Carracci, and the sublimity and grand
contorno of Michael Angelo ; with all the rest of the
cant of criticism, which he emitted with all that volu-
bility which generally those orators have who annex
no ideas to their words. As we were passing through
the rooms in our way to the gallery, I made him
observe a whole length of Charles the First by Van-
dyke, as a perfect representation of the character as
well as the figure of the man. He agreed that it

was very fine, but it wanted spirit and contrast, and
had not the flowing line without which a figure could
not possibly be graceful.   When we entered the
gallery, I thought I could perceive him recollecting
his rules by which he was to criticise Raffaelle.   I
shall pass over his observations of the boats being
too little, and other criticisms of that kind, till we
arrive at St. Paul preaching.   This, says he, is
esteemed the most excellent of the Cartoons ; what
nobleness, what dignity there is in that figure of St.
Paul !   And yet what an addition to that nobleness
could Raffaelle have given had the art of contrast
been known in his time !   But above all the flowing
line which constitutes grace and beauty !   You would
not then have seen an upright figure standing equally
on both legs, and both hands stretched forward in
the same direction, and his drapery to all appearance
without the least art of disposition.   The following
is the charge to Peter :—Here, says he, are twelve
upright figures—what a pity it is that Raffaelle was
not acquainted with the pyramidal principle !   He
would then have contrived the figures in the middle
to have been on higher ground, or the figures at the
extremities, stooping or lying, which would not only
have formed the group into the shape of a pyramid,
but likewise contrasted the standing figures.   Indeed,
added he, I have often lamented that so great a

genius as Raffaelle had not lived in this enlightened
age, since the art has been reduced to principles, and
had had his education in one of the modern academies.
What glorious works might we have then expected from
his divine pencil." In this essay the word *connoisseur*
is used satirically. In the following passage, which is
taken from the notes on Dufresnoy, it is used seriously;
the half-learned connoisseur is the connoisseur of the
preceding discourse. " The only opinions of which
no use can be made, are those of half-learned connoisseurs who have quitted nature and have not
acquired art. Of many things the vulgar are as competent judges as the most learned connoisseur ; of
the portrait, for instance, of an animal, or of the truth,
perhaps, of some vulgar passions." (Notes on Du
Fresnoy's *Art of Painting*, by Sir J. Reynolds, Note
xlix.) These passages show clearly what Sir Joshua
Reynolds thought, and how much he was misunder-
stood when quoted as an authority for the rejection
of artistic testimony. Artists, according to him, are
the true connoisseurs, and their opinion alone is valuable ; next in order come the vulgar, who can judge
whether a picture is a faithful imitation ; lastly, at
the bottom of the list, the professed critic, whose
opinion is always worthless.

We may proceed now to the more general question. Though in this trial the point to be decided

was one about the execution of a bust, the controversy generally is about the art of painting, and
most of the arguments offered, and testimony quoted
at the time and afterwards, had reference to painting.
When an application was made for a new trial in the
spring of the following year, it had, apparently, been
discovered that it was rash to appeal either to Aristotle or Sir Joshua Reynolds, and a far more suitable authority had been found. An extract from
Macaulay's *Essays* was substituted in support of the
same view, which seems, curiously enough, to have
been written for the express purpose of refuting
Reynolds. In this extract, Macaulay uses the word
connoisseur, which was not a very common term
when he wrote, and though he begins with a general
statement about all the arts, and men of genius, he
ends with an illustration from, and an argument about,
the art of painting alone. The passage is the following :—" It is neither to the multitude nor to the few
who are gifted with real creative genius that we are
to look for sound critical decisions. The multitude,
unacquainted with the best models, are captivated by
whatever dazzles them. A man of great original
genius, on the other hand—a man who has attained
to mastery in some high walk of art—is by no means
to be implicitly trusted as a judge of the performances
of others. The erroneous decisions pronounced by

such men are without number.   It is commonly supposed that jealousy makes them unjust.   But a more
creditable explanation may easily be found.   The
very excellence of a work shows that some of the
faculties of the author have been developed at the
expense of the rest, for it is not given to the human
intellect to expand itself widely in all directions at
once, and to be at the same time gigantic and well-
proportioned.   Whoever becomes pre-eminent in any
art or style of art, generally does so by devoting
himself with intense and exclusive enthusiasm to the
pursuit of one kind of excellence.   His perception
of other kinds of excellence is therefore too often
impaired.   Out of his own department he praises
and blames at random, and is far less to be trusted
than the mere connoisseur, who produces nothing,
and whose business is only to judge and to enjoy.
The more fervent the passion of each artist for his
art, the higher the merit of each in his own line, the
more unlikely it is that they will justly appreciate
each other.   Many persons who never handled a
pencil probably do far more justice to Michael
Angelo than would have been done by Gerard Douw,
and far more justice to Gerard Douw than would
have been done by Michael Angelo." (*Times*, June 5,
1883.)   When Macaulay wrote this he was thinking
of the sneers of Sir Joshua, and was doing battle

in behalf of his fraternity.   His literary skill deserves
all praise.   The pointless antithesis with which he
begins between the multitude who are captivated by
whatever dazzles them, which seems to mean, are
pleased with whatever pleases them, and the genius,
on the other hand, who is by no means to be implicitly trusted, does not lead up to the conclusion
which is derived ; but the bad logic is hidden by an
interposition of platitudes, such as that it is not given
to the human intellect to expand itself widely in all
directions at once.   He does not tell us at first who
the sages are whose judgment may be implicitly
trusted, because they are not so weak as to be pleased
with whatever pleases them.   But it turns out that
they are many who have never handled a pencil.
This is mysterious.   It would seem that after all the
multitude are the trustworthy judges.   It is, however,
clear that Macaulay's modesty deterred him from
saying exactly what he meant.   We must put a gloss
on these words, and read, " Some who have handled
a pen," instead of " many who have never handled a
pencil."   There is then no difficulty.   The purport
of the passage is, that if Michael Angelo were still
alive, it would be foolish to take his opinion about
the merit of a picture, when a sounder opinion could
be obtained from an eminent handler of the pen.
The words that " out of his own department," the

artist "praises and blames at random," are very true. Macaulay was an artist in language, and had studied the use of words with "an intense and exclusive enthusiasm." It is implied in his argument that artists who do not paint in the style of Michael Angelo are in the habit of denying the beauty and excellence of his works. It would be hard to find a more ill-founded accusation, or a better illustration of the truth that artists praise and blame at random when they quit their own department to offer opinions on matters which they have not studied.

The view in support of which Macaulay's words were quoted in the Belt trial was that the multitude give safer, broader, and juster judgments than artists. Macaulay, it will be observed, does not say this— indeed, says the exact opposite of this. The multitude are captivated with whatever dazzles them. Nevertheless the barrister who quoted the passage was right, and the real point is the quarrel between artists and non-artistic critics, as to which Macaulay and the anti-artistic faction are quite in unison. Sir Joshua Reynolds gave a tripartite classification of opinion under the three heads, Artists, Critics, and the Vulgar. Macaulay, having in his mind what Reynolds had said, also gave a threefold division ; but the true division at the present day is the dichotomic division which the presiding judge gave. The

connoisseur described by Sir Joshua Reynolds as a
half-learned connoisseur has vanished, and his place
has been taken by a wholly ignorant connoisseur,
between whom and the multitude there is no dis-
crepancy of opinion.   It is obvious that Macaulay's
premisses lead up to a result which he would not
have admitted, and which is a *reductio ad absurdum*
of them.   He says that every one is the best judge
in his own province, and that random opinions are
formed outside it.   It follows that painters are the
best judges of pictures.   But he also says that very
eminent artists cannot be trusted.   It follows that, if
painters are consulted about pictures, care must be
taken to select unsuccessful painters.   But he does
not draw this inference, and did not wish to draw it.
He wished to show that Reynolds was mistaken in
thinking that the proverb about every one being the
highest authority in his own art can be applied to
painting.   It is, therefore, indisputable that a good
selection was made when Aristotle and Reynolds
were dropped, and Macaulay put in place of them.
The question appears in its true aspect in his argument, though the reasoning does not support the
inference.   The real question is, whether one who
writes on the art of painting, not having practised it,
is, or is not, a higher authority than an artist?   This
question is, from the nature of the case, the same as

the question whether painting is a kind of science. Macaulay does not attempt to assert this. He does not attempt to deny directly the contention of Reynolds that rules or fixed principles are out of place, and it is exceedingly significant of the truth that he should have abstained from making this attempt. If he could have shown that any sort of demonstration is possible, he would have made his case good. Authority vanishes in the presence of demonstration. High as the authority of Newton is in science, it would be ridiculous to say that the wave theory of light must be rejected because Newton held the emission theory. If painting is a science, if it is a Liberal Art, academies must bow their heads and artists must admit that theoretical lecturers are their superiors. This, therefore, is the position of critics and essayists. It is necessary for them in some way to keep up the pretence that demonstration is possible, for without this they have no *raison d'être ;* but they find it exceedingly difficult to maintain this fiction, and the result has been that a very simple question has been kept out of sight by a lavish use of rhetoric and metaphor. An oracular air and an abundance of fine words are made to defend an untenable position.

Reynolds, in his essay on criticism, derives the wisdom of the connoisseur from two sources. He

first learned some rules of the Academy by convers-
ing with artists, and then matured his powers by a
tour in Italy.   Tours in Italy and other parts of the
continent have become more common since those
days, and travellers have ceased to prepare their
minds by a study of academic rules before starting.
The majority of the more recent travellers have taken
little interest in, and paid small attention to, art. A
hasty annual visit to the exhibition of the Royal
Academy has been for most of them their only
discipline.   At home they have been free to consult
their own tastes.   Not caring for pictures, they have
not thought it necessary to affect an interest which
they did not feel, and have been busied with other
matters.   Circumstances are changed on the continent.   Time hangs heavily on hand, and a tyrannical
guide-book declares that there are galleries to be
visited which are full of celebrated pictures.   The
traveller who would confess without compunction at
home that he does not know how many works of
Titian, or Rubens, or Velasquez, our national collection contains, fears, when abroad, the cross-ques-
tioning to which he may be exposed at *table d'hôte*,
and explores, partly out of curiosity and partly from
a sense of duty, the treasures which he is assured
are so admirable.   He finds, to his surprise, that
among these works, which are said to be priceless,

there are many as to which he can only perceive
that the subjects selected are uninteresting or improbable, and he is irritated and perplexed by the discovery.   He can understand that the bunch of roses
which his daughter has painted on a screen should
be admired, but cannot conceive why any one should
be enthusiastic about compositions, the colours of
which are gloomy and the themes unlikely or disagreeable.   This feeling had reached an acute stage
when Mr. Ruskin's *Modern Painters* was published.
A general sensation of relief was felt when there
appeared an authoritative declaration that it was not
necessary to admire all the pictures which, up to that
time, it was supposed good taste admired, and that
a free ridicule of such errors, real or supposed, as
could be discovered, was the surest sign of an enlightened mind.   It was for this reason that an
attack on Sir Joshua Reynolds was welcomed.   Of
those who applauded this attack not one, probably,
in a thousand knew precisely what Reynolds had
said or which the painters were that he admired
or disliked.   But his name represented the odious
academical authority which insisted that works devoid
of all apparent merit were excellent, and it was
pleasant to hear that he was inaccurate in his facts
and false in his principles.   But the argument was
based on the universal doctrine that pictorial instruc-

tion is theoretical in kind, and that artists are the
slaves of rules. We have seen what Sir Joshua
Reynolds thought about this. It seemed to him
that these rules are only provisional guides for
beginners, such as the rules which are sometimes
given in schools for the composition of themes, and
that the application of them to works of art was a
mistake of the connoisseur. If he was right, the
mistake made by the connoisseur was such as would
be made by an ignorant person, if, having examined
an Oxford prize poem, he were to infer that no
other form of poetry is legitimate. A mistake of
this kind is of course natural and even inevitable.
The problem being to ascertain why a composition
is admired which does not seem to be admirable,
the natural explanation which offers itself is that
there must be in it a strict conformity to some
theory. The attack on conventionalism which Mr.
Ruskin made was misdirected. It applies to an
earlier species of art-critic, not to true artistic
opinion; for, as Guido and Sir Joshua Reynolds
agree about the artistic view, their testimony must
be accepted. But it was superfluous, though just,
if applied to art-critics. The kind of criticism
described by Reynolds is obsolete, and a new kind
has taken its place. The connoisseur, we are told,
as he entered the gallery and before he had recol-

H

lected and begun to apply his rules, remarked that the boats were too little, and made some observations of that kind which Reynolds did not think it worth while to record. This kind of criticism has since that time been developed into a system, and is called realism. This word, used in this sense, is itself a proof that the system is, as a formally recognised method, a novelty. Realism is a term which, until quite recently, has borne in metaphysical speculation a totally different meaning. It is evidently now required in artistic criticism in a new sense, owing to the popularity of a new system of criticism.

I must once more introduce a quotation. A string of quotations makes, no doubt, a composition tedious ; but this cannot be helped. It is impossible without their assistance to make the points clear. I have put my view of the difference between artists and theorists. The latter indirectly maintain that painting is a kind of science, and that those who write on it are more likely to judge rightly than those who practise it. The passage which is appended shows that Alison had observed that a difference exists, but understood the question differently. He wrote as follows in the Introduction to his *Essay on Taste :*—" The various theories of philosophers may, and indeed must, be included in the two following classes of suppositions :—

" 1. The first class is that which resolves the emotion of taste directly into an original law of our nature, which supposes a sense or senses by which the qualities of Beauty and Sublimity are perceived and felt as their appropriate objects, and concludes therefrom that the genuine object of the arts of Taste is to discover and to imitate those qualities in every subject which the prescription of nature has made thus essentially either beautiful or sublime. To this class of hypotheses belong almost all the theories of Music, of Architecture, and of Sculpture, the theory of Mr. Hogarth, of the Abbé Winkelman, and perhaps in its last result also the theory of Sir J. Reynolds. It is a species of hypothesis which is naturally resorted to by all artists and amateurs, by those whose habits of thought lead them to attend more to the causes of their emotions than to the nature of the emotions themselves.

" 2. The second class of hypotheses arises from the opposite view of the subject. It is that which resists the idea of any new or peculiar sense distinct from the common principles of our nature ; which supposes some one known and acknowledged principle and affection of the mind to be the foundation of all the emotions we receive from the objects of taste, and which resolves, therefore, all the various phenomena into some more general law of our intellectual or moral constitution. Of this kind are the hypotheses of M. Diderot, who attributes all our emotions of this kind to the perception of relation ; of Mr. Hume, who resolves them all into our sense of utility ; of the venerable St. Austin, who, with nobler views a thousand years ago, resolved them into the pleasure which belongs to the perception of order, design, etc. It is the species of hypothesis most natural to retired and philosophic minds ; to those whose habits have led them to attend more to the nature of the emotions they felt, than to the causes which produced them." Alison's *Essay* is, as may be supposed, intended to support the view which he describes as the favourite hypothesis of the philosophic mind. It is unfortunate for him that he should be obliged to admit in his introduction that a different theory of causation is usually adopted by those who have most attended to the causes. The only comment, however, which need be made here on his statement is that Sir Joshua Reynolds did not contend that there is a " peculiar sense distinct from the common principles of our nature " by which beauty and sublimity are perceived, but thought only that ordinary perceptions may be quickened by cultivation, and may operate more satisfactorily when free than when oppressed by critical rules. It may be added that although

speculation about such questions was alien to the
philosophy of Greece, Lucian observed that artists
and the multitude are not at one about the mode
in which pictures should be estimated.   Zeuxis, he
tells us, once painted a picture of a centauress with
her cubs, of which he was vain.   He determined to
exhibit it, and invited the public to the spectacle.
Crowds came to gaze and all applauded ; but Zeuxis
after a time grew angry, and directed his servant to
remove the picture and allow no one in future to
look at it.   "These men," he said, "are admiring the
mere dregs of art, and all the real excellence is lost
on them."   οὗτοι γὰρ ἡμῶν τὸν πηλὸν τῆς τέχνης
ἐπαινοῦσι, τῶν δ' ἐφ' ὅτῳ, εἰ καλῶς ἔχει καὶ κατὰ
τὴν τέχνην οὐ πολὺν ποιοῦνται λόγον.   Lucian gives
what he conceives to be the explanation of Zeuxis'
grievance.   He may be right or wrong about this,
and there may be even no truth in the story ; but it
shows that Lucian had observed that artists and the
multitude judge from different points of view, and
that irritation may be excited by foolish praise as
well as by irrelevant blame.

There are, therefore, two views or theories about
the nature of painting, and a dispute which is not
found with regard to the other arts.   It extends
partially, but only partially, to statuary.   The chief
reason of this limitation is that there is in this art no

question of colour ; another reason is that painting
is the more popular of the two, and attracts more
attention.   Alison, describing the first class of hypotheses, observes that it includes almost all the
theories of music, architecture, and sculpture, and
adds, without naming painting, that to it belong
the theories of Hogarth, Winckelman, and perhaps
Reynolds.   This implies that the dispute is chiefly
about the art of painting, and in some measure
about sculpture.   It would be a great exaggeration
to affirm that the two factions or parties are distinctly separated.   In such matters absolute divisions
of opinion are not found.   But the tendency may be
observed, and the two parties may be described as
the artistic and literary.   Many artists belong to the
latter, though it is doubtful whether many *littérateurs*
belong to the former.   The essential characteristic
of the literary view is that it assumes a theory or
general principle which can stand as the major premiss of an argument.   A theory on which argument
can be based is not necessarily a universally-true
proposition, such as are found in strict or mathematical science, but if the theory is sound, must be one
which is ultimately true.   The principle now assumed
in criticism of painting is the realistic principle that
the most exact imitation is the best work of art.
It is the connoisseur's remark that the boats are too

little aggrandised into a system.   This, as Reynolds observed, is the way the multitude judge, and as this method has completely vanquished the earlier type of criticism, there is no longer any difference between the connoisseur and the multitude, except that the former may be more confident or skilful in the use of words.   The public are now supposed to form broader, safer, and juster judgments than artists, because it is well understood that the connoisseur agrees with them rather than with the artist.   This is because it is taken for granted that a kind of demonstration of the qualities of pictures can be given, and a definite test applied.   It may easily be observed how universal this opinion is.   If one who is supposed to be an authority in such matters, having expressed an admiration of some picture, were asked what he found in it so admirable, and were to answer that the forms and colours pleased him, but that he could say no more about it, it is certain that to most this would seem a foolish answer, and he would probably be given to under-stand that he would do well in future to abstain from expressing opinions which he could not justify. If, indeed, circumlocution were called in to help him out of the difficulty: if he were to envelop his answer in phrases about æsthetic grace, plastic power, and subtle harmony, it might be accepted, and the

listener might try to think that he had learned
something though he did not know exactly what.
But this only shows what language can effect.
These phrases are nothing more than a roundabout
way of saying that the forms and colours give an
indefinite satisfaction, the nature of which cannot
be exactly analysed.

CHAPTER III.

REALISTIC THEORY.

THOUGH Horace first put the comparison between painting and poetry in such a shape as to make it permanent, Aristotle had anticipated him in a more philosophic investigation of the relation of these arts to each other. There are, in his Poetic Art, the rudiments, though only the rudiments, of a theory of the Fine Arts. Creative, or poetic, art was, it is there said, born of the union of two tendencies which are innate in mankind. ἐοίκασι δὲ γεννῆσαι μὲν ὅλως τὴν ποιητικὴν αἰτίαι δύο τινὲς καὶ αὖται φυσικαί. τό τε γὰρ μιμεῖσθαι σύμφυτον τοῖς ἀνθρώποις ἐκ παίδων ἐστί, καὶ τούτῳ διαφέρουσι τῶν ἄλλων ζῴων ὅτι μιμηκώτατόν ἐστι καὶ τὰς μαθήσεις ποιεῖται διὰ μιμήσεως τὰς πρώτας, καὶ τὸ χαίρειν τοῖς μιμήμασι πάντας. σημεῖον δὲ τούτου τὸ συμβαῖνον ἐπὶ τῶν ἔργων· ἃ γὰρ αὐτὰ λυπηρῶς ὁρῶμεν τούτων τὰς εἰκόνας τὰς μάλιστα ἠκριβωμένας χαίρομεν θεωροῦντες, οἷον θηρίων τε μορφὰς τῶν ἀτιμοτάτων καὶ

νεκρῶν. αἴτιον δὲ καὶ τούτου ὅτι μανθάνειν οὐ μόνον
τοῖς φιλοσόφοις ἥδιστον ἀλλὰ καὶ τοῖς ἄλλοις ὁμοίως,
ἀλλ' ἐπὶ βραχὺ κοινωνοῦσιν αὐτοῦ. διὰ γὰρ τοῦτο
χαίρουσι τὰς εἰκόνας ὁρῶντες, ὅτι συμβαίνει θεω-
ροῦντας μανθάνειν καὶ συλλογίζεσθαι τί ἕκαστον, οἷον
ὅτι οὗτος ἐκεῖνος, ἐπεὶ ἐὰν μὴ τύχῃ προεωρακώς, οὐχ
ᾖ μίμημα ποιήσει τὴν ἡδονήν, ἀλλὰ διὰ τὴν ἀπερ-
γασίαν ἢ τὴν χροιὰν ἢ διὰ τοιαύτην τινὰ ἄλλην
αἰτίαν. There is, Aristotle says, a double propensity in human nature. 1. Man delights in imitating
and is the most imitative of animals ; 2. He loves to
compare things together and to observe similitudes.
Both these statements seem to be just. It has been
said by some that imitations were first introduced as
a kind of pictorial language, and that subsequently
a split took place, whence on the one hand arose
hieroglyphic writing and on the other painting and
sculpture. But the rude essays of prehistoric man
which have been discovered, make it probable that
Aristotle gave the true account. They seem to be
the result of an imitative tendency, and were not
meant for language. There is nothing unlikely in
this. As some birds imitate sounds, and as monkeys
imitate gestures, a further tendency to imitate forms
might display itself in a more highly developed and
more perfectly organised animal. But there was
joined to this an intellectual pleasure in making

comparisons. A proposition, which is a product of
the understanding, is a kind of comparison. Two
distinct ideas are in it set in relation to each other,
and when Aristotle says that man loves to perceive
that this one is that one, he is affirming that the
gratification which art affords is in part an intellectual gratification. This, he says, is the explanation of the fact that a pleasure is caused by imitations
of objects which are in themselves displeasing. The
problem to which Aristotle here calls attention has
ever troubled theorists, and is still unsolved. It is
indisputable that among the most admired of works
of art are found representations of objects and scenes
which, as realities, would be uninteresting in some,
and exceedingly offensive in other cases. In many
instances the attractive quality of a work of art may
be explained by the theory that it reminds the
spectator of some scene or object which would be
pleasant if beheld as a reality. This is notably the
case with many landscapes. Natural scenery soothes
and cheers the wanderer, and the painted landscape
operates in the same way, though in a less degree.
Johnson has expatiated on this topic in his Preface
to Shakespeare, and has shown how the memory of
pleasant hours spent under trees and by the river-
side may be revived by the painter's art. "Imitations produce pain or pleasure, not because they are

mistaken for realities, but because they bring realities
to mind. When the imagination is recreated by a
painted landscape, the trees are not supposed capable
to give us shade or the fountains coolness ; but we
consider how we should be pleased with such fountains playing beside us, and such woods waving
over us." Another kind of explanation is sometimes possible. Mankind are curious to know how
celebrated persons and places appear, and the
painter's art gratifies this curiosity. Johnson has
also advocated this view, and has said in one of his
essays that Reynolds would do well to abstain from
mythological scenes and keep to portrait painting,
not on the ground that he was more successful in
the latter style, but because likenesses of celebrated
persons are interesting, while no one could care to
know how Reynolds might imagine a scene which
was admitted to be purely imaginary. Johnson's
views are consistent with the realistic theory. It is
obvious that if the sole end of the art of painting is
to recall to the spectator's memory objects which
have afforded him pleasure, or to put before him
likenesses of realities which he might desire to see,
but has no opportunity of seeing, the most exact
representation must be the best work of art. Johnson
could put this view consistently and unhesitatingly,
because he never admitted the existence of the Fine

Arts as a class different from other arts, and did
not trouble himself about the *a posteriori* argument.
But those who have attended to the question cannot.
They cannot forget such pictures as Guido's St.
Sebastians, and such statues as the Laocoon, and
they cannot pretend that all who have admired such
pictures and statues have been pleasantly reminded
of the realities which correspond. Nor can they
easily contend that the sole test of merit in a work
of art is the degree of resemblance of the imitation
to the thing imitated. This is the realistic principle ; but when stated without disguise it deprives
the term Fine Art of all meaning. The careful
cabinetmaker who has made a chair or a table after
a given pattern has satisfied this test exactly as well
as the painter or sculptor. It leaves no distinction
between fine art and mechanical art. Yet every
modern theory contains this principle. All theories
come under one of two heads. They are either
some form of the theory which Reynolds ridiculed—
that is, are based on rules which are supposed to be
established by academic authority—or are based on
the principle that the most exact imitation is the
best work of art, which principle is supposed to be
established by common sense. The former kind of
theory is now effete, and all contain the realistic
principle, with the accompanying difficulties. There

is, indeed, an exception. Some theorists are content to play with words, wholly disregarding facts, and these encounter no difficulties. Diderot was one of this kind. His theory is that any perception of any relation produces a sense of the beautiful. " Le rapport en général est une operation de l'entendement, qui considère soit un être, soit une qualité, en tant que cet être ou cette qualité suppose l'existence d'un autre être, ou d'une autre qualité." (*Dictionnaire Encyclopédique*, Le Beau.) " Placez la beauté dans la perception des rapports, et vous aurez l'histoire de ses progrès depuis la naissance du monde jusqu'aujourd'hui : choisissez pour caractère différentiel du beau en général, telle autre qualité qu'il vous plaira, et votre notion se trouvera tout à coup concentrée dans un point de l'espace et du temps." " La perception des rapports est donc le fondement du beau : c'est donc la perception des rapports qu'on a désignée dans les langues sous une infinité de noms différents, qui tous n'indiquent que différentes sortes de beau." It would be superfluous to refute this definition of *le beau*, but Diderot has kindly provided a refutation, in case one should be wanted. Before stating his paradox he elaborately demonstrates that a perception of utility is not the same as a perception of beauty, and having triumphantly proved that this particular *rapport* does not

produce *le beau*, he goes on to affirm that any relation of any kind suffices. Some writers had argued
that there must be two kinds of beauty, one of which
belongs exclusively to the Fine Arts ; but when the
speculation which was fashionable in the eighteenth
century had called Burke's attention to the question, he reproduced the Aristotelian explanation.
Aristotle's words are the frame on which his *Essay
on Taste* is constructed. He does not, it is true,
avow this ; but he has in one place referred to the
Poetic Art, and his words so far resemble Aristotle's
as to make it probable that the latter was their
origin. It must be added that he could not well
have maintained a theory so palpably false, if he
had not been misled by a semblance of authority.
This essay was not an early or hasty effort. It was
written after an investigation of the Sublime and
Beautiful had forced it on his observation that there
was something mysterious in the charms which
painting and sculpture possess for their votaries, and
it is said that when he was urged subsequently to
expand and amend it, he replied that he had done
his utmost, and must leave it as it was. It is an
attempt to work out Aristotle's hint, and to show
that the realistic principle accounts for the peculiarity which Aristotle had recognised but Johnson
ignored. It admits that the nature of the thing

represented cannot adequately account for the qualities of the representation, but asserts that a sufficient explanation is found in the quasi-intellectual
gratification which is attached to the process of
comparing two things together.   This position, however, is narrower in Burke's than in Aristotle's statement.   The latter had the advantage or disadvantage
of writing in a language which confounded representation and imitation under one term, and though
his wider proposition is undoubtedly true, at least in
part, it certainly has not the truth which was required
for Burke's purpose, narrowed as it is in the *Essay
on Taste.*   He disfigured Aristotle's statement in
another way.   The latter did not profess in the
passage quoted above to offer a complete theory of
art as it is in a mature and fully developed condition, but was narrating its birth only, and added the
qualifying clause, "except workmanship, colour, or
something of that kind."   Burke omits this, and
turns a rational and probable account into an extravagant paradox.   He puts his argument as follows :—
" But in the imagination, besides the pain or pleasure
arising from the properties of the natural object, a
pleasure is perceived from the resemblance which
the imitation has to the original.   The imagination,
I conceive, can have no pleasure but what results
from one or other of these causes."   "When two

distinct objects are unlike to each other, it is only
what we expect : things are in their common way,
and therefore they make no impression on the
imagination. But when two distinct objects have a
resemblance we are struck, we attend to them, and
we are pleased." (*Essay on Taste*, p. 105, ed. 1826.)
A moment's thought shows that Burke had bid
adieu to common sense when he wrote this. If it
were true that objects which are unlike other objects
make no impression, eclipses, meteors, the aurora
borealis would be the most uninteresting of spectacles. On the other hand, if the perception of
resemblance is so potent as he says, a citizen of
London, as he walks down the Strand and looks
first at the houses on one side the street and
then at those on the other, should be in a con-
tinual state of ecstasy : when seated in his own
room his enjoyment should become more intense
as he glances first at the pattern of the paper
on one of his walls and then on the other, and
as he examines first one of his chairs and then
another. Or if it should be said that in these
instances he has been surfeited, and satiety has
blunted his sense of delight, he ought certainly,
according to Burke, to be flung into raptures whenever he meets twin brothers, and to feel as if he
were in the presence of a masterpiece, for the

I

resemblance in this instance frequently takes the beholder by surprise. Nevertheless, Burke adheres to his theory, though he cannot avoid incessant self-contradiction, and gives the following illustration :—"A man to whom sculpture is new sees a barber's block, or some ordinary piece of statuary ; he is immediately struck and pleased because he sees something like a human figure, and entirely taken up with this likeness he does not at all attend to its defects. No person, I believe, at the first time of seeing a piece of imitation ever did. Some time after we suppose that this novice lights upon a more artificial piece of work of the same nature, he now begins to look with contempt on what he admired at first, etc." (p. 107). This is a sample of the way in which Burke argues the case throughout. He has to prove that an increased admiration for works of art is the same as an increased perception of resemblance, and having cited instances where an improved faculty of detecting inaccuracy destroys the admiration which might otherwise be felt, assumes that he has made his point good. In support of this fallacy he urges that the term "improved taste " is inaccurate, and that "increased knowledge " would be more appropriate. "It is from this difference in knowledge that what we commonly, though with no great exactness, call a difference in taste proceeds."

" That the critical taste does not depend upon a superior principle in men, but upon superior knowledge, may appear from several instances." He is here asserting the view which Alison said was characteristic of retired and philosophic minds. The latter said that artists attribute to themselves a peculiar sense or senses, the existence of which is not recognised by the philosophic mind. Burke in like way implies that some believe in "a superior principle," and denies the existence of this principle. His theory, therefore, is the one which Alison incorrectly described as a theory which does not take into consideration the causes of the emotions, but investigates rather the emotions themselves. Alison thus described it because in his essay he made a futile attempt to bring music into the philosophic theory. The realistic theory does, in fact, erect a barrier between music and architecture on the one hand, and painting and sculpture on the other. Mr. H. Spencer has put forth a form of this theory in his *Essays on Education,* and it will be seen in the following passage that he is unable to fortify his argument by an illustration taken from music or architecture. " As we have above asserted, science is necessary, not only for the most successful production, but also for the full appreciation of the Fine Arts. In what consists the greater ability of a man than of a child to perceive the beauties of a picture, unless it is in his more extended knowledge of those truths in nature or life which the picture renders? How happens a cultivated gentleman to enjoy a fine poem so much more than a boor does, if it is not because his wider acquaintance with objects and actions enables him to see in the poem much that the boor cannot see? And if, as is here so obvious, there must be some familiarity with the things represented before the representation can be appreciated, then the representation can be completely appreciated only when the things represented are completely understood. The fact is that every additional truth which a work of art expresses gives an additional pleasure to the percipient mind, a pleasure that is missed by those ignorant of this truth. The more realities an artist indicates in any given amount of work the more faculties does he appeal to, and the more numerous ideas does he suggest, the more gratification does he afford. But to receive this gratification the spectator, listener, or reader, must know the realities which the artist has indicated, and to know these realities is to have that much science." (*Education, Intellectual, Moral, and Physical,* p. 44.) Music and architecture are, in Mr. H. Spencer's opinion, as appears elsewhere in his writings, Fine Arts as much as painting and sculp-

ture and poetry ; and the argument which he has
here given is instructive as showing that theories of
art, as they are called, are only theories of the
mimetic arts. The way in which Alison twisted
the literary theory and the facts of the case in order
to bring music into the "philosophic" view shall be
described hereafter. It is a solitary and unsuccessful
effort, and may be passed over for the present. Mr.
H. Spencer, however, is straining a point when he
brings in poetry. John Stuart Mill was not one
who would be disposed to underrate the claims of
science, and he has recorded the growth of his own
taste for poetry in a way which accords ill with
Mr. H. Spencer's account. "The result (of reading
Wordsworth's poems) was that I gradually, but completely, emerged from my habitual depression, and
was never again subject to it. I long continued to
value Wordsworth less according to his intrinsic
merits, than by the measure of what he had done
for me. Compared with the greatest poets he may
be said to be the poet of unpoetical natures possessed
of quiet and contemplative tastes. But unpoetical
natures are precisely those which require poetic
cultivation. This cultivation Wordsworth is much
more fitted to give than poets who are intrinsically
far more poets than he." (Mill's *Autobiography*, p.
149.)

Mr. H. Spencer has said elsewhere that a complete theory of the Fine Arts will not be found in his writings, and that he only takes such points as come before him from time to time in the exposition of his scheme of philosophy. There are, I think, other passages which show that he would in some way have modified these words if it had been necessary for him to discuss the Fine Arts as a whole. Some qualification is plainly necessary. Ideas and realities are often painful, and it cannot be universally true that the works of art which indicate and suggest most realities and ideas afford the greatest pleasure. More of these would be suggested to a half-ruined speculator than to another by a picture of a rich man reduced to poverty, more to one whose friend had committed suicide or been murdered by a picture of a suicide or murder than to another. But it would be inexplicable, if true, that the gratification which art affords is enhanced in this way.

As the realistic theory cannot be defended by Burke's principle that a perception of resemblance affords a mysterious pleasure, other writers have endeavoured to invent modifications which may give it plausibility. One of these is represented in the *Laocoon* of Lessing. His theory is in form, but only in form, of the kind to which the connoisseur of

Sir Joshua Reynolds clung. Lessing begins by declaring that the authority of the ancient Greeks
cannot be controverted in artistic questions, and that
the research of the beautiful was their guiding prin-
. ciple.   This is nominally an appeal to artistic opinion.
But the substance of the *Laocoon* is composed of a
kind of equation between poetry on the one hand,
and painting and statuary on the other, and as the
possibilities of this equation are limited by the possibilities of language, the literary theory asserts itself
in spite of his intention.   Johnson took for granted,
without arguing the question, that painters should
imitate only pleasing or interesting objects.   Lessing's theory is the same, with the difference that he
insists more on the necessity of selecting such objects
as may be called beautiful, *i.e.* the forms and colours
of which are pleasing.   It is the same theory, but
put more ambiguously, and put in this shape it has
been often cited as a wise and profound saying.   Its
chief superiority over Johnson's is, in truth, that it
has less meaning.   Infinite confusion has arisen in
artistic speculation from an inaccurate use of the
epithet " beautiful."   The word is primarily applied
to forms and colours.   I do not mean that this is
the etymological meaning, for it is said to be derived
from *bene*.   But in common use the strict meaning
of it is a combination of forms or colours which

pleases. We can even speak of an isolated colour as beautiful, though one musical sound by itself would be called pleasing rather than beautiful. It is then employed metaphorically of other combinations which please in other ways. A piece of music, a poem, or even a scientific demonstration, may be called beautiful. But the use of the word is figurative in these instances, though so common as to have almost ceased to be figurative. Lessing in his argument first employs it in the literal sense, passing over the fact that scenes and objects cannot be classified as beautiful and ugly. Diderot discussing the theory of Batteux, who composed an essay called *Les Arts réduits à un même Principe*, observed " M. L'Abbé Batteux rappelle tous les principes des Beaux Arts à l'imitation de la belle nature, mais il ne nous apprend pas ce que c'est la belle nature." ("Le Beau," p. 445.) This objection applies to Lessing. But he extricates himself by that fertile cause of fallacy, the use of abstract instead of concrete terms. " Die Malerei," he says, "als nachahmende Fertigkeit kann die Hässlichkeit ausdrücken : die Malerei, als schöne Kunst, will sie nicht ausdrücken. Als jener gehören ihr alle sichtbaren Gegenstände zu : als dieser schliesst sie sich nur auf diejenigen Gegenstände ein, welche angenehme Empfindungen erwecken." (*Laocoon*, chap. xxiv.) It sounds reasonable to say that the artist must not express ugliness ; but it is not practicable to arrange objects in composite scenes so that all which may be called ugly shall be excluded. This may, perhaps, be accomplished in portrait painting, and the absurdity of the' result is here evident. No one would call the old men and women whom Rembrandt painted beautiful, and all, or almost all, Rembrandt's portraits would be rejected from the list of works of Fine Art if Lessing's definition were accepted. In like manner, if the general impression produced by a scene is taken as the test, Rembrandt's picture of the Anatomical School would be excluded. Any one who had just quitted a dissection would be thought insane if he were to comment on the beauty and the charm of the spectacle, and, according to Lessing, this picture does not come under the category of Fine Art. He would, apparently, not shrink from this result. The modern artist is, in his opinion, depraved in his tastes, and we must revert to ancient Greece to find human nature immaculate. Yet, even ancient Greece, he says, was not quite faultless. It had its Pauson and its Pireicus, who turned aside from the pursuit of the beautiful. But Pauson, he adds, was rightly punished for his depravity. He lived despised, and died in poverty and contempt. Those who have read Lessing's biography will see here a singular illustration of the sway which a pet theory exercises on its owner.   He spent the earlier part of his life in protesting against the doctrine that worldly success can be taken as a criterion of merit, or that a scholar should be diverted from his pursuits by mercenary considerations ; but because this poor painter neglected the path which might have led to fame and riches, to follow the bent of his own genius, Lessing exults ferociously at the thought of his failure. But Lessing was perverting history.   He took for granted that a Pauson whom Aristophanes names was Pauson the painter, a conjecture which nothing supports.   Both Lucian and Aristotle speak of the painter in a way which makes it probable that he was successful.   It is allowed by all that Pireicus was famous and wealthy.   But scanty as our know-ledge of Greek painting is, other cases may be found which refute Lessing, and are omitted by him. Lucian, in the *Dialogue on Calumny*, has left a de-scription of a picture by Apelles, in which the prin-cipal figure was one of Envy, personified as a man pallid and hideous, ὠχρὸς καὶ ἄμορφος, who advances to address another with monstrous ears.   Lessing. might say that the Greeks would not have counted this as a work of art.   But where is the evidence ? Again, in the famous series which Polygnotus painted in the Lesche at Delphi, there was, Pausanias tells us, a demon of a bluish-black colour, like that of a blue-bottle fly, who displayed his teeth. How would Lessing get over this? Would the grinning demon suffice to condemn the composition, or would it be all a work of art with the exception of the demon? Lessing's strange obliviousness of the plainest facts is remarkably illustrated in the following passage :—

" Der Dichter der die Elemente der Schönheit nur nach einander zeigen könnte, enthält sich daher der Schilderung körperlicher Schönheit, als Schönheit, gänzlich. Er fühlt es dass diese Elemente, nach einander geordnet, unmöglich die Wirkung haben können, die sie, neben einander geordnet, haben : dass der concentrirende Blick, den wir nach einer Enumeration auf sie zugleich zurück senden wollen, uns doch kein übereinstimmendes Bild gewähret, dass es über die menschliche Einbildung gehet sich vorzustellen was dieser Mund, und diese Nase, und diese Augen zusammen für einen Effect haben, weun Man sich nicht aus der Natur oder Kunst einer ähnlichen Composition solcher Theile erinnern kann." (*Sämmtliche Werke*, 1824, ch. xx., vol. iii., p. 212.) It is impossible to put two interpretations on this passage. Lessing declares that the reason why a description in words of the human countenance is less effective than a painted likeness is that in the former case an effort of memory and imagination is required which transcends human ability. The mouth, the nose, the eyes, are described separately, and the imagination fails to reunite the separate items. The truth of this can be easily tested. All which human ingenuity can effect in the way of describing the human countenance has been done by police agents, when it was usual to append descriptions to passports. If an agent had been endeavouring to verify such a description in the presence of a suspected traveller, what would have been his answer, if Lessing had explained to him that the feebleness of his memory and imagination was the sole cause of the difficulty, and that if he would verify the mouth, the nose, and the eyes, successively, the truth could be established as perfectly as by a well-painted portrait? It is manifest that this point of which Lessing makes so much is a minor and secondary one. The poet often describes the complexion of his mistress as whiter than snow ; compares the blue of her eyes to the blue of the sky, her hair to gold or the plumage of the raven, and adds that roses bloom in her cheeks. It is easy to remember these details and imagine the union of them ; the objection is, that they produce a monster when remembered and united. The proposition, moreover, with which Lessing begins, is as false as the explanation which he adds. The poet is not wholly precluded from physical beauty. Every thought and feeling which can be clothed in language

is the property of the poet, physical beauty among
them. He inserts the words *als Schönheit.* But
physical beauty is not excluded in itself more than
any other quality. All the world has admired
Dante's description of the distant bell which seems
to lament the dying day, which Gray purloined, and
physical beauty belongs to poetry in the sense in
which sound belongs to it. The amorous poetry of
every age would be robbed of three-fourths of its
contents if physical beauty were taken away. But
Lessing's misstatements are no incidental blot in
the *Laocoon.* They are the logical results of a de-
termination to frame a scientific equation, where an
exact analysis is impossible.

The earlier essayists stated their case and their
arguments plainly and failed in consequence. Their
speculations have amused their occasional readers ;
but every one has divined that they are only displays
of dialectical ingenuity, and they have produced little
practical result. The realistic or philosophic theory
has since been taught by experience, and, conscious
that it cannot stand alone, has summoned the artifices
of rhetoric to support it. Lessing was satisfied with
a brief declaration that there is a base propensity in
artists ; but this point has in more recent writings
become more prominent and been put more plausibly.
The art-critic has now his own school, and affirms

that his *protégés* and their works are more honest
and noble and conscientious than others.   The word
conscience has no meaning except in connexion with
a mental conflict.   A person who always follows his
own inclinations is not said to be conscientious,
however virtuous his inclinations may be.   When
an artist is commended as conscientious it is implied
that he has fought against and overcome some propensity.   The propensity in question may be the
almost universal propensity to indolence ; and, doubtless, it may be a merit in an artist, as in any one
else, to overcome this.   But the only way in which
a critic can judge about this is by an examination of
the work in order to see whether much labour has
been spent on it.   A great deal of the writing which
passes for art-criticism is made up in this way.
Works are often condemned as slight, and others
are praised on the score that there is in them evidence of care and labour.   Such criticism is not
applied to poetry.   The presumption is rather against
the poem, which is manifestly laboured.   This kind
of criticism, therefore, though not uncommon, needs
some disguise.   It too obviously leaves no distinction between the artist and the painstaking or conscientious artisan who makes chairs and tables.
The propensity, accordingly, which the realistic
artist overcomes is understood to be in part this

universal tendency to indolence, and in part a tendency to a vicious conventionalism, and in this manner his superior moral *status* is affirmed without too plain a negation of the characteristics of his pursuit. The question then obtrudes itself, why and how the practice of painting (for this is the art chiefly affected) should generate in artists corrupt propensities which can only be overcome by a virtuous self-denial? why they, if left to their own instincts, and deprived of the lamp of the art-critic, should be always wandering and deserting the right path? It would seem that Mr. Ruskin, after he had composed his *Modern Painters*, was perplexed by · this phenomenon, for he added a kind of explanation. Sir Joshua Reynolds advised the artist to generalise the forms of his foliage. This is downright heresy in the philosophic theory, and the question naturally offered itself, how Sir Joshua could have fallen into it. Mr. Ruskin gave a quasi-explanation in these terms:—" Is it to be supposed that the distinctions of the vegetable world are less complete, less essential, or less divine in origin, than those of the animal? If the distinctive forms of animal life are meant for our reverent observance, is it likely that those of vegetable life are made merely to be swept away?" This implies that the propensities of the " conventional " artist

are connected with a want of piety; but this is not
satisfactory, for it does not show why Sir Joshua
should only display this irreverent tendency in dealing with landscape.   Would Mr. Ruskin admit that
the practice of landscape painting is for some unknown reason specially apt to engender irreverence,
and that portrait and figure painting do not have
a similar effect?   The only other clue which can
be discovered is in a note about Sir George Beaumont, who has been made immortal by the unhappy
question, "Where do you put your brown tree?"
and the still more disastrous assertion that a landscape ought to resemble an old fiddle in general colour.
"Sir G. Beaumont," Mr. Ruskin says, "furnishes in
the anecdotes given of him in Constable's *Life* a
melancholy instance of the degradation into which
the human mind may fall when it suffers human
works to interfere between it and its master." These
passages are in the Preface to the second edition,
and they indicate that Mr. Ruskin felt a difficulty
about the hypothesis which his argument demanded.
It is, I believe, understood that he has withdrawn
them; but it is not sufficient to withdraw them and
put nothing in their place.   His theory crumbles to
pieces if he cannot explain the phenomenon which
he admits, and give some rational account of the
conventionalisms which he attacks, and which are

typified in the statements of Sir J. Reynolds and
Sir G. Beaumont.   The note on the latter shows
where Mr. Ruskin's theory lands him.   The expression "to suffer human works to interfere between it
and its master" is, as the context shows, a meta-
phorical description of the practice of collecting and
studying pictures.   Mr. Ruskin is an iconoclastic art-
teacher, who affirms that a taste for pictures produces
a degradation of the human mind.

Alison in his *Essay on Taste* has explained how
it is that artists corrupt the arts, and has given his
explanation with much clearness and a courageous
defiance of history worthy of a better cause.   Their
excessive vanity is the root of the evil, and the lash
of the critic is wanted to repress this foible.   "However obvious or important the principle which I have
now stated may be (*i.e.* that it is wrong to sacrifice
the beauty of character or expression to the meaner
and less permanent beauty which may arise from a
display of skill), the Fine Arts have been unfortunately governed by a very different principle, and the
undue preference which artists are naturally disposed
to give to the display of design has been one of the
most powerful causes of that decline and degeneracy
which has uniformly marked the history of the Fine
Arts, after they have arrived at a certain period of
perfection.   To a common spectator the great test

K

of excellence in beautiful forms is character or expression, or, in other words, the appearance of some interesting or affecting quality in the form itself. To the artist, on the other hand, the great test of excellence is skill ; the production of something new in point of design, or difficult in point of execution. It is by the expression of character, therefore, that the generality of men determine the beauty of forms. It is by the expression of design that the artist determines it.   When, therefore, the arts which are conversant in the beauty of form have attained to that fortunate stage of their progress—when this expression of character is itself the great expression of design—the invention and taste of the artist take, almost necessarily, a different direction.   When his excellence can no longer be distinguished by the production of merely beautiful or expressive form, he is naturally led to distinguish it by the production of what is uncommon or difficult ; to signalise his work by the fertility of his invention, or the dexterity of his execution, and thus gradually to forget the end of his art in his attention to display his superiority in the art itself.   While the artist thus insensibly deviates from the true principles of composition, other causes tend also unfortunately to mislead the taste of the public.   In the mechanical arts, whose object is utility, this utility is itself the principle by which we determine the perfection of every production. Utility, however, is a permanent principle, and necessarily renders our opinion of this perfection as permanent. In the Fine Arts, whose object is beauty, it is by its effect upon our imagination alone that we determine the excellence of any production. There is no quality, however, which has a more powerful effect upon our imagination than novelty. The taste of the generality of mankind, therefore, very naturally falls in with the invention of the artist, and is gratified by that continued novelty which the art affords it. In the mechanical arts, which are directed to general utility, all men are in some measure judges of the excellence of their productions, because they are in some measure judges of this utility. But in the Fine Arts, which seem to require peculiar talents, and which require, at least, talents that are not generally exerted, all men neither are, nor conceive themselves to be, judges. They willingly, therefore, submit their opinions to the guidance of those who, by their practice in these arts, appear very naturally the most competent to judge with regard to their beauty; and while the arts amuse them with perpetual novelty, very readily take for granted that what is new is also beautiful. By these means ; by the preference which artists are so naturally disposed to give to the ex-

pression of design above the expression of character ;
by the nature of these arts themselves which afford
no permanent principle of judging ; and by the disposition of men in general to submit their opinions
to the opinions of those who have the strongest
propensity and the greatest interest in their corruption, have the arts of taste in every country, after
a certain period of perfection, degenerated into the
mere expressions of the skill and execution of the
artist, and gradually sunk into a state of barbarity
almost as great as that from which they first arose."
(*Alison*, vol. ii., p. 110, ed. 1825.)   The lamentable
readiness of the public to submit their opinions to
those of artists who " have the strongest propensity
and the greatest interest in, the corruption of the
arts " has been, since Alison's day, in some measure
corrected, and it is understood now that the handler
of the pen, and not the handler of the pencil, is the
true authority.   But the regeneration of the arts is
still not quite accomplished, and some even now are
found who think that the proverb *cuique in suâ arte
credendum* may hold good in painting as in other
matters.   Those who think this have a right to
demand some better explanation than Alison has
given of the exception in which they are expected
to believe, and of the strange and unfortunate cir-
cumstance that there must be artists for the produc-

tion of works of art, and yet that the artist, if he is not constantly checked, will do all that he can to degrade the arts. Lessing gave this same explanation of artistic degeneracy. The artist, he said, is greedy of praise, and neglects the beautiful in order that his skill may be admired. But Lessing did not expand his theory as Alison has done, and did not explain why or how the artist could best secure the praise which he covets by neglecting the beautiful. The beautiful is the difficult, χαλεπὰ τὰ καλά, in the Greek proverb. Why should the artist neglect the difficult and accomplish the easy if he desires to be admired? We know, and Lessing must have known, that history answers him. Phidias did not neglect the beautiful, and the honour which Phidias received from his contemporaries might have satisfied the most inordinate appetite. But Alison built his theory on a false account of the birth of the arts, and in this way gave it an apparent consistency. The passage which has been quoted had been preceded by the following statement :—" In the infancy of society, when art was first cultivated, and the attention of men first directed to works of design, it is natural to imagine that such forms would be employed in those arts which were intended to please as were most strongly expressive of design or skill." Here Alison assumes that the arts of

design came into existence as arts which were intended to please.   It is true that the bare rudiments
may have had such an origin in the sense that the
inventor meant to amuse himself.   The designs of
prehistoric man seem to be of this kind.   But it is
untrue in Alison's sense.   The early Greek statues
were made in honour of the Gods, and the early
Italian pictures were painted in honour of the Saints,
and were intended to kindle the devotion and confirm the faith of the spectator, not simply to please
him.   Although, therefore, it may be "natural to
imagine that such forms would be employed as were
most strongly expressive of design or skill," history
forbids this pleasure of the imagination.   "This," he
goes on to say, "would take place from two causes.
1. From their ignorance of those more interesting
qualities which such productions might express, and
which the advancement of the arts could alone un-
fold.   2. From the peculiar value which design or
art itself, in such periods, possessed, and the conse-
quent admiration which it raised."   The ignorance
of these "more interesting qualities " (viz. the sanctity
of the Gods and Saints) did not exist, and the minds
of the spectators were, like the mind of an Italian
peasant at the present day, occupied with devout
thoughts in the presence of the image or statue, and
attached no "peculiar value " to the art or design.

On this unstable foundation, however, Alison con-
structs his edifice. "When," he proceeds, "any art
was first discovered among a rude people, the cir-
cumstance that would most strongly affect them
would be the art itself, and the design or skill which
it exhibited—the real capabilities or consequences of
the art they must be ignorant of. What the artist
would value himself on would be the production of
a work of skill. What the spectator would admire
would be the invention or ingenuity of the workman
who was capable of imagining and executing such a
work. What the workman, therefore, would study
would be to give his work as full and complete an
expression of this skill or design as he could."
(*Alison*, vol. ii., p. 69.)

The facts are inverted in this account. Though
the oddities of the Pre-Raphaelite painters were,
probably for the most part, simply the result of a
want of skill, the name given rightly indicates the
theory which justified them. The movement was
avowedly retrograde, and an attempt to restore
painting to the condition in which it was before
painters had corrupted it. The principle against
which Pre-Raphaelite art was a protest was this one
which, according to Alison, prevailed in the early
period. Undoubtedly, as regards the historical facts,
those who gave the name Pre-Raphaelite were right,

and Alison is wrong. The more interesting qualities, as he calls them, are supreme in the first period,
and the artistic considerations come later. But it
was only by some such perversion as this that he
could make his theory hold together, for it would
otherwise have been incumbent on him to explain
why artists allow the arts to progress up to a certain
point, and then begin to pervert them. There is,
according to him, no change in the artistic nature.
It is from the beginning to the end made up of pure
undiluted vanity; but the multitude, which is dazzled
and therefore captivated, as Macaulay would say, by
novelty, gives a fatal turn to this vanity after a
certain time. We return, accordingly, to the threefold division of opinion in Alison's theory. The
handler of the pen alone is trustworthy. Finally,
the arts decay in a mysterious manner. The decay
of the arts in Greece means principally, though not
exclusively, that after a time Greek artists ceased to
produce statues so excellent as had been produced
in the previous period. The decay of the arts in
mediæval Italy means that after a time such artists
as Raphael, Michael Angelo, and Titian, were not
found. This happened, according to Alison, because
in Greece all sculptors were the equals of Phidias ;
all painters in Italy the equals of Raphael, Michael
Angelo, and Titian. An excess of food caused a

famine ; a superabundance of water caused a drought.

The theory of mimetic art (commonly called Fine Art) is one and the same everywhere. Its principle is that the most exact imitation is the greatest work of art. This theory ends inevitably in some absurdity, because it is an attempt to account for a phenomenon by a denial that the phenomenon exists. The phenomenon to be explained is that painting and sculpture are Fine Arts. They are reduced to the status of mechanical arts, when the only merit which is allowed them is accuracy of imitation. But it will be said that there must be some other principle, and that all the speculative writers who have directly said or indirectly implied that theoretical discussion and criticism are possible, must have some profounder theory than this. Dogmatical treatment must not be confounded with theoretical treatment. Any one can dogmatise. But whenever it is admitted that criticism is dogmatical, credentials are needed. The lectures of Sir Joshua Reynolds are, in great part, avowedly dogmatical. His opinion was not disguised that artists of eminence, himself among them, have a right to say what they think, and that those whose experience is less would do well to listen deferentially. But if a critic cannot produce testimonials such as Reynolds could show,

his words can have little value if they are nothing
more than confident expressions of opinion. In
fact, however, critics do not admit that they are
only dogmatising when they write about pictures.
Their criticism is, or claims to be, rational or argumentative. When Mr. Ruskin attacked a certain
number of so-called classical landscape painters, he
offered a kind of argument, and his writings would
have attracted little attention if he had simply said
that he disliked these painters. The argument contained one fallacy which may be summarily dismissed.
He examined the works of the artists to which he
objected with a view to the discovery of every possible error ; described these errors with much exaggeration of language ; and assumed that he had
made his case good. Such a method as this is too
convenient to be legitimate. If the plays of Shakespeare are ransacked with a view to the discovery of
every blemish or flaw in the language or plot—if
every fault is catalogued, and every merit ignored—
if, then, Shakespeare is taken to represent the
Romantic Drama, it is easy to prove that the
Romantic Drama is vicious, and that Shakespeare
is the shocking example. But as it is impossible
to wade through all which has been written about
the principles of so-called Fine Art, in order to show
that there is in it only one principle (viz. the real-

istic), a different method must be adopted to settle this point. Let the writings of any author of repute, which have any bearing on questions of this kind, be examined in order to find some principle which can in any way be applied, so as to frame an argument. There is no English author whose works better answer to this description than Mr. Herbert Spencer's. I am, however, tolerably confident that the most general proposition of the kind required which can be found in his writings is the proposition that variety is agreeable. This, in his argument, illustrates the connexion between psychology and physiology. Moderate nervous exercise is, like moderate muscular exercise, pleasant ; exercise continued till fatigue supervenes causes discomfort. But when this principle—that variety is agreeable—is made the basis of a theory of art, it turns out to be a failure. It was part of the obsolete theory of Sir Joshua's connoisseur, and was Hogarth's theory, which has also passed away. Alison, upholding the "philosophic" theory, was obliged to dispute Hogarth's, and spoke of it as follows :—" The conclusions seem to lead to a very different rule for the compositions of beautiful forms from that which Mr. Hogarth has laid down in his *Analysis of Beauty*. ' The way,' he says, ' of composing pleasing forms is to be accomplished by making choice of variety of lines as to their shapes and dimensions, and then, again, by varying their situations with each other by all the different ways that can be conceived, and at the same time (if a solid figure be the subject of the composition) the contents or space that is to be enclosed within those lines must be duly considered and varied too, as much as is possible with pro-priety.' " (*Alison*, vol. ii., p. 36.) The saving clause, " as much as is possible with propriety," destroys the whole value of the theory. This is, perhaps, more evident in architecture than in painting. If the theory were worth anything, it would be an im-provement in the nave of a cathedral if every suc-cessive column and arch differed, not only from those which stand beside it, but also from those which are opposite ; and a room in which no two walls were parallel, and no two angles of equal magnitude, would be superior to a symmetrically-shaped room. Though it is not necessary that the proposition on which a theory is founded should have the universal truth of an axiom of Euclid, it must, if the theory is sound, be ultimately true. The principle on which political economy is based is that every one seeks his own interest. No one denies that there are ex-ceptions, and that philanthropy, conservative preju-dice, indolence, or other motives may interfere. But those who believe in political economy maintain that ultimately the egoistic motive asserts itself and triumphs. Those who deny this deny the claims of political economy to be considered a science. The principle that variety is agreeable is true, but has not the triumphant truth which a theory requires. It cannot be made the premiss of an argument, and consequently cannot form a theory. But, besides this, the only principle which can be found is the general proposition that the most exact imitation is the best work of art.

CHAPTER IV.

ARTISTIC OPINION.

IF it is granted that there is even a *modicum* of truth in the description of the two theories—the literary and the artistic—which has been given above, it will be allowed that the two parties fight on unequal terms. The one wields that all potent weapon, the pen ; the other makes a half inarticulate protest. The artist when he attempts to argue his case is of necessity a traitor to his own party, and has put on the colours of the adversary. The ridicule which Reynolds cast on the theory of the flowing line was intended for Hogarth, as true, and perhaps as great, an artist as himself. But Hogarth the painter was not Hogarth the *littérateur*, and his pictures prove that when his brush was in his hand he forgot his theory, and did not trouble himself about the flowing line. As the art of music is not an art of representation, the literary theory could not make so good a fight when it opposed the develop-

ment of instrumental music ; but reiterated assertions
always tell at last, and there has been of late a resus-
citation of the view for which Steele and Addison
contended, and which for a time the composers of
the eighteenth century overcame. Wagner's is the
great name which is cited in support of the literary
theory at the present day ; but when Wagner's name
is cited, it is well to remember that as Hogarth the
painter was not Hogarth the " speculatist " (as Johnson would have called him), so Wagner the composer and Wagner the speculatist are not necessarily
one. The argument which has been put without
any disguise about the advance of music is that as
the sonatas of Beethoven, and above all the later
sonatas, produce on those who listen to them the
effect which is produced by a fine poem, the cul-
minating point of music must be the union of poetry
and music. It is creditable to the vitality of the
literary theory that such a *non-sequitur* should pass
for an argument. If a name for this theory were
invented to correspond to the name Pre-Raphaelite
in painting, it should be called Pre-Bachian or Pre-
Handelian ; for Bach and Handel began the revolution of opinion which the work of Beethoven completed, and first silenced the enemy who sought to
oppose the progress which music was making.
There may be many who are attracted by a com-

bination of verse and music, who find little to gratify
them in music alone ; but it does not need much
observation or thought to see that when poetry and
music unite, each art must sacrifice something.   It
is allowed by all that at present Beethoven is king,
and that his compositions are unrivalled ; while none
can say that the *libretti* of operas and oratorios are
excellent specimens of poetry.   But as Alison alone
has attempted to argue the case at length, we will
see what he has to say.

This is his introductory statement.   " If I am
not mistaken, the real extent of musical expression
coincides in a great degree with this account of it.
The signs in the human voice are general sounds.
They express particular classes of passion or emotion, but they do not express any particular passion.
If we had no other means of intercourse or information, we might from such signs infer that the person
was elevated or depressed, gay or solemn, cheerful
or plaintive, joyous or sad ; but we could not, I
think, infer what was the particular passion which
produced these expressions.   Music, which can avail
itself of these signs only, can express nothing more
particular than the signs themselves.   It will be
found, accordingly, that it is within this limit that
musical expression is really confined ; that such
classes of emotion it can perfectly express, but that

when it goes beyond this limit it ceases to be either expressive or beautiful." (Vol. i., p. 262.)

With one exception, nothing can be clearer or more consistent than this statement. But having said that music cannot go beyond a certain limit, Alison is illogical when he adds that, if it does go beyond this limit, it ceases to be beautiful or expressive. Granting that two and two cannot make five, it is nonsense to add that two is a comparatively useless number when added to itself it does make five. Nevertheless this little logical escapade was absolutely necessary for his purpose. The literary principle is that the most perfect imitation is the greatest work of art. In Greek this can be applied to music without any change of words, but in modern language representation must be substituted for imitation. The principle applied to music must be that the most perfect representation is the greatest work of art. Having, accordingly, begun by saying that music can only represent classes of feeling, and cannot indicate particular passions, the logical inference in the literary theory would be that music is a worthless art. But the essay was written solely because in Alison's time it had become manifest that music is an important art, and some explanation was required of this fact. It was therefore necessary for him to contradict himself

L

in some way.   Having done this, he sails in smooth
waters, eluding the difficulty by a quotation from
Beattie.   " The general emotion," he continues, " of
gaiety, elevation, solemnity, melancholy, or sadness,
it is found every day to express, and with regard to
such general expressions there is never any mistake ;
but when it attempts to go farther—when it attempts
to express particular passions : ambition, fortitude,
pity, love, gratitude, etc.—it either fails altogether
in its effect, or is obliged to have recourse to the
assistance of words, to render it intelligible.   ' It is
in general true,' says Dr. Beattie, ' that poetry is the
most immediate and the most accurate interpreter of
music.   Without this auxiliary, a piece of the best
music, heard for the first time, might be said to
mean something, but we should not be able to say
what.   It might incline the heart to sensibility, but
poetry or language would be necessary to improve
that sensibility into a real emotion, by fixing the
fancy upon some definite and affecting ideas.   A
fine instrumental symphony well performed is like
an oration delivered with propriety but in an unknown tongue : it may affect us a little, but conveys
no determinate feeling.   We are alarmed, perhaps,
or melted or soothed, but very imperfectly, because
we know not why.   The singer, by taking up the
same air, and applying words to it, immediately

translates the oration into our own language. Then all uncertainty vanishes, the fancy is filled with determinate ideas, and determinate emotions take possession of the heart.'" This passage quoted from Beattie contains what Alison wished to say, but did not dare to say in his own words. He knew that his essay was composed because it was no longer possible to affirm that instrumental music can only " incline the heart to sensibility," and that words are necessary " to improve that sensibility into a real emotion." But the principle which he had undertaken to establish was that which is implied in Beattie's antithesis, " may affect us a little, but conveys no determinate feeling." He was resolved to assert that whatever conveys no determinate feeling is worthless in art, and it was incumbent on him to escape in some way from his own admissions and the obvious truth. He therefore got over the difficulty by quoting Beattie for the position which he required, denying the phenomenon of which his essay was a professed explanation. Having thus obtained what he wanted, he proceeds to argue the case on the assumption that music can and cannot express particular passions or feelings. The following passage is a sample of his method :—" If the Passion of Revenge, for instance, were expressed by the most beautiful composition of sounds conceivable, which either naturally or from habit were considered as expressive of tenderness, every man, instead of being affected with its beauty, would laugh at its absurdity." (Vol. i., p. 282.) Having already said that music cannot express a particular passion, such as revenge, he would not, if he were consistent, put this case. But the case being taken as it stands, what he says is untrue. Every man would laugh, if he laughed at all, at the folly of the composer who chose to spoil both the poetry and the music by an incongruous combination, but the absurdity would not belong to the music more than the words. Alison ends his argument with the words, " There cannot well be a stronger proof that the beauty or sublimity of music arises from the qualities which it expresses, and not from the means by which they are expressed." Perhaps he is right in this, but if so, his theory demands no further refutation.

We may pass now to the other side of the question and examine the artistic or anti-literary theory. It is, as put by Guido and Sir Joshua Reynolds, negative in kind. Artists deny the application of rules—the rule that the most exact imitation or representation is the greatest work of art—among them. The accusations made by the other side are various, though they generally take the shape of a sweeping charge that artists, as represented by

Academicians, are full of prejudices. These arise, in the theories of Lessing and Alison and many other writers, from vanity, and the extreme desire of the artist to obtain applause. On the one hand, it is said, the more interesting qualities of the object which is represented are admired—this is the legitimate kind of beauty ; on the other, the skill of the artist— this is the meaner beauty, and the artist is desirous that this meaner beauty should monopolise the spectator's attention. It would have been well if Alison had explained why, when mankind discuss works of art, they conspire to misuse words with the meaning of which they are familiar ; or why, if they do not misuse words, they should make a mistake about the nature of their own feelings which they do not ordinarily make. In every case, except in works of art, it is allowed that an admiration of skill and an admiration of beauty are distinct. When a natural object—a beautiful face or a beautiful land-scape—is admired, no one objects that a mistake has occurred, and that the spectator is in reality admiring the skill of the maker. Some, indeed, may have said that the perfect skill of the maker of all things ought to be admired rather than the product ; but it is not said that in point of fact there is a mistake. If, therefore, we waive for the moment the question whether artistic quality is or not a meaner beauty, it must be granted that there is a singular misapprehension prevalent, if it lies in an exhibition of skill. It is, moreover, a proof that Burke had reflected more deeply than Alison on this, that the former did not endeavour to give this explanation. Undoubtedly, the Aristotelian explanation which he substituted is equally false and more paradoxical; but this alone shows that Burke felt it impossible to fall back on the doctrine that the skill of the artist is admired. It must have occurred to him. To recur to an illustration given above, if one who had expressed an admiration for Rembrandt's picture of the anatomical school were asked why he admired so disagreeable a subject, the answer usually given would undoubtedly be, that he admired the skill of the artist in spite of the subject. The natural inference is the one which Alison draws, that the vanity of artists corrupts the arts. But though many who have gazed with admiration on this picture might give this explanation, it does not follow that it is the true one. The truth finds its way out in impulsive expressions rather than in after-thoughts which come when a reason is demanded. How fine! is the natural exclamation, not How clever! Again, if a visitor at some strange place were invited to make an excursion to see a beautiful scene, and were shown at the end of his journey a

half-ruined cottage, with an old woman seated in the
doorway, he would think that he had been made the
victim of a practical joke. The same person, if he
found hanging on the wall of the room a well-painted
picture of the same scene, might exclaim, How
charming! Here too, if pressed to explain why he
thought the representation charming, though he found
no beauty in the reality, he might say that he admired the skill of the artist. But, if so, why should
the words "how charming" rise to his lips, rather
than "how clever"? The admiration of skill is a
distinct feeling. The feats of the pickpocket and
the swindler sometimes excite it in a high degree ;
but no one falls into the error of calling their conduct fine or charming. It is not likely that such a
mistake should be made elsewhere. The solution,
however, of the qualities of works of art into the
more interesting qualities of the object, on the one
hand, and the meaner quality of skill, on the other,
is a part of the literary theory, though the form in
which it is put may be varied. As the theory is
that painting is a purely imitative art, and is not in
any way poetic or creative art, it has in the literary
theory all the characteristics of useful art. One of
these is this double interest. A watch, for instance,
may be regarded either as a machine useful for
marking the time—this is what Alison calls the more

interesting quality—or it may be examined and the ingenuity of the workman admired—this is what he calls the meaner quality. Now a poem contains a *residuum* quality. When *Paradise Lost* is laid down, or any other poem which may suit the reader, the sentiment which is left does not resolve itself into the feeling that on the one hand something has been learned, and on the other, that Milton, or whoever the poet may be, is a very ingenious writer. Moreover, although Alison, writing on music, for which he did not care, could wind up his argument with the assertion that "the beauty or sublimity of music arises from the qualities which it expresses, and not from the means by which they are expressed," no critic of poetry has said this. Horace tells us that when a poem is broken up, we find in the fragments of language (*i.e.* in the means by which thoughts are expressed) the scattered limbs of the poet, and it would be strange if Alison or any other competent writer were to deny that all the great poets—with Shakespeare at their head—are distinguished by beauty of language. This beauty in poetry is not said to be a mean beauty, and is not said to be vainglorious display of cleverness. Nor is it said that poets corrupt their own art. Alison's theory of music, worked out on lines parallel to the argument about painting, would lead up to the result that the

great musical composers of the last century corrupted the art of music.   Perhaps, even now, some
who do not like classical music, though they enjoy
operas, think in secret that musicians are prejudiced
or affected, and that academical propensities interfere
with the true development of the art.

It is impossible to find a better test of the value
of artistic opinion than the nature and origin of Sir
George Beaumont's brown-tree and old-fiddle theory.
Though no one will maintain that the most classical
and conventional of artists have literally obeyed this
rule ; though it is certain that if Sir G. Beaumont spoke seriously, he fell into the error of the
connoisseur, and cannot be taken as a representative
of artistic opinion ; though it is, on the face of it,
unfair to take Sir G. Beaumont, who was not a
professional artist, to be the mouthpiece of Academicians, and Constable, who was a professional artist,
to be the spokesman of the opposite party, still it
must be granted that there is described in the celebrated question and assertion a tendency which may
be observed.   Among recent artists Copley Fielding
is an instance.   There is no doubt that he had a
weakness for a brown tree.   We will examine the
facts in order to see whether a more probable
account of the matter cannot be given than that a
study of pictures engenders a depraved taste.   It

must be observed that in this question, as in Sir
Joshua's bad advice to generalise the forms of vegetation, landscape art alone is interested.   Sir G.
Beaumont was speaking of landscape alone when he
insisted that the general colour should be that of an
old fiddle.   Moreover, it will, I suppose, not be disputed that he was speaking of the nearer parts of
the landscape, and did not mean that the sky or the
distant parts should have this inexcusable quality.
Now the great distinction between figure or portrait
painting on the one hand, and landscape on the
other, is that in the latter greater differences of
distance are found than in the former.   In addition
to which the latter is a representation of things seen
in the full light of day ; the former, commonly,
though not necessarily, of things seen in the subdued
light of a room.   When the whole case is examined,
it will be found that a partial departure from the
natural colouring is required in landscape, which is
not requisite when the differences of distance and
the degree of illumination are less.

Leonardo da Vinci, of whom Hallam has said
that his scientific intuition strikes us with the awe of
præternatural knowledge, first announced that the
atmospheric blue is caused by minute particles which
reflect certain of the rays of light.   The interception
of the minor waves, which cause the sensation of

blue, tinges the setting sun red, because the interposed volume of air, in which these particles float, is
greater than when the sun is higher in the heavens.
Of objects which are seen by reflected light the
moon is almost the only one which is affected in
like manner. It is not absolutely the only one.
The snow-mountain irradiated by the setting sun
is of a more pure rose colour when beheld from a
distance than when seen from a nearer point of view.
The first and immediate effect of the atmosphere is
to colour distant objects red, not by an addition to
the red rays, but by a diminution of the blue. But
the particles which intercept the blue as it travels
from the distant object to the spectator reflect at
the same time the blue which is found in the
scattered daylight. This latter effect overpowers
the former, unless the distant object is much more
strongly lighted than nearer objects. Although,
therefore, the setting sun or moon, and the distant
snow-mountain, are tinged with red, the ordinary
effect is that distance turns objects blue. But the
blue which has been intercepted is not exactly
replaced by the blue which the intervening atmosphere causes. The former was a varying quantity
determined by the nature of the thing, the latter is
a uniform quantity determined by the distance, or
volume of air which is interposed, and is in excess

of the former.   The latter, therefore, is practically
a ˜translucent screen, which not only causes a blue
tone, but also diminishes the light.   It is evident
that there is a diminution of light besides the addition of blue, for though the sun becomes crimson, it
is less dazzling than at mid-day.   But the painter
can only imitate the blue, and cannot also give the
stronger light of the foreground, yet, if he would give
a true representation, must take note of differences of
illumination as well as differences of colour.   Professor Helmholtz shows how this is done, and shows
at the same time, without intending it, how much
more valuable the true science of optics is than the
spurious science of painting.   The crowning victory
of the realistic principle has been in this question of
the brown-tree doctrine.   The honesty of the realistic
artist has been shown in a lavish use of pure green
in defiance of academical prejudice.   When the
point is examined it is found to illustrate the
warning of Sir Joshua Reynolds that when rules are
uppermost the perceptions are wrong.

I must refer the reader to the Lecture on Optics
and Painting, by Professor Helmholtz, for a full
elucidation of the principle.   He points out that
there are in natural objects different degrees of light
and dark which cannot be reproduced in a picture,
and though he has not discussed the question which

we have here, his argument may be transferred to it. Briefly put, it is that an increase of the red or yellow tones produces much the same effect as an increase of light. It is immediately obvious that the desire to make the foreground parts of a landscape, and especially the trees in the foreground, browner than they are in nature is justified by science. The artist is bound to imitate natural colours, but at the same time, if he altogether ignores differences of light and dark, the effect is false—false, at least, for the cultivated eye which has learned unconsciously and instinctively to require the twofold representation. The natural tree, before the leaves begin to fade, is green. Green with an infusion of red becomes brown. The brown tree in the foreground represents the greater illumination of the foreground. The only explanation, so far as I know, which has ever been given of Sir George Beaumont's doctrine (besides the explanation, which is no explanation, of academical prejudice) is that artists have a hypochondriacal taste for melancholy ideas, and love autumnal tints as suggestive of decay. The sentiment is rather of the opposite kind, derived from the vivifying influence of the sun's rays. The necessity for a departure from the natural colours exists in a less degree, if at all, in portrait and figure painting. Though it is not

scientifically accurate to say that there is no green
or blue in the human countenance, it is true so far
as colours can be classified and named. As, moreover, the differences of distance are so small in the
countenance that they have no practical effect on
the colour question, a direct imitation is possible
which renders the degrees of light and dark without
a departure from the natural colours. Thus it is
that the portrait painter has not been taxed with
conventionalism. The violation of natural colour is
apparent only where the complementary green is
charged with red. Clearly, therefore, no test or rule
can be applied. Taste alone can judge whether the
compromise is just. In any given instance it may
seem to one eye that too much has been conceded
to the illumination, and that the qualification of
natural colour has been excessive ; to another, that
the natural colour has been imitated with an excessive fidelity and the relations of light ignored.
Theory cannot teach the artist to steer between
Scylla and Charybdis, but, as Sir Joshua says, he
must have his perceptions right.

As a general proposition, it would be allowed on
all hands that perceptions are cultivated by exercise.
No one would dispute that the blind, obliged to
rely on the sense of touch, acquire an unusually nice
tactual sense, and can by touch discern much which

those who habitually use their eyes cannot feel.
Moreover, it would be allowed that the faculty improved by special exercise is, whatever the faculty
may be, for the most part more trustworthy than
the uncultivated faculty.   For instance, few or
none would deny that the professional taster of
wine is more probably right about the respective
merits of two bottles of claret, than the total
abstainer who has never tasted wine, or the boor
who has drunk nothing but beer.   But all general
propositions are reversed in the literary theory of
painting, and in the cry that academies are the
upas tree of this art, it is assumed that cultivation
perverts the taste, and that the natural (by which is
meant the uncultivated) taste is the true taste.   Yet
if the educated writers who repeat this cry would
reflect on their own art of literature and the patent
facts, they would see that the styles which they
admire are distasteful to those who have spent little
time over books.   The taste which admires Horace,
or Dante, or Milton, is an artificial taste, and seems
to the ignorant a perverted or conventional taste.
There is a presumption, derived from analogy, that
a practical study of colours improves the perceptions,
as other exercises do.   Nevertheless, there is a point
with regard to which a digression into a technical
question is necessary in order to remove a mis-

understanding, as it seems to me to be. It is quite certain that there have been many painters who have, in spite of an assiduous cultivation of their art, remained to the last bad colourists, or relatively bad colourists. The fact cannot be disputed because artists agree with professional critics about this. Critics commonly explain this by saying that such artists have no eye for colour, and this explanation is put as if it were so self-evident as to require no argument for its support. The critic lets it be seen that he is sure that if he practised the art, he would be, at least in this respect, superior to the artist whom he condemns. A closer examination of the facts would, I believe, show that some, if not all, bad colourists have had a very keen eye and an enthusiastic appreciation of colour, and that the defect in their own style is caused by a technical difficulty, and is not the result of a defective sense./

If any natural objects, remarkable for the beauty of the colouring, such as the plumage of birds, shells, butterflies, are examined closely, it will be seen that the colour is not absolutely homogeneous, but is, in the language of artists, broken. If, moreover, the colours are imitated artificially, with a neglect of the breakage of the tones, the combinations which are in the natural object so admirable become crude and offensive. But it is not easy in oil-painting to give the play of more or less complementary colour which is found in natural objects, and the difficulty is greater for those artists whose style is precise and hard than for those whose manner is comparatively indefinite. An inspection of a number of paintings will prove both these points. It will show that different artists employ different artifices, and that the same painter sometimes breaks the colour in one way in one place, in another in another place. It will, moreover, I think, show that the bad colourists have usually been artists who have aimed at great precision of outline. The difficulty in this matter which the oil-painter encounters is the exact opposite of that which the water - colourist finds. A mechanical painter can cover the wall of a room with a perfectly "flat" colour without the slightest difficulty. The water-colourist cannot obtain a square foot of flat colour without a long and tedious process. When water-colours are employed the tones break themselves, and one reason why a sketch is often more attractive than a laboured water-colour drawing is that in the finishing process the slight inequalities which add to the beauty too often disappear. Consummate skill and admirable taste, such as David Cox possessed, are needed to finish the water-colour

M

without impairing the effect which chance gave when it came to assist art. Although, therefore, it might be rash to affirm that there is no difference among artists of colour perception, it is equally rash to take for granted that a defective sense is common. It is more likely that a technical difficulty is the real cause. When the colour is not effectively broken some combinations which might otherwise be possible are impossible, and all are less pleasing than they would otherwise be.

Constable ridiculed Sir George Beaumont, and the accepted view about Constable seems to be that, although he was a professional artist, he was superior to the common prejudices of his order, and that the day which was dawning had dissipated some of the mist which usually obstructs the artistic vision. It is thought that he at least was guided by the realistic principle that the most exact imitation is the greatest work of art, and Mr. Ruskin hints that he even went too far in this direction. We have Constable's word for it that he did not obey the realistic principle. He said that his practice was to subordinate all other considerations to the massing of the lights and darks, and he made a number of studies which were entirely devoted to this end. But to mass the light and dark is to omit intentionally many of the forms

which can be observed in natural objects. This is
not realism. His sin was one of omission; Sir G.
Beaumont's one of commission; and this is the only
difference. Professor Helmholtz has discussed this
question as well as the previous question. He
shows, illustrating his argument by a reference to
Rembrandt, that the massing of the light and dark
is an artifice of which the purpose is the same as
the modification of natural colour. It is another
way in which the artist surmounts the difficulty
caused by the fact that the scale of light and dark
which he commands is narrower than the scale in
natural objects. Constable consciously employed
one artifice, Sir George Beaumont another; but
though the former ridiculed the doctrine that trees
should be brown, or landscapes have the colour of an
old fiddle, I do not think that Constable loved in
practice crude greens any better than his friendly
antagonist.

These questions do not go to the bottom of the
dispute between artists and non-artistic critics. The
two parties are separated by a wider chasm, and
apparently both have been reluctant to let the real
question appear. The real question is whether a
pleasure in colours or combinations of colours and
forms, of which no rational explanation is forthcoming, is or not contemptible. Artists have

hesitated to affirm consistently and plainly that their chief object is to produce such a pleasure, and that they select such themes for their pictures as are suitable for this purpose, rather than such as are interesting in other ways, because it is universally understood that intellectual pleasures are of a higher kind than other pleasures, and it has seemed to them that their art is lowered in dignity, if it is allowed that this is their chief end. On the other hand the "speculatist" who affirms that painting, as rightly understood, does not condescend to produce "a mere pleasure of sense," but causes an intellectual pleasure, comes into collision with facts which display their proverbially disagreeable attribute. He therefore shrinks from plain and candid statements, as well as his opponent, though for a different reason. He cannot help observing that for some reason, whatever it may be, there is a tendency in human beings to admire some colours more than others, and some forms more than others. The former of these tendencies is more plainly observable than the latter. Not only do human beings exhibit a preference for certain colours, which seems to be innate, as when infants or savages are attracted by bright colours, or when a quite uncultivated person admires the beautiful hues of a window of stained glass, but there is some reason to

think that the lower animals, as they are called, share
this taste. The fact therefore that preferences of
this kind may exist is indisputable. It is equally
clear that, the principle that intellectual pleasures
are the highest pleasures being granted, there is a
danger lest the art of painting may be degraded, if
it is conceded that any preference of this kind is
allowed to affect the judgment. The literary theory
is obliged for another reason to deny the legitimacy
of any test of this kind. When the test is accuracy
of imitation, argument is applicable. The representation may be compared bit by bit with the
thing represented, and it may be demonstrated, as
in the inductive sciences, that a given opinion is
right or wrong. No demonstration of error is possible, when colour preferences are admitted, inasmuch as it is impossible to prove that a gratification
is not felt which the spectator professes to feel.
But though the advocates of the literary theory
cannot admit that "a mere pleasure of sense" is
legitimate in painting, they cannot explain the
phenomenon which they undertake to explain (*i.e.*
the popularity of this art) when they deny it. They
cannot show why, if painting is, as it is in their
theory, nothing more than a kind of hieroglyphic
writing, any one should resort to so clumsy and
antiquated a device, when language would serve the

purpose better. It being granted that intellectual pleasures are the highest, the answer is obvious that if this is taken to mean that they alone are permissible, they can be obtained by the study of books much more effectually, and there is no reason why any one should paint pictures. The fact remains that pictures are painted and are highly esteemed. When a theory is in a difficulty of this kind, the greatest kindness which a well-wisher can do it, is to present it with a sonorous word which has no well-ascertained meaning. Germany has conferred this favour on the literary theory of painting. It has invented the word *æsthetic*, almost as blessed a word as Mesopotamia, and far more useful to the art-critic than the latter has ever been to the theologian. Vehemently as the friends of the literary theory have asserted that academical authorities are inaccurate in their facts as well as false in their principles, and that it is idle to hope for sound judgments except among the many who have never handled the pencil, they have never quite convinced themselves, and are conscious that they have not convinced others so perfectly as might be desired. They have at the same time been partly awake to the fact that the rudimentary colour-taste which animals and savages display is, in a more complex and developed condition, strong in the artistic nature, and is in some measure the secret of the vicious artistic propensity. The word æsthetic has enabled them to admit the fact without a repudiation of their own cardinal doctrine. It is understood that æsthetic is a science. It is defined in Roget's *Thesaurus,* as the science of taste, in Mr. Hay's *Essays,* as the science of beauty. Some, among whom I think Professor Helmholtz must be counted, appear to be sceptical ; but the German nation seems to have persuaded the greater part of mankind that there is a science called æsthetic. This discovery has been invaluable to the literary theory. It could not admit a mere pleasure in colour, but, as æsthetic is a science, it has no objection to an æsthetic sentiment. Thus the difficulty is kept in the background, and a scientific appearance preserved, while a non-scientific element is admitted.

The objection to a recognition of colour-taste is not simply the negative one that it is non-intellectual, but is in part positive, and is connected with the ascetic sentiment. The word asceticism usually appears in connexion with religion, and is the name of extreme self-abasement and self-denial. But the ascetic temper is found in atheistical philosophy no less than in religious creeds, and wherever civilisation extends the doctrine or sentiment that pleasures of sense are reprehensible is more or less manifest. So

widely spread and so deeply rooted a sentiment is
not easily intelligible, and the theological doctrine
that pleasures of sense are the favourite weapon of the
author of evil shows that a need of some explanation
is felt. It has been said by some who reject the
theological explanation that the ascetic sentiment
has its root in the desire of self-abasement in presence
of human potentates ; but though it may be true
that this is in part the origin of the feeling, this
account does not seem to be quite adequate if
taken by itself. Antagonists of the theory of evolution have adverted to this and some points connected
with it, and though they have not disputed the *a
priori* argument as enunciated by Mr. Herbert
Spencer, have insisted that there is a difficulty when
an attempt is made to reconcile with the theory the
facts which are observed. By the word evolution
most understand the one point in the theory which
most interests them, viz. the doctrine that mankind
are descended from an ape-like animal ; but the
general theory, as we find it in Mr. Herbert Spencer's
volumes, is a far wider one, and includes much as to
which the general principle is conceded by all. Although asceticism, as part of a religious creed, is
explicable as a display of self-humiliation in the
presence of a superior, it is found where this explanation of its origin is unsatisfactory. Sir Alexander

Grant, in his essays on Aristotle's philosophy, and in his *Essay on the Ancient Stoics*, has described the ascetic temper as a part of an extreme self-assertion. The philosopher would not condescend to a pleasure of sense lest he should degrade himself, and although it is undoubtedly true that moral sentiments become in time so purely instinctive that their ultimate application may be a contradiction of their origin, it may reasonably be doubted whether self-negation can so entirely change into self-assertion. But as the theory of evolution is that the five senses have been developed out of the sense of touch in conformity with the nature of things, it is a blot in this theory that a pleasure of sense should be repudiated, and it does not appear why a philosopher, who must admit that his senses are part of himself, should separate them from himself as a lower and relatively ignoble part. The evolutionist philosopher cannot fall back on the answer which so many have given, that the understanding is a divine *particula*, and that human nature has a double origin. In addition to this the facts do not fit in exactly. Shaftesbury has plainly put the argument, which many other authors have put indirectly, against the legitimacy of colour-taste. "If brutes, therefore, be incapable of enjoying and knowing beauty, as being brutes, and having sense only (the brutish part) for their own share, it follows that neither can man by the same sense, or brutish part, conceive or enjoy beauty; but all the Beauty and Good he enjoys is in a nobler way and by the help of what is noblest—his mind and reason." (*The Moralists: a Rhapsody, Characteristics,* vol. ii., p. 425.) Now among the pleasures of the brute creation there is not one which has been so often observed and described as the delight of the female parent in nursing and protecting its young. But the inference has never been drawn that this tendency is brutish and unworthy of a rational being. Why should the senses be condemned on the score that brutes have senses, if parental affection is laudable which the brutes so strongly feel? Obscure as this question is, an explanation—though perhaps only a partial explanation—suggests itself when the theory of evolution is closely followed. It is certain that either by the influence of the law of the survival of the fittest, or of some other law, the various races of animals adapt themselves in course of time to the circumstances in which they are placed. In conformity with this principle it is found that instincts are a sure guide when they are exercised under conditions which have been long unchanged, but are treacherous when the animal is placed in unfamiliar surroundings. It is almost superfluous to offer examples of a fact so well known. A striking example

is seen in the tendency of moths to burn themselves
in a lighted candle.   In the natural condition which
determined the instincts of the moth the only bright
lights which it could see were the stars and the moon.
It could not burn itself in these, and if they attracted
it and caused it to fly upwards, this habit might, by
facilitating the meeting of the sexes, or in some
other way, be beneficial.   When the lighted candle
—a novel element in the " environment "—is introduced, the instinct is false and injurious.   If, then, we
suppose that the moths could observe, remember, and
reflect on what occurs, and that lighted candles were
during a long period of time frequently found in their
favourite haunts, it is evident that a sentiment might
be formed that it is perilous to allow the instinctive
love of a bright light to influence their conduct, and
with this a general feeling that pleasures of sight are
dangerous.   Further, as the different senses form one
connected group, and moral sentiments are greatly
affected by the association of ideas, there might arise
ultimately the doctrine that all pleasures of sense are
evil in their nature.   Now, whatever theory may be
adopted about the origin of the human race, it is too
late to argue that man was created a civilised being.
It is certain that a long period elapsed before art
changed the environment, and that his physical
nature and instincts were immutably determined in

their more general characteristics, while the conditions
in which he existed were those which nature provided.   In order, therefore, to ascertain why, consistently with the doctrines of evolution, human
beings should think pleasures of sense evil, we must
ask whether man ever did for himself what he does
for the moth when he produces a lighted candle.   It
is evident that he did this.   When he invented
fermented liquors, with which nature had not provided
him, he kindled a torch which has burned ever since,
and in the flames of which mankind have never
ceased to singe their wings.   The direct and immediate effect of intoxication — the temporary loss of
reason and the temporary excitement of unbridled
passion — would in itself be enough to cast discredit
on the sense of taste and on the other senses by an
association of ideas.   But this was not the only way
in which the invention of fermented drinks affected
the moral sentiment.   It went hand in hand with
the art of cooking, and these two arts together have
given to banquets a degree of importance in the
ceremonies of civilised life which they could not
otherwise have obtained.   Though the moralists of
ancient Greece, like the moralists of the present day,
direct their invectives against the immediate effects,
all history shows that the remoter results of intem-
perate feasting have engendered a profounder anger.

The extravagance of the despots of antiquity and of
the kings and nobles of modern Europe has been
connected with revelry, of which feasts have been
the nucleus.   The oppressed and over-taxed peasant
or tradesman who could forgive the expenditure
which was caused by war could not pardon the wanton
self-indulgence which caused him and his children to
starve.   The connexion between tyranny and the
indulgence of the pleasures of sense is perhaps more
plainly seen in the history of France than anywhere
else.   But it is in some shape discernible everywhere,
and it is not strange that a passion, which begins by
stealing the brains and ends by robbing others of
their rights, should have stamped with an ineffaceable
stigma the whole family of the senses.   Among
irrational animals the laws of evolution work surely
and swiftly.   When savages are brought face to face
with an abundant supply of fermented liquor they
are speedily killed off, and if the art of making it had
been suddenly perfected before the moral sentiment
had time to ripen, it is probable that all would have
been destroyed, or a few left whose descendants
might either dislike or be uninjured by alcoholic
liquor.   But the intelligence which invents interferes
to thwart the summary execution of the law that the
fittest survive.   It may be that at some distant
period alcohol will cease to be injurious, or will cease

to be attractive or attractive in excessive quantities. But there is no sign that this consummation is at hand, and the instinct which is so trustworthy when nature's one drink is present has not yet adapted itself to the novelty which art has produced. Inasmuch, therefore, as the pleasure of eating and drinking is the most universally experienced and most influential of all the pleasures of sense, when the whole period of human life is surveyed, there is an ever-present and ever-increasing disposition to condemn all pleasures of sense ; and, paradoxical as it may seem to connect the cry that academies of painting are mischievous with the evil effects of intoxication and feasting, perhaps there is a connexion. There is no evidence that artists suppose a peculiar sense, which was Alison's account, but there is evidence and a general probability that they attach value to qualities of form and colour, for which they cannot give an intelligible reason. Although in the arguments which are framed the point to which prominence is given is that any preference of this kind is unintellectual, there is a secret assumption that any pleasure which is unintellectual is evil.

Shaftesbury drew a distinction between form and colour. It was proper, he said, that the artist should study form, and rational beings might without self-degradation admire the various qualities of form ; but

too much was conceded to the "brutish part" when
colours were studied or admired. It is not likely
that any critic at the present day would say this, and
most would indignantly refuse to admit that such a
doctrine is part of their creed. Yet I think that any
one who has been in the habit of scrutinising the
criticisms which are published in newspapers and
magazines must have observed traces of this opinion.
It is, however, noteworthy that a greater philosopher
than Shaftesbury drew a different line. It happens
that Plato touched this question, and expressed a
different opinion. " I do not mean by the beauty of
form such beauty as that of animals or pictures,
which the many would suppose to be my meaning ;
but, says the argument, understand me to mean
straight lines and circles, and the plane or solid
figures which are formed out of them by turning
lathes, and rulers, and measurers of angles ; for these
I affirm to be not only relatively beautiful, like other
things, but they are eternally and absolutely beautiful, and they have peculiar pleasures quite unlike the
pleasures of scratching. And there are colours which
are of the same character and have similar pleasures."
(*Philebus, Dialogues of Plato,* Jowett, vol. iii., p. 203,
ed. 1871.) This is a very different account. Plato
implies that the pleasures attached to some kinds of
forms are like the pleasure of scratching, *i.e.* belong

to the brutish part, and that colours are divisible in a like manner. Which of these two opinions is the sounder is a question which can only be answered by an inquiry into the origin of taste. But there are some comments on Plato's statement which may be appropriately made here. It is quite manifest that the eternally beautiful forms of which he speaks are the geometrical forms which can be exactly expressed in technical language. When he adds that a like distinction holds good among colours it must, I think, be supposed that he recognised the fact that some colour-names are more definite than others, but had not observed that even the most exact names of colours lack the mathematical precision which distinguishes some forms from others. The eternally beautiful forms are clearly the forms which belong to science. Not having carefully investigated the point he took for granted that the primary colours resemble them in this. But the passage is chiefly significant, as showing that statuary was not in Plato's opinion a fine art. Whatever may be the exacter definition of fine art, it must be allowed that it means generally admirable art. Statuary proper, however, as distinguished from architectural sculpture, absolutely repudiates the truly beautiful forms, and appropriates the forms which give a pleasure like that of scratching. It is impossible that Plato could have thought such

an art an admirable art. But, as will be more
perfectly shown presently, Plato held the literary
theory of statuary. It was in his eyes valuable solely
as a means of representation.

Although these distinctions have been drawn between colour and form, and between two kinds of
form, all writers on Ethics unite in affirming that
the two senses of seeing and hearing are of a nobler
kind than the three other senses of touch, smell, and
taste. There is a dispute about the relative rank
of the latter. Touch is commonly put at the bottom
of the list, but Professor Bain contends that it
ought to be placed above the other two. Writers on
these topics have not arrived at any certain grounds
for the relatively high estimation in which the
faculties of seeing and hearing, with their annexed
pleasures, are held. The question is intricate, but
I will endeavour to put briefly the points which
seem to have been most effective in giving them
their higher rank. The pleasures of seeing and
hearing are for the most part felt more feebly than
those of physical taste, and the ascetic sentiment
for this reason admits them to be less culpable.
But taste is more nearly identical with smell and
touch than with seeing and hearing. Touch com-
prehends many sensations of different kinds; but
except in the instance of heat sensation, which is

N

caused as colour sensation is caused, the three
senses of touch, taste, and smell, recognise only the
matter which is known to touch, and ignore the
hypothetical matter which transmits the waves of
light. The faculty of hearing resembles them in
this, but resembles sight in the peculiarity that distant objects are connected with it by a series of
vibrations. The two senses of seeing and hearing
are in this way specially connected with the understanding, which in theological theory is the highest
part as a *divina particula*, in evolutional theory, as
the most potent instrument in securing the means
of life. For though the sensation of warmth is
caused as colour sensations are caused, there is the
difference that temperature does not subdivide itself
into distinct sensations as colours and sounds do,
but is always of one kind existing in different
degrees. The two senses of seeing and hearing are
then connected with the understanding in two
different ways which has raised the reputation of
both. As knowledge advances, sight is ever taking
the place of touch. The ignorant person tests the
temperature of a fluid by putting his finger into it ;
the chemist puts a thermometer in, and observes the
rise or fall of the mercury. The savage estimates
the weight of a thing by the sense of muscular effort ;
the civilised man takes a balance and trusts to his

eyes.   Sight, therefore, is a higher sense than touch.
Different considerations give a dignity of a different
kind to the faculty of hearing.   The infant and the
savage think—rightly or wrongly—that the kind of
knowledge which the combined exercise of the
faculties of touch and sight provides for them is of a
poor and worthless kind in comparison with the
traditional knowledge of religious truths, family feuds
and friendships, benignant and maleficent spirits,
and all the general principles which determine the
conduct of life.   Knowledge of this kind is orally
given, and the faculty which is its recipient is raised
in esteem by the association.   It may often be
observed how strong the resulting sentiment is.
Some philosophers have thought that it would be
improper to commit to writing the profounder parts
of their wisdom.   Most pious persons think that a
sermon which has been read is an inadequate substitute for a sermon which has been heard.   Even
learned universities hold that the knowledge which
is contained in books acquires an added value when
imparted in professorial orations.

CHAPTER V.

TASTE.

IT has often been observed that opinions remain with some life in them long after the decay of the arguments which gave them their being. Few like to think that what has often been said can be altogether false. When physical science was in its infancy and the causes of the intermittent phases of the moon were not understood, nor how it affected the tides, it was natural to attribute to its influence variable phenomena for which no better cause could be found. Experience has slowly expelled the doctrine that the moon is the origin of lunacy; but inaccurate observers persist in thinking that it determines the changes of the weather. A similar persistence of false opinion may be observed in mental science, and though the kind of theory on which the science of taste is founded is obsolete, it is commonly said and thought that there is such a science. A few quotations must be introduced in order

to show what is said and thought about this. Burke
built his argument on the following foundation :—
" On a superficial view we may seem to differ widely
from each other in our reasonings, and no less in
our pleasures; but notwithstanding this difference,
which I think to be rather apparent than real, it is
probable that the standard both of reason and taste
is the same in all human creatures. For if there
were not some principles of judgment, as well as of
sentiment common to all mankind, no hold could
possibly be taken either of their reason or their
passions sufficient to maintain the ordinary correspondence of life. It appears, indeed, to be generally
acknowledged that with regard to truth and falsehood there is something fixed. We find people in
their disputes continually appealing to certain tests
and standards which are allowed on all sides, and
are supposed to be established in our common
nature. But there is not the same obvious concurrence in any uniform or settled principles which
relate to taste. It is even commonly supposed that
this delicate and aerial faculty which seems too
volatile to endure even the chains of a definition
cannot be properly tried by any test or regulated
by any standard." This argument may be put more
briefly as follows :—" With regard to a certain class
of questions, we find disputants ' continually appeal-

ing to certain tests and standards which are allowed
on all sides.' This is a proof that there is 'something fixed.' With regard to another class, it is
supposed that they cannot be 'tried by any test or
regulated by standard,' and there is not 'the same
obvious concurrence in uniform or settled principles.'
This is a proof that the latter opinion is erroneous."
But though it suited Burke to say that taste is a
word which seems to be too volatile to endure the
chains of a definition, this excessive volatility is not
usually attributed to it. Many have said, and all
except the advocates of the science of taste have
thought, that taste can be defined as a preference
about which argument is impossible. The proverb,
de gustibus non est disputandum, is in substance a
definition, for every one understands that the *gustibus*
are likings or preferences. The figurative use of the
word taste is, in fact, one of the many pieces of
evidence of the importance of the physical taste.
Metaphors are borrowed from the stronger and
transferred to the weaker. Different shades of
colour are called tones because sounds have greater
effect on feeling than colours, and likes or dislikes
are called tastes and distastes, because the preferences and aversions which are connected with food
are stronger, more diverse, and more constantly experienced than any others. As these preferences are

inexplicable, taste is the name of an inexplicable
preference. It is no answer to this to say that
science has explained some, and perhaps may ultimately explain all. Undoubtedly it may. But the
meanings of words are fixed by the opinions of
those who use them, and "taste," with its equivalents
in other languages, has been defined without any
thought of physiological theories. The term *science
of taste*, is, therefore, a self-contradiction. Science
explains phenomena, *i.e.* connects certain particular
propositions with wider propositions. A science of
taste is an explanation of the inexplicable. We
cannot say with propriety that a mother has a taste
for her own infant, because the general law that
parents love their offspring explains the preference ;
nor that a man has a taste for his own horse,
because it is known that most persons esteem highly
that which belongs to them. But class preferences
of which there is no apparent explanation are called
tastes. As children have a taste for sweet things,
so it is said that some men have a taste for horses,
some women for children. The true meaning of the
assertion that there is a science of taste is, accordingly, that there ought to be no tastes, and as a
whole series of inconvenient facts intrudes when this
is said, it is not surprising that the world should
have eagerly adopted the use of the word æsthetic,

which it owes to Germany.   No one knows precisely
what this term means, and it can be employed without too plain an implication that there are no tastes
or ought to be no tastes.   Burke announced himself
as the founder of the science, and thought it necessary to demonstrate the possibility and utility of it.
An advance had been made when Coleridge composed a Preface for the *Encyclopædia Metropolitana*,
and he assumed, or affected to assume, that no doubt
could exist, though the more pliant word æsthetic
had not come into fashion.   He wrote as follows :—
" The relations of Law and Theory have each their
method.   Between these two lies the method of the
Fine Arts, a method in which certain great truths,
composing what are called usually the Laws of
Taste, necessarily predominate ; but in which there
are also other laws, dependent on external objects
of sight and sound, which these arts embrace.   To
prove the comparative value and dignity of the
first relation, it will be sufficient to observe that
what is called ' tinkling ' verse is disagreeable to the
accomplished critic in poetry, and that a fine musical
taste is soon dissatisfied with the harmonica or any
similar instrument of glass or steel, because the body
of the sound (as the Italians phrase it), or that effect
which is derived from the materials, encroaches too
far on the effect derived from the proportions of the

notes, which proportions are in fact Laws of the
Mind, analogous to the Laws of Arithmetic and
Geometry." Unfortunately Coleridge did not think
it necessary to specify a Law of Taste, but, leaving
the reader to find one for himself, informs him that
such a relation would be in the opinion of the accomplished critic of more value and dignity than
some other relation. This seems to show that if
there is a science of taste it must differ greatly from
most other sciences ; for it certainly is not usual to
consult the accomplished critic about the relative
value and dignity of the relations of hydrogen to
oxygen, and of two angles of a triangle to each
other. But in the latter part of the paragraph Laws
of Taste disappear, and Laws of Mind are substituted. The singular statement is then made that
the proportions of musical notes are in fact laws of
mind. Now a musical note may mean—1. A
certain musical sensation ; 2. A certain set of
vibrations which causes the said sensation ; 3. A spot
of ink on a sheet of paper which represents both the
sensation in question and the vibrations which cause
it. In which of these three senses the proportions
of notes can be laws of mind, is a question as
obscure as that more celebrated problem, whether a
chimæra buzzing in a vacuum can feed on second
intentions. The fact is that Coleridge was distorting

the undoubted truth that there is a mathematical science of music so as to make it seem to support his case, and it must be remarked that although he introduces the words "external objects of sight" in the first part, implying thereby that what he says is applicable to the arts of sight, he does not attempt to give an illustration which bears on painting or statuary. We will now come down to our own time. It is a curious and suspicious fact that although Burke undertook to frame a science of taste, and Coleridge thought there was such a science, a French author who died not long ago imagined that it had been reserved for him to enunciate the principles of this science. M. Charles Blanc has explained in the Introduction to his *Grammaire des Arts du Dessin*, why he thought it necessary to compose this treatise. The conversation at a dinner party had turned on the Fine Arts, and after some discussion—"Cependant parmi les hommes éminents de la compagnie il s'en trouva qui, un peu confus de ne pas avoir les notions les plus élémentaires de l'art, demandèrent s'il existait un livre ou ces notions fussent presentées sous une forme simple, claire, et assez brève pour ménager le temps du lecteur. Nous répondimes que ce livre n'existait point, et qu'au sortir du collége nous eussions été heureux nousmême de le rencontrer; que beaucoup d'ouvrages avaient été composés sur le

beau ; qu'on avait écrit de traités sans nombre sur
l'architecture comme sur la peinture, et plusieurs
volumes sur la statuaire, mais qu'il restait encore à
conçevoir un travail d'ensemble, un résumé lucide de
toutes les idées que le monde a remuées ou que la
meditation peut faire naître touchant les arts du
dessin." If a science of taste can be constructed, it
is strange that at so recent a period M. Charles Blanc
should have sought in vain for an elementary treatise,
and that these *hommes éminents* should have been in
doubt on the subject. An elementary treatise on
Chemistry or Hydrostatics would have been easily
found. The excessive volatility which Burke thought
was an attribute of the word taste seems to be a
peculiarity rather of the science.

The term " laws of taste " is now old-fashioned, and
" canons of criticism " is found instead of it. This
change of phraseology is recommended by the same
considerations which make the word *æsthetic* desirable.
A law of taste is a self-contradiction, but the term
" canon of criticism " is free from this objection. It
is a term which, outside the province of taste, has a
well-ascertained meaning, and does not provoke an
instinctive revolt of the understanding, if such a
phrase may be excused, by its false ring. But the
improvement thus effected is only superficial, for
there cannot be canons without laws. An example

of a true canon of criticism is the rule, which seems at first paradoxical, that when two readings are found in ancient manuscripts, that one must be preferred which gives the less satisfactory meaning. This canon is derived from the law that all changes must have a cause. A cause can be imagined for the change from a less to a more intelligible reading in the desire of the scribe to make the passage intelligible ; but as such a cause cannot be imagined for a change in the opposite direction, the presumption is that the unintelligible reading is the older and more genuine. The law on which all modern canons of artistic criticism are based, is the supposed law that the most exact imitation is the greatest work of art. But the truth is cleverly disguised. Among the artifices which are employed for this purpose two merit a special notice. The first is, to lay down one or two trite maxims of morality, and to pretend that these are laws of taste. The art teacher lays a stress on the indisputable fact that careless and hasty work is less satisfactory than work which is carefully executed, and exhorts the artist or artisan to be honest and industrious. If teaching of this kind could be effective there is no doubt that it would be valuable, and other things besides the Fine Arts might profit by it. But the cart is here put before the horses. Good morals and honest enthusiasm may make good art, but cannot themselves be created by lamentation about the decay of art. Impotent, however, as such teaching is for good, it can work, and has worked, mischief. Artists and artisans who refuse to change their nature for one occasion only, in order to please æsthetic sentiment, are willing to compromise the matter by an imitation of the styles which are held up to them for admiration. Let the lecturer on taste make a bygone style fashionable, and they will not refuse to produce a superficial imitation which saves them the trouble of invention. Principles of morality are not laws of taste ; and, when dressed up as such, inflict an injury on morals as well as taste. Another disguise which laws of taste sometimes assume is that of self-evident and meaningless propositions. An example of this is the rule that colour should be harmonious. Such a rule applied to sound has a meaning because the harmonies of sound can be calculated, but applied to colour it only means that the combinations of colour should be pleasing, and is worthless. The test of colour-harmony is the effect which it produces on feeling, and it is understood that the colouring should be pleasing. But this rule, like the moral precept which gives birth to an incongruous mixture of different styles, may be mischievous, though powerless for good. A discord implies the presence of at least two elements. One colour by itself cannot be discordant, nor one musical note. The rule, therefore, that colour should be harmonious is not wanted if the colouring is mono-chromatic. When applied to polychromatic colour-ing its practical meaning is, that the risk of discord should be avoided by an exclusion of all well-marked tones, and that colour should be mono-tonous, if not absolutely monochromatic. The greater the variety, the greater the danger, and the decorator or artist who remembers this seeks safety by avoiding variety. With this rule uppermost his taste has not free play, and his perceptions lose their value.

The principles of the science of taste were first pro-mulgated when it was not understood that the likes and dislikes which circumstances form in individuals may be transmitted to later generations. Writers on this question thought that they had to choose between two alternatives: that either the natural causes which affect each individual must account for all the tastes of the individual, or that tastes have a supernatural origin. They had not observed that there is a process of hereditary accumulation, and that a faint influence extending through long periods of time may ultimately form strong preferences and distastes, for which there is no apparent reason. The inference which Burke drew was natural. If some

of the sentiments were shared by all, and were, as
was assumed, part of a prearranged design, it was
reasonable to suppose that there must be some way
by which minor differences could be reconciled to
each other. So long as this theory was deemed
incontrovertible, and one party endeavoured to prove
that the individual's experience of utility determined
the individual's tastes, the other, that an experience
of utility has no effect on tastes, and that they have
all a supernatural origin, the truth could not be
ascertained. Hutcheson, maintaining the view, sound
in itself, that the tastes of each individual cannot be
explained by the experience of each individual, overstated the case as follows :—" Custom can never
give us any idea of a sense different from those
which we had antecedent to it. It will never make
the blind approve objects as coloured, or those who
have no taste approve meats as delicious, however
much they might approve them as strengthening or
exhilarating" (p. 88, ed. 1726). "Our sense of
pleasure is antecedent to advantage and interest,
and is the foundation of it" (p. 113). It is, of
course, true that custom can never make the blind
approve objects as coloured, as there can be no
custom in this case ; and, in like manner, those who
have no taste (if by this is intended those who are
incapable of distinguishing by taste) cannot learn to

approve meats as delicious which they cannot distinguish from other meats. But the point which he is endeavouring to establish is, that taste cannot be affected by an experience of utility, and in this he is mistaken. An experience that a given kind of meat is strengthening or exhilarating does tend to make it agreeable to taste, and even many drugs lose at last their nauseous quality when the patient has often found that they relieve a sense of pain or discomfort. Hutcheson overstated his case, because his adversaries overstated theirs, when they endeavoured to prove that the tastes of the individual are formed by the individual's experience. This alternative has now vanished, and a rational theory of taste must admit two laws: 1. That a true cause operating during long periods may, though a feeble cause, produce at last, by a process of hereditary accumulation, results which it is at first sight inadequate to produce. 2. That a more potent cause, operating during a shorter period, may produce equally great results. But in both it must be assumed that a true taste, or purely instinctive preference, has a remote origin. For instance, in the example given above, although the medicine which is at first extremely distasteful becomes less offensive as its good effects are felt, the consciousness that this is the reason of the change of taste is not entirely lost. It

does not become a purely instinctive preference.
Another example of a taste which is being formed
may be found in architecture.   A wall which is not
vertical is displeasing to taste, but at the same time
there is a consciousness that the distaste is produced
by a sense of insecurity.   The taste is partly formed,
for no intellectual conviction that the slanting wall
is made secure by an external buttress, or some device
of this kind, suffices to make such a wall pleasant to
the eye ; but the taste is not perfectly formed, since
it can be explained, and is not a pure instinct.   An
instance of a genuine taste is the desire to make a
building symmetrical.   In many public buildings the
architect sacrifices convenience for the sake of putting
the chief entrance in the centre, with two sides which
exactly correspond, and all approve this arrangement.
This taste is so genuine or instinctive that no one
asks whence it comes.

Since all true tastes must have a remote origin,
we are obliged to suppose that all have their seat in
what Shaftesbury called the pleasures of the brutish
part.   If they are directly traceable to physical causes
brutes must share them, and the natural causes which
have been effectual in man must be those which
affect irrational animals.   The first question, therefore,
which offers itself is, what are the chief pleasures of
irrational animals ?   These come under three heads :

O

1. The sexual passion ; 2. The pleasure of eating and drinking ; 3. The general pleasure which accompanies health and vital energy or vigour. The second of these pleasures, which has in the human race been unnaturally developed by the arts of cooking and making fermented liquors, does not seem to have contributed to the development of colour or sound taste directly, though it has aided indirectly, as both music and the arts of sight have been pressed into the service of festivity. But there is reason for thinking that in the insect tribe this pleasure has directly formed the colour-taste. Much has been written about the way in which the insects have given their colours to the petals of flowers, and flowers in return have formed the tastes of insects. The theory of evolution, however, does not admit that the vertebrates are descended from the articulates, and though many reject what this theory affirms, none will dispute what it denies about descent. Consequently human beings cannot have inherited colour-tastes from the insects. The origin of these tastes must, accordingly, be sought under one of remaining heads, or both of them. The first suggestion which occurs is that the vertebrates generally are active in light and are sluggish in the dark, and that in this way the third origin must be in some way the source of these tastes. This, more-

over, to some extent suits the facts of the case.
The colour-tastes are not strong or pronounced, but
are such as might be formed by an association with
the pleasure of moderate activity.　If there could be
developed a race of artists in the insect tribe, it is
likely that there would be a keen and passionate
delight in bright colours, corresponding to the strong
passion for food and the brilliant hues of the flowers ;
but though it is beyond all question that the primary
colours are more attractive than others to human
beings, and perhaps to other animals (to wit, the
bower-birds of Australia) this preference is not
very strongly marked.　Still an objection occurs
when the colour-tastes are referred to the influence
of light.　It seems to be thought by those who have
studied the question that the earliest progenitors of
the human race lived in woods and climbed trees.
If this is true we might expect to find a decided
preference for green, as the colour most constantly
present.　Even if no weight is attached to this
theory, green is a colour which is conspicuous in
summer and rare in winter, is frequent in such
places as are suitable to life, and unknown in arid
regions where life is hard and unpleasant.　Yet
language testifies to the fact that green is not a
very attractive colour.　Pure or true greens are
qualified as " coppery," " raw," and " crude."　These

epithets imply that there is a distaste for pure green, and they suggest an explanation. Their testimony to the fact cannot be disputed, but it does not follow that the implied explanation is true. An abundant experience proves that even at the present day a knowledge of the poisonous quality of most metallic greens is not common, and cases frequently occur of deaths and illness caused by pickles and sweetmeats which attract by their bright green colour. Nor is the implied explanation that uncooked vegetables are indigestible any more satisfactory. On the contrary, it is an object in cooking to preserve the true green colour; and raw green lettuce excites no feeling of repugnance. Some different association must have determined this distaste; for it seems to be highly improbable that any direct physical cause can be assigned. If red were a displeasing or relatively unattractive colour, it might be thought that the greater magnitude of the waves which provoke the sensation accounts for the fact. But as green stands in the middle of the scale, an explanation of this kind cannot be the true one. If, however, we pass to an examination of the other colours, it is apparent that an adequate cause can be found for the beauty of at least one of them. This is blue. This colour is only found in nature when the sun shines, and the vivifying influence of the direct rays of the sun is felt by almost all the animal world. When the clouds collect and intercept the rays of the sun the pure blue disappears and a canopy of lead takes its place. At the same time the vital energy feels the loss. Perhaps it is this association which has made "a leaden disposition" proverbial as a term of disapprobation, rather than the weight or poisonous quality of the metal. Maritime races have, it must be supposed, been more strongly affected than any others. The ocean reflects in deeper tones the azure blue of the sky, and all things conspire to make it a grateful colour to those who do business in the great waters. But the inhabitants of inland districts have felt the charm as well as the dwellers on the coast. Even in tropical climates blue is welcome, and gray is the companion, sometimes of oppressive heat, sometimes of superabundant rain. It is true that when the colours are arranged in order as more or less warm and cold, blue must stand at one end and red at the other. But practically the colours which cause a sentiment of coolness are those which incline to blue. Pure blue is lavishly displayed in the pictures of Titian and P. Veronese. It heightens the value of the other colours by contrast, but does not mar the sunny effect of the composition. Fromentin is an example of a modern painter whose taste for tropical

scenery and subjects was accompanied by a passion
for blue.   But the sunshine, which comes with the
blue sky as an invariable companion, annihilates the
pure greens of nature by an augmentation of the
yellow and red tones.   In rainy and gloomy weather
the foliage greens are true greens : when the sun
darts forth his rays they acquire an orange tint.
This seems to be true reason why a pure green
colour excites an instinctive antipathy.   It is the
artist who talks of crude and coppery greens as if he
disliked them ; and, as is shown by the practice of
colouring pickles, preserved vegetables, and sweetmeats, they are not repugnant as symptomatic of
poison or indigestibility.   They are emblematic of
the absence of the sun, as blue is the emblem of its
presence, and are suggestive of a malignant influence.
A blue eye is counted a beauty ; but Shakespeare
describes jealousy as a green-eyed monster.   This
same association is sufficient to account for the
milder charm which subdued or qualified greens
possess.   The warmth of the sun is not always
desired, and a colour which typifies its absence may
be agreeable.   An observation which Sir Frederick
Leighton made in an address delivered at Burlington
House bears on this question : " This is worthy of
notice, that we see in Egyptian painting the first use
of that combination of green and blue which was to

be the dominant note of so much that is most beautiful in Eastern coloured decoration." (*Times,* December 11, 1883.) A taste for a combination of blue and green, it must be observed, cannot be explained by the law of the decorator that the complementary colours form the colour-harmonies. Sir Frederick Leighton describes this taste as one peculiar to Eastern nations. I suppose that it cannot be thought a violent construction of the meaning, if we understand by Eastern nations the inhabitants of hot climates. It is inconceivable that a mere difference of longitude can have an influence, and it is generally allowed that green and blue do not form a combination which pleases the eye of the inhabitant of colder countries. But this taste which contradicts the accepted theory of colour-harmony perfectly suits the view that the warmth of the sun forms the colour-taste. Blue is universally desirable: green especially welcome to the inhabitant of a tropical country; and thus a concord is formed for the latter by the junction of two colours which harmonise less perfectly elsewhere. It seems to me that if it were true that the harmonic quality of colouring is determined by the composition of light, a pure colour should be distasteful when the complementaries are absent. This feeling, however, that something is wanting, does not arise. When any one is seated in a boat on the sea at a distance from the shore, he sees, if the day is fine, only blue of different shades.   But there does not arise a feeling that this uniformity of colour is offensive, unless the monochromatic quality is connected with a sense of weariness and a desire for change.   As a part of the desire to be on dry land again there may of course be a desire to escape from the all-surrounding blue. A single musical sound differs, as Professor Helmholtz explains, from a single colour with regard to this.   In the musical sound there are concords. There is, to borrow a term from physiology, a superfoetation of harmonics.   This does not occur in colour, and the total absence of harmonic quality in each separate colour makes it unintelligible that a single colour can please the eye, on the hypothesis that colour-harmonics are determined by quantity.   The difficulty entirely disappears when it is assumed that the warmth of the sun is the determinant cause, and that the sense of harmony is formed exclusively by an association of ideas.   Some of the rules which authorities give are completely justified when tried by this test.   For instance, orange and blue is said by Mr. Hay (*Principles of Colouring,* p. 57) to make a harsher contrast, and one which stands in greater need of modification than any other junction of complementaries.   (Orange and blue are complementaries in the artistic though not in the scientific arrangement.) These two colours are the chief emblems of sunshine. The flag which the sun unfurls in the heavens is of azure blue, and at the same time the increase of light colours all visible objects orange. The supposed harshness may be the excessive sentiment of glare and heat. But the truth is that it is almost a waste of time to discuss a question where sure *data* are wanting. Some other authority may have said—and I think it has been said—that blue and orange produce a specially agreeable mixture. The whole value of the theory of complementary colour is destroyed by the fact that science gives a different list of primaries. Though yellow and blue pigments mixed together produce green, the green rays cannot be resolved into yellow and blue. These colours united form white, and yellow itself is formed by the union of green and red. If the composition of the composite ray determines the harmonic effect, yellow and blue should form a satisfactory combination. The received opinion is that this combination is unsatisfactory.

Archæologists have proved that in Peru, as well as in the old world, gold was the emblem of the sun, and have reasonably conjectured that the yellow colour of this metal made it appropriate for this

purpose.   It is the colour which most nearly represents white, and is visible at a greater distance than
any colour except white.   Nevertheless it is the
symbol of melancholy.   To see things yellow is, in
French, as well as to see things black, the proverbial
description of a melancholy view.   This counter-
association must, I suppose, be derived from the
yellow tints of decaying leaves, and of the human
body in disease or after death.   But blue is in this
country the commoner symbol of melancholy, and
an Englishman in a depressed frame of mind is said
to have a fit of the blues.   Though this association
of melancholy and blue cannot be directly explained,
it may be understood as an instance of the law of
contrast, into which Darwin has resolved many of
the expressions in his volume on the *Expression
of the Emotions.*   Red and blue stand at opposite
extremes of the list of colours, and as red is the
emblem of joy, blue becomes the sign of melancholy.
Pink is a colour which must be put under the head-
ing of red, and a rose-colour is everywhere emblematic of cheerfulness.   There is a beautiful Greek
epigram, the sentiment of which has been expressed
in a thousand ways—

"τὸ ῥόδον ἀκμάζει βαιὸν χρόνον, ἢν δὲ παρέλθῃς
ζητῶν εὑρήσεις οὐ ῥόδον ἀλλὰ βάτον."

Johnson translated this—

" Soon fades the rose ; once past the fragrant hour,
  The loiterer finds a bramble for a flower."

But the epithet *fragrant* which is introduced does
not appear in the Greek, and the colour, not the
scent, of the rose has made it the symbol of pleasure.
Scotland's great poet gives us the clue to this
mystery.   The line—

" O, my luve's like a red, red rose "—

contains the history of the supreme attraction which
this colour possesses, and which has been transferred
to the whole class of red colours.   Both sexes have
submitted to the spell, and acknowledged the charm
of the ruddy hues of youth and health.   When the
Daughters of Jeruṣalem in the Song of Solomon
questioned their companion about the extraordinary
merit of her Beloved, she replied, " My beloved is
ruddy and white, the chiefest among ten thousand."
A more potent influence than the warmth of the
sun's rays has been at work here, and ancient history
reveals some singular traces of it.   Both in Italy
and other countries the archaic images of the Deities
were painted red, and the traditional practice was, in
some cases, long continued.   It has been said that
this practice was intended to please " the colour-
sense," by which is meant that these images were
regarded as pretty gewgaws.   This is not likely, and

the true explanation is that the colour red was sacred. All pristine creeds can, with some probability, be traced ultimately to two origins. They are, in different disguises, the worship of the sun and the worship of humanity. Yellow is the sacred colour of sun-worship ; red is consecrated to the worship of humanity. Red became, therefore, an exceptionally odious colour when the ascetic temper gained . possession of religion. The author of the *Wisdom of Solomon* betrays a profound antipathy in the following passage :—" Or made it like some vile beast, laying it over with vermilion, and with paint colouring it red, and covering every spot therein." The coating of vermilion was plainly offensive to him, and he describes in another place the voluptuary as crying, " Let us crown ourselves with rosebuds before they are withered." Afterwards a fresh association was added, and scarlet typified not only the sins of Babylon, but their punishment. When Dante in his Vision approached the Infernal City, he saw that the towers in it were scarlet, as if they were just out of the furnace. The universal custom of sacrifice is, perhaps, connected with this feeling. The pouring out of the blood represents the submission of man to a higher power, because red is the emblem of humanity. Philological research has supplied a curious confirmation of the view that red was a sacred colour

in primitive life. In the Ilchester Lectures delivered
at Oxford on the Slavic and Latin languages by Dr.
Carl Abel, it is said that in the Great Russian dialect
there was one word for *good* and for the colour red.
"Khoroschi, probably an etymological development
of the root 'kras,' meaning red, in the Little Russian
mostly keeps to the sensuous sphere, and, getting no
farther than a very slight metaphor will carry it,
signifies 'pleasing,' 'beautiful'; in Great Russian, on
the other hand, the word at a leap passes from the
signification 'pleasing' into that of 'good.'" (*Slavic
and Latin*, Carl Abel, Ph.D., 1883, p. 35.) This
shows that it is not an extravagant conjecture that
red was a sacred colour wherever the ascetic temper
had not triumphed. At the same time an association with warmth has always contributed to the
same result. Although pure reds are comparatively
rare in nature, the relatively high value which they
obtain, as light becomes more intense, and they are
contrasted with a blue background, tends to increase
their reputation. Such bright reds as may be seen,
as for instance in the petals of flowers, become more
brilliant, and all visible objects acquire a reddish
tinge. The fires of Phœbus and of Cupid are alike
symbolised by the reds. Bacchanalian songsters
have felt the instinct, and " red " or " ruby " is the
favourite epithet of wine. Anacreon in one of his

Odes declares that he will seek inspiration in draughts of red wine, πίνων ἐρυθρὸν οἶνον, θέλω θέλω μανῆναι, and the epithet "red" is not simply ornate, but indicates a fiercer passion. Though it is not easy to test the tastes of savages or children, a bright red is, I imagine, the most attractive of colours. It may be added that, if Darwin has rightly explained how nature has painted the birds, some influence must have been at work in the history of man which has not touched them. Though all the colours, scarlet among them, are displayed in the plumage of birds, this colour is not so common as it would be if they had ever identified good and red.

The taste of landscape painters for sombre colours may be in part a sentimental preference for red ; for they cannot altogether disregard the natural colours, and most of these become brown when infused with red. But the necessity, explained by Professor Helmholtz, of qualifying the tones in order to make the representation true, has most influence. They are compelled by their limited scale of light and dark to reject pure colours where these violate the relative truth. For this reason yellow is the colour which is most valuable where rightly used, most fatal when misapplied. It is composed of green and red, which contain all the larger waves, and is for this reason the aptest representation of light. The fashionable taste for sombre colours in dress has a different origin. It is in part caused by a just desire to select such colours as give the greatest value to the natural colours of the complexion, but is also a protest against the natural taste. Fashions are always in part artificial distinctions between the rich and poor, or the reputable and disreputable classes. The fashion of tight-lacing in women has this origin. Lecturers on this subject point to the Greek statues to enforce their maxims ; but it appears from a passage in the *Eunuchus* of Terence that a similar practice was usual in Athens, and that the natural shape was not thought genteel.

The tastes for form must have, like all others, a remote origin, and as the forms of the human body alone interest the untutored savage, these alone can have given them. Two peculiarities which distinguish animal organism are especially conspicuous in the human body. 1. There is an absolute bilateral symmetry. The eyes, the ears, and the limbs are pairs, of which the outer and inner forms differ, but which correspond as wholes to each other. The head, the nose, the mouth, the trunk, which do not form pairs, are characterised by the bilateral equality. A constant contemplation of this mysterious synthesis gave rise in early speculation to the belief that there is in the nature of things a law that " all things are double one against another." Many fantastic theories were formed in this way. It was supposed in one form of Pythagorean philosophy that there is a counter-world, ἀντίχθων, on the opposite side of the sun which corresponds to this world. The sun was supposed to stand in the centre, like the trunk of the human body, and to have on each side of it a world—two arms, that is. This idea of a centre with two symmetrical sides is the fundamental idea of architectural construction. Taste is shocked when it is violated in an important building, and even a lopsided room, though it may be quite convenient and quite secure, is displeasing to taste. But a large part of the architectural tastes are dependent on mechanical laws, and are semi-rational preferences which admit logical or rational criticism. Even colour may be rationally treated, within certain limits, by a reference to mechanical considerations. An association has been formed by experience between dark colours and solidity. The only translucent substances which are very common are the fluids air and water. As the solid substances which intercept light become in this way associated with dark colour, it is more suitable to taste that the lower parts of a structure should be dark and the upper light, than that this arrangement should be

reversed. I do not know whether this principle
would be conceded; but we have in London a
celebrated work of art which allows it to be tested.
In the Albert Memorial in Hyde Park a dark mass
is superimposed on a white basis. If this arrangement pleases the spectator's taste the principle is
worthless for him; if he thinks that the structure as
a whole wants dignity, this may be the explanation.
2. The second peculiarity of animal organism, which
is conspicuous in man, is the long series of curves of
different shape and magnitude which the muscles
form as they overlap each other. I think that the
mysterious attraction of "the flowing line," about
which so much has been written, must be derived
from this, and that Plato's instinct was true when
he said that artistic forms give a pleasure which
resembles the pleasure of scratching; for he meant
by this phrase what Shaftesbury intended by the
term "the brutish part." Hence the serpent has,
like the colour red, a double significance in religion.
Its folds represent the flowing line, and it was the
symbol of health in Greek mythology, and has been
deified in various creeds which are not historically
related to each other.

The musical taste is the most mysterious, and has
caused the most speculation. The popular theory is
described in the language of poetry by Dryden in

the ode on St. Cecilia, called "Alexander's Feast."
Cecilia drew an angel down: that is, the taste for
music has a supernatural origin.   The most faithful
adherents to the theory of evolution seem reluctant
to allow that Darwin's theory contains the truth; but
if it is rejected a supernatural cause of some kind
must be assigned to the taste for music.   The first
sentence of the passage which follows has reference
to the theory of musical taste which Mr. H. Spencer
gave : "This remark holds good whether we believe
that the various qualities of the voice originated in
speaking under the excitement of strong feelings, and
that these qualities have been subsequently transferred to vocal music, or whether we believe, as I
maintain, that the habit of uttering musical sounds
was first developed as a means of courtship in the
early progenitors of man, and thus became associated
with the strongest emotions of which they are capable
—namely ardent love, rivalry, and triumph.   That
animals utter musical notes is familiar to every one,
as we may daily hear in the singing of birds.   It is
a more remarkable fact that an ape, one of the
Gibbons, produces an exact octave of musical sounds,
ascending and descending the scale by half-tones, so
that this monkey alone of brute animals may be said
to sing.   From this fact, and from the analogy of other
animals, I have been led to infer that the progenitors

of man probably uttered musical tones before they had acquired articulate speech, and that consequently when the voice is used under any strong emotion it tends to assume, through the principle of association, a musical character." (*Expression of the Emotions,* p. 87.)

It must, I presume, be understood in this theory that a musical sound has an effect on feeling peculiar to itself, antecedently to, and apart from, any effect which association forms. It is certain that it may have, for dogs—at any rate some dogs—are made restless by musical notes, and testify to their feeling by howling, if they are not accustomed to them. The theory, then, is that the deeper effect which music has on emotion is the result of an association. Some peculiarities may be observed in musical tastes which suit this theory, but which cannot be, or at least have not been, explained in any other way. The most remarkable of these is that although women are keenly sensitive to music, have admirable taste,—being perhaps superior to men in this respect, —and are at least equal to men as executants, the long bead-roll of composers does not contain a single female name which would in the opinion of most judges be put even in the second rank. There have not, it is true, been many female sculptors or painters of high repute, but there have been and are some. But the singularity is that the art of music is

the one which women have chiefly cultivated, while
etiquette and custom have interposed some difficulties
in the practice of painting and sculpture. Let the
article on Pianoforte Music in Grove's *Dictionary* be
explored, and it will be seen that even in this department—the specially female province—composition is
almost entirely a masculine faculty. What can be
thought of this except that the males were the
composers when the taste was fixed, and have
retained their primæval privilege? A second peculiarity is that the taste for music displays itself in an
unaccountably capricious manner, and that we find
an absolute insensibility in one and a violent passion
in another, although nothing in accidental circumstances of life or education explains this difference.
Shakespeare, whose love of music was strong, seems
to have thought that a deficiency of this taste was a
symptom of moral depravity; but he was certainly
mistaken about this. Many amiable and illustrious
men, of whom Alison seems to have been one, have
been perplexed by the evidence of a feeling to which
they were strangers; and a distinguished author, no
longer alive, whom his very enemies, if he had any,
would not have accused of a turn for treasons and
stratagems, once told me that he was absolutely
insensible to musical quality. All the facts which
Darwin collected to prove the uncertain reappearance

of the characteristics of ancestors tend to give probability to the view that the uncertainty of musical
taste is an instance of this law. No scheme of
supernatural causation accounts for this caprice of
nature, nor can it be connected with natural causes
otherwise than by the supposition that these causes
have long ceased to operate. But intermediate
between the lover of music and the cynical adversary,
to whom it is " no better than the rattles of children,"
stands the doubtful friend, who is said to have a "bad
ear." This defect is of a wholly different kind from
the one known as colour-blindness. The latter
defect is caused by an insensibility of the nerves of
the eye to vibrations of a certain magnitude. The
unfortunate owner of a " bad ear " recognises the
intervals of the musical vibrations, but for some
reason does not recognise them correctly. As it is
impossible to compare one person's feelings with
another's, it is impossible to gauge the amount of
satisfaction which those whose ear is bad derive from
music. But as the defect seems to be an intermediate
stage between the true taste and the total extinction,
the presumption is that the gratification is fainter.
Unfortunately for the rest of the world it is frequently
sufficient to inspire a misplaced ambition to sing or
whistle tunes, and most persons must sometimes have
endured the torment of a prolonged melody in which

every note was false. It is a curious fact that
persons with a defective ear sometimes attempt to
study instrumental music.   When a keyed instrument
is selected the radical defect may escape notice for a
time, but is certainly detected where mechanism has
not fixed the intervals.   Professors of the violin have
often been obliged, either by a regard for their own
nerves or by conscience, to explain to their pupil that
there is a *pons asinorum* which he cannot pass.
False notes in singing are of course not always a sign
of this defect, but may be simply a vocal defect.

The science of taste was invented in Germany by
Alexander Gottlieb Baumgarten, and the oblivion
into which his name has fallen is a notable instance
of the ingratitude which mankind have often shown
to great discoverers.   It has, however, been in this
instance more pardonable than in some others, for
Baumgarten has, in his barbarous and uncouth Latin,
revealed the truth with a *naïveté* which must be inconvenient to those who would fain think that a
valuable addition was made to the list of sciences
when Æsthetic was introduced to the world.   " Æsthetica," he begins "(theoria liberalium artium, gnoseo-
logiâ inferior, ars pulchre cogitandi, ars analogi
rationis) est scientia cognitionis sensitivæ."   In this
passage we find the misuse of the term Liberal Art,
which has played so great a part in the dissemination

of this theory. "Æsthetic," he says, "the theory of
the Liberal Arts, inferior to *gnoseology* (*i.e.* true
science), the art of beautiful thought, the art of something which is analogous to reason, is the science of
sense-cognition." One step is made in this sentence : "Æsthetic is the science of sense-cognition."
The original meaning of the word *æsthetic* justifies
this ; but as this assertion would not by itself assist
him, he slips in the words, "the art of beautiful
thought." He must then connect sense-cognition
with "beautiful thought." This union is effected in
the following manner :—"Æsthetices finis est per-
fectio cognitionis sensitivæ, quâ talis ; hæc autem est
pulchritudo." "The end of æsthetic is the perfection
of sense-cognition as such ; but this is beauty." In
this manner poetry is connected with the other Fine
Arts, which was his object. The assertion that beauty
is the end of sense-cognition might, of course, be
disputed; but we will here pass over this question for
the sake of considering the question whether the
beauty of beautiful thought and the beauty of sense-
cognition are, as is assumed in Baumgarten's argument, one and the same, or whether this is only a
play upon words. An objection presents itself, even
if we take the case as stated by him. Æsthetic, he
says, is the *art* of beautiful thought, and the *science*
of sense. He is conscious of this difficulty, but gets

out of it by the help of an imaginary dialogue, the
most convenient way of conquering objections which
ὁ θέσιν διαφυλάττων has ever invented.   An imaginary opponent says: "Æsthetic is an art, not a science."
He reduces this supposed antagonist to silence by
saying, " These are not *oppositi habitus.*   For a great
many occupations which were formerly arts are now
sciences."   Nevertheless, as he progresses in his
argument, he becomes very candid, and makes the
following curious admission :—" Est, ergo, veritas
æsthetica a potiori dicta verisimilitudo, ille veritatis
gradus, qui etiamsi non evectus sit ad completam
certitudinem, tamen nihil contineat falsitatis observabilis."   (*Æsthetica*, S. 483.)   Other writers have
been bolder, and by affecting a complete certitude
have admitted a *falsitas observabilis.*   But his theory
is that science comes under two heads, which he
names respectively *Logico-dogmaticum* and *Æsthetico-
dogmaticum.*   The *dogmaticum* of the latter class
subsequently waxed very great, and swallowed up
the *æstheticum.*   Baumgarten's invention, however,
remained in obscurity until Richter adopted it, and
Carlyle seems to think that Richter's treatise on
Æsthetic is the one which will do most to keep his
reputation alive.   The treatise of Baumgarten was
not finished, and is, as it stands, little more than a
verbose recoction of the work known as *Longinus*

on the Sublime, dealing exclusively with poetic literature ; but his intention was to make good with regard to the other arts what he borrowed from Longinus about poetic quality. Richter's Æsthetic resembles it in this, though it differs in style, and the chief difference between the German and English modes of defending the science of Taste is that our writers hide in tortuous phrases their meagre principle that exactness of imitation is the test of excellence; the German writers discuss poetic literature, and tell their readers that whatever holds good of literature holds good of music, painting, statuary, and architecture. The most popular definition of the Fine Arts is derived from Baumgarten's treatise. They are said to produce The Beautiful, or the sense of The Beautiful. Although a pedantic fidelity to the original use of words is absurd when a change of meaning is wanted, it is not irrational to ask how it can have happened that the Greek nation never required such a use of the term *æsthetic* as was introduced by him. It is no answer that science has made great progress. The sciences which have advanced have been the physical sciences ; but if there is an æsthetic science in the modern sense, the Greek philosophers must have been blind to an elementary truth of mental philosophy. It is far more probable that facts have been strained in order to frame an explanation of a newly-observed phenomenon. Baumgarten's essay was written in the early part of the eighteenth century, when the strange fascination which the arts of music and painting exercise on their votaries was first observed, and was intended to account for this. Though he does not name Bach, and though Bach's great fame was not then established, it is not impossible that the wave of feeling which his genius had stirred had reached Baumgarten and prompted his speculation, as it is certain that Burke's *Essay on Taste* was the result of an attempt to discover what is the meaning of "the beautiful" in music.

Bouillet, influenced, like many French authors, by the fact that poetry is not included in the list of subjects which belong to the Académie des Beaux Arts, leaves it out, and defines the other arts as follows :—" On réunit sous ce nom tous les arts qui ont pour but de charmer les sens par la culture du beau. Les arts du dessin (Peinture, Sculpture, Gravure, Architecture), La Musique, La Danse." (*Dictionnaire des Sciences, des Lettres, des Arts— Les Beaux Arts.*) Definitions like this have been given of all the arts, including poetry, and Baumgarten's first point is that this definition takes in poetry. But if we omit poetry for the moment, and examine Bouillet's list alone, it is plain that the word "beautiful" is employed in an unusual manner.

Kant, Burke, and other writers, who have investigated the nature of "the beautiful," uninfluenced by
a desire to define the Fine Arts, have drawn a distinction between the Sublime and the Beautiful, which
is dropped in this definition.   Burke, who was free
from prejudice or bias in his investigation of "the
beautiful," arrived at the following result :—" The
beautiful in music will not bear that loudness and
strength of sounds which may be used to raise other
passions, nor notes which are shrill or harsh or deep.
It agrees best with such as are clear, even, smooth,
and weak."   It is not necessary to insist on the
perfect accuracy of this, and it might be varied in
some way ; but some distinction of this kind is drawn
by all who allow a difference between the Sublime
and Beautiful.   It is, however, quite obvious that
Burke's definition, even if modified, would entirely
condemn and exclude from the list of works of art
a large part of the compositions of Handel.   What
would he have said if informed that the Fine Arts
produce the beautiful, and that this in music agrees
best with notes which are clear, smooth, even, and
weak ?   But the objection does not end here.   The
Fine Arts produce emotions which exist only as
contrasted states of feeling.   The odes of Collins
and the music of Chopin cause a sentiment of melancholy ; John Gilpin and the music of Offenbach a

feeling of gaiety. When two contrasted states of mind are united under one term, all meaning is lost. At the same time it is clear that, unless this definition contradicted the common use of words, it would be worthless. Let us take a particular instance. Every one will admit that the word beautiful is employed consistently with usage when a face is called beautiful. But if one who had admired a beautiful face were to ask a philosophical friend to tell him why it was beautiful, and were to receive for answer the statement that it was beautiful because it excited a sense of the beautiful, the futility of such an explanation would be obvious. The definition that the Fine Arts produce a sense of beauty is satisfactory because as words are commonly used they produce some feeling besides the sense of beauty. Consequently the definition is not of a purely verbal kind, but has some meaning. The question then is what is the information which this definition conveys? Is it solely that the speaker chooses to use the word beautiful in an unusual manner, or does it cast any light on the nature of the Fine Arts? If the former is the answer, the definition is plainly worthless. If the only answer given when a definition is required of the word "beautiful," is that whatever the Fine Arts produce is beautiful, the whole problem remains exactly where it was. We learn nothing except

that the speaker chooses to call some things beautiful which are not usually so described. But if the
answer is that the definition casts a light on the
nature of the Fine Arts, this can only be true on
the hypothesis that there is some quality in works
of art called beauty, common to them all, which
makes them attractive ; in other words, that there is
an entity called beauty.   In this manner the science
of æsthetic requires a hypothetical sense called the
æsthetic sense.   If there is a " beautiful " common
to the sublime and the beautiful, and also common
to mental perception and to sense perception (which
is the assumption), there must be, besides the
ordinary mental perceptions and sense perceptions,
some other faculty which detects the beautiful in its
various modes of being.   The philosophers of Greece
were ignorant that there is an æsthetic sense, and
the acquisitions of modern science make it hard to
understand how there can be an entity called The
Beautiful.   There was a time when it was supposed
that sounds, heat, and colours, have what Coleridge
would have called an objective existence.   It was
thought that there were qualities in things which
correspond to feelings, and that sound, heat, and
colour might continue to exist after all sentient
creatures had been annihilated.   It is very well
known now that this is not true, and that these

sensations are caused by molecular movements of different kinds. Some metaphysicians go so far as to think that nothing would be left if sentience were annihilated ; but the doctrine that only motion of different kinds would be left is a deduction from ex- perimental science, and not a metaphysical specula- tion. . If, therefore, we must suppose that beauty is an entity, and that when the word beautiful is used something more is meant than that a given combina- tion of sounds, colours, or thoughts, produces a sense of gratification, we must suppose that the beauty of music can exist when no sound is audible, and of pictures when nothing is visible. This is the alter- native which meets the definition that the Fine Arts produce a sense of beauty. It either means that in works of art combinations are found which in some way gratify the spectator or auditor, in which case the definition is worthless, for it is admitted *ex hypothesi* or *vi terminorum* that the Fine Arts gratify ; or else it means that if all sentient beings were destroyed, there would remain, sole occupants of the universe, a number of vibrations and The Beautiful. The truth is that both this definition and the science of Beauty grow out of the ill-repute into which the physical sense of taste has fallen. Poets and artists present combinations which please the understanding and the senses of seeing and hearing ; cooks present combinations which gratify the palate. The former set of combinations may be called beautiful with propriety, but it is thought vulgar to call a good dinner beautiful. It is therefore supposed that there is a something called "beauty" in the former set of combinations, which does not exist in the latter, and the further inference is drawn that this something must have an appropriate science and be discoverable by a peculiar sense. But this kind of argument is unworthy of this enlightened age. The doctrine of modern philosophy is that words are an indication of the opinions of those who use them, but are no proof of the nature of things. The fact that the educated half of mankind agree to call poems, pictures, and pieces of music beautiful, though they refuse to call agreeable combinations of food beautiful, is only an indication that they recognise a general similarity in the feeling of gratification which the former class produce, and that they are unwilling to apply the same eulogistic epithet to the pleasure of eating and drinking. The *a posteriori* proof that there is no science of æsthetic, is as complete as the *a priori*. The word was introduced with the pretence that intellectual beauty is the same as sensuous beauty. There is absolutely no reason or excuse for the word *æsthetic* except this. Nevertheless writers on æsthetic are obliged to separate

the two uses, and take one or the other. The
German treatises on the rules of literary criticism
may be valuable or worthless, but there is not the
slightest reason for calling them æsthetic. The
term was introduced by Baumgarten with the pretext
that it was possible to lay down a set of rules which
would be equally applicable to poetic literature and
to the arts of sense. Neither he, nor any one else,
has yet done this.

CHAPTER VI.

POETRY AND PAINTING.

ATTEMPTS are sometimes made to distinguish between the meanings of the words fancy and imagination, though there does not seem to be any definite
distinction commonly recognised. We can speak of
the poet's fancy or the poet's imagination, where the
terms are eulogistic; and, on the other hand, the
ailments of the hypochondriac may be called either
fanciful or imaginary, where the epithets are contemptuous. Generally, however, imagination is a
word of more honourable meaning than fancy. It
is rather more contemptuous to describe the troubles
of the hypochondriac as fanciful, than to call them
imaginary. The chief difference is that imagination
is a term commonly applied to the fabrication of a
complete mental series, while the word fancy is used
when the images or sensations which occur are
separate and unconnected. Hippolyta, in the *Mid-
summer Night's Dream*, having heard the story of

the lovers who spent the night in the wood, observes that it grows to something of great constancy and witnesseth to more than fancy's images. Nevertheless, this story was, in fact, only a tissue of fancy's images which had grown to great constancy in Shakespeare's mind. But Shakespeare had in the previous passage employed the term imagination when describing the process by which such scenes are manufactured. The test, therefore, in this case is that the products of fancy want a rational connexion, while those of imagination are coherent. As the words are commonly used, this difference may be observed. If, for instance, some one thinks that he hears a sound which bystanders do not hear, supposing no explanation is forthcoming, the term fancy is usual ; but if some explanation can be suggested, if, for instance, the supposed sound is the voice of an absent friend, who is known to be in danger, the term imagination suggests itself. The delusion is here connected with the fact that there was a previous interest in the friend's safety, and, a cause having been found, imagination is the more appropriate term. There results from this difference a kind of antagonism between the two terms, as is implied in Shakespeare's words. Coherence is a test of truth, and though imagination as a mode of fancy gives to airy nothing a local habitation and a name, this airy nothing must be allowed to exist when all things conspire to affirm its reality. Science, accordingly, as well as art, employs imagination. A familiar instance is in astronomical observations where the existence of a planet has been imagined in order to explain a deviation from the calculated path of other planets, and observation has subsequently proved that the imagined planet is not imaginary. Even in a wider sense imagination may be allowed a place in science. If etymological propriety were strictly observed, the term would be employed only when the corresponding term *image* can be employed. But it is not thus restricted in ordinary language, and fallacies of argument always find their way in, when words are used in unusual senses. It is impossible to deny that sounds can be imagined, though sounds are not images. It is impossible to deny that the *gourmand*, who thinks with satisfaction of the approaching dinner, enjoys a pleasure of the imagination, though it cannot be said that the pleasure of eating and drinking constitutes an image. Ideas are imagined as well as images. Newton imagined a universal attraction extending through all space, and all who adopt the Newtonian theory exercise their imagination. They imagine not only suns and worlds which form images, but also attraction which exists as an idea. Those who insist on the identity

of art and science make the most of this fact. Great
discoverers, they say, are indebted to their imagination, like great poets ; and the inference is drawn
that Wordsworth and other poets who have betrayed
an anti-scientific sentiment are the victims of prejudice and ignorance. Nevertheless, an unbiassed
examination of the facts will prove that this sentiment is well founded. Science employs imagination
in so far as it is a part of every mental operation,
but always restricts its province as much as possible,
and does not allow fancy's images to be permanent.
Let it be granted that the thought of a universal
attraction extending through all space implied imagination, and that it has been invaluable in science.
It is not the less true that its value lies in the fact
that less is laid on the imagination in this theory
than any other. To take one instance out of many.
Nature was formerly said to abhor a vacuum.
Imagination was asked to credit an unknown something called "nature" with the feeling of hatred ;
then nature was credited with a power of pushing
matter in order to gratify this feeling of hatred.
Imagination rebelled when it was found that either
nature did not hate very large voids, or could not
gratify its feeling in such cases. If all the earlier
theories of every kind of motion are examined, it
will be found that, as in this instance, the imagi-

native element is greater than in the Newtonian
theory, and science accepts the latter for the sake of
what it excludes, not for what it adds.   Again, it
may be said that Darwin was indebted to imagination, that facts and observations may be accumulated
for ever, but would remain sterile if imagination did
not lend her aid.   The answer is still the same.
More was required of imagination when separate acts
of creation were supposed, and Darwin's theory was
welcome because it removed the necessity of imagining
these.   If imagination plays the same part in science
and art, the description of the creation must be a
blot in *Paradise Lost*.   It is, indeed, so obvious that
the imaginary is not co-extensive with that which
can be imagined, that an apology seems to be due
to the reader for adverting to this elementary truth ;
but so much misplaced ingenuity has been exercised
to prove that the Fine Arts, and especially the art of
painting, are arts of the understanding and not of the
imagination, that the point could not be omitted.
A foolish kind of optimism prevails everywhere, and
the heir of all the ages tries to forget that there is a
law of compensation, and that qualities have their
defects while defects have their qualities.   He hears
the praises of science chanted, and he will not endure
the suspicion that he is unscientific.   Art also is
lauded, and he cannot bear to have it thought that

he is unartistic. Every device is employed to bridge over the chasm, but the truth cannot be suppressed, and art and science protest in turns against the in-trusion of the other. Goethe was the incarnation of the modern sentiment, and he had what is called " the courage of his opinions." He declaimed angrily against Newton's application of mathematical science to the investigation of light, because he saw that science in Newton's hands was unpoetical. In his own theory, if it deserves to be called a theory, a number of *idōla*, or airy nothings, were forged, and he could not forgive the dry light which cast a doubt on their existence. He had imagined different kinds of colours, and he clung to the belief, that what he had imagined was not imaginary. Carlyle's senti-ment about history was similar. Dryasdust was his Newton. Dryasdust represents in Carlyle's writings the exact and laborious inquirer whose researches were inconvenient, because they cast discredit on the theory that history is moulded by heroic characters of an extraordinary type, and Carlyle wished, like Goethe, to leàve the imagination unfettered. We can distinguish between three uses of the word im-agination. There is first the sense in which the word fancy is more common. Here imagination is the supposed cause of the imaginary ; it is that which gives birth to a delusion. In the next place, there

is the poetic or artistic imagination, which, accepting
the imaginary as such, permits fancy's images to be
fertile, and thus connects them with other images.
There is, lastly, the imagination of science which
discards the imaginary, when proved to be such.   It
is with reference to the fertility of the artistic imagination that Shakespeare puts into one class the lunatic,
the lover, and the poet ; but inasmuch as the rational
connexion is less perfect in the lunatic, who does not
recognise the imaginary as such, than in the poet,
who does, the former would more usually be called
the slave of fancy than of imagination.   Poetry is
called creation, because in it the imaginary is accepted.
Science is not creation, because it rejects the imaginary.   But the theory of poetry does not end here.
The materials of thought must be found, and a true
or complete creation is impossible.   Imagination is
only a form of memory.   All systems of philosophy
agree in this.   Some, like Plato's, suppose a prior
stage of existence, or a supernatural origin ; others
derive the materials which imagination employs from
the actual state of existence, and allow only a natural
origin ;   none suppose the possibility of making
thought out of nothing.   The theory of poetry as
creative art, accordingly, takes two forms.   On the
one hand, the poet is supposed to be a channel
through which a stream flows whose source is un-

known.   The poet is said to be inspired.   On the
other hand, he is supposed to possess a faculty of
seeing more than others see, and of painting what he
sees.   The poet is called a painter.   The former of
these two views prevailed in classical Greece.   This
does not imply that all the Greeks seriously believed
that the poet was inspired; but the doctrine was
current as a formal explanation of poetic quality, and
was accepted, just as many persons now accept theological explanations about which they may feel sceptical from time to time, when they reflect on them.
But this doctrine had lost all meaning when the
civilisation of Rome succeeded to that of Greece.
Roman authors repeated it, but it was only a trick
of words in their mouths.   Horace calls the poet a
vates sacer, but was perfectly conscious that he himself owed everything to the literary file and the
midnight lamp, and nothing to a divine phrenzy.
At the same time another change had occurred.
A spirit of historical criticism has been aroused.
The Greeks, with some few exceptions, did not
trouble themselves about historical evidence.   They
took the plays of Æschylus for history, without
curiously inquiring how Æschylus could know all
which he seemed to know.   This acquiescent faith
was a natural accompaniment of the doctrine that
the poet was inspired.   The Romans were more

rationalistic, and understood that narrative is not
always history. Simultaneously with the notion of
lyrical poetry as pure art, was formed the notion of
epic poetry, and Virgil rewrote the *Iliad* with a
perfect consciousness that he was not a historian,
as Horace rewrote the lyrics of Greece with a
perfect knowledge that he was not inspired.   A
void was thus left in the theory of poetry. The
older doctrine remained only as a fashionable phrase
without meaning, and it was necessary to find a
substitute. This substitute was imagination. The
poet became a painter, who described what he saw,
and ceased to be the mouthpiece or irresponsible
instrument of the Deity.   At the same time, it was
impossible to forget that the difficulty was only
shirked in this way, and that the question still remained why the poet saw more than others. Genius
—*ingenium*—was accordingly introduced as the
primary supposed cause of poetic quality.   In this
vaguer and obscurer shape the doctrine of inspiration
was tolerated.   The poet was credited with genius—
genius gave him imagination—imagination enabled
him to paint. The Roman theory is contained in
the treatise on the *Sublime*, which bears the name of
Longinus, and the difference between the Greek and
Roman theories is apparent when the language of
Longinus is compared with classical Greek.   Three

distinctions were wanted for the argument which
classical Greek did not provide : 1. A distinction
between imitation and representation ; 2. Between
genius and skill ; 3. Between imagination and fancy.
The first of these three defects was irreparable.   The
second was imperfectly remedied by an occasional
use of the word φύσις or nature, sometimes by a
periphrasis, such as τὸ περὶ τὰς νοήσεις ἀδρεπήβολον,
sometimes an equivalent, such as τὸ μεγάλοφρον or
τὸ μεγαλοφυές.   The third deficiency was easily
rectified by a slight expansion of the meaning of the
word *phantasia.*   It would, perhaps, be an exaggeration to affirm that phantasia never bore the meaning of imagination in writings of the earlier period.
It is exceedingly unlikely that any absolute demar-
cations can be found in general questions ˋof this
kind.   Stobæus reports Aristotle's opinion as follows :—'Αριστοτέλης φαντασίαν δ' εἶναι πάθος τι καὶ
κίνησιν τῆς κατ' ἐνέργειαν αἰσθήσεως.   Ὠνομάσθαι δ'
ἀπὸ μιᾶς τῶν αἰσθησέων τῆς ὁράσεως, τῷ φαίνεσθαι
παρὰ τὸ φάος ἔχειν τὴν ἐπίρρησιν.   τοῦτο δ' οἰκεῖον
εἶναι τῆς ὄψεως διατείνειν δ' εἰς πάσας τὰς αἰσθήσεις
καὶ τὰς διανοητικὰς κινήσεις, καὶ γὰρ ταύτας ὁμωνύμως
λέγεσθαι φαντασίας. (*Physica,* vol. i., p. 505, ed.
Gaisford, 1850.)   These terms are perhaps wide
enough to cover all the uses of imagination.   *Phantasia,* Aristotle says, though originally a word used

of the sense of sight, is used metaphorically of all
the senses, and even of intellectual operations. It is,
nevertheless, the fact that, practically, *phantasia* was
the equivalent rather of fancy, which has been derived from it, than of imagination, which is a Latin
word. But in Longinus it is distinctly imagination.
Shakespeare's definition is anticipated with remarkable completeness in the following passages :—καλ-
εῖται μὲν γὰρ κοινῶς φαντασία πᾶν ἐννόημα λόγου
γεννητικὸν, ὁπωσοῦν παριστάμενον, ἰδίως δὲ ἐπὶ
τούτων κεκράτηκε τοὔνομα, ὅταν ἃ λέγῃς, ὑπ᾽ ἐνθου-
σιασμοῦ καὶ πάθους βλέπειν δοκῇς, καὶ ὑπ᾽ ὄψιν τιθῇς
τοῖς ἀκούουσιν. "Every thought, however it may
arise, which is creative of oratory is called *phantasia*,
but the name has come into use as especially appropriate when, under the influence of mental excitement
and strong feeling, you seem to see the things which
you are describing, and set them before the eyes of
the auditors" (sect. xv.) Again, 'Ενταῦθ᾽ ὁ ποιητὴς
αὐτὸς εἶδεν 'Ερινύας. ὃ δὲ ἐφαντάσθη, μικροῦ δεῖν,
θεάσασθαι καὶ τοὺς ἀκούοντας ἠνάγκασεν. "There
the poet (Euripides) himself saw Furies ; and what
imagination had formed, he almost compelled his
auditors to see." These passages answer to the
words of Shakespeare: "The poet's eye in a fine
phrenzy rolling doth glance from heaven to earth,
from earth to heaven, and as imagination bodies

forth the forms of things unknown, the poet's pen turns them to shapes." It is worth while to observe that the most modern in spirit of Greek poets, Euripides, is selected by Longinus to illustrate his theory, and it is evident that in these passages, as throughout his treatise, *enthusiasmus* has insensibly glided from the classical sense of inspiration to the sense of the modern enthusiasm, *i.e.* mental excitation. This change in the theory brought in its train a new criterion by which poetic merit could be judged. So long as the view prevailed that poetry was an uncontrollable torrent of inspired words, the obvious test was the effect produced on the emotions of the hearer. It might be granted, if the hearer were strongly stirred in feeling, that he had heard divine words, though no definite images or conceptions had resulted in his mind. When, however, imagination took the place of inspiration, this test was not sufficient. The contention of the poet was now that he saw things which others did not see, and it was necessary that he should prove this by enabling others to see them. He could no longer reply that he was the irresponsible instrument of a higher power, and that it did not belong to him to paint. The accepted theory identified him with the painter, and the condition of his art was, that he should give an intelligible representation. There was still in the background *ingen-*

ium or genius, which allowed a partial escape from
this obligation ; but genius was theoretically subordinated to imagination, and poetry became almost
identical with word - painting. This view existed
theoretically down to a very recent period, when a
revulsion of sentiment occurred. Darwin has described the change which took place at the close of
last century, in the biography of Erasmus Darwin
which is prefixed to the translation of Krause's
Erasmus Darwin. "Notwithstanding the former
high estimation of his (E. Darwin's) poetry by men
of all kinds in England, no one of the present generation reads, as it appears, a single line of it. So
complete a reversal of judgment within a few years
is a remarkable phenomenon. . . . But the sudden
downfall of his fame as a poet was in great part
caused by the publication of the well-known parody,
the 'Loves of the Triangles.' No doubt, public
taste was at this time changing and becoming more
simple and natural. It was generally acknowledged,
under the guidance of Wordsworth and Coleridge,
that poetry was chiefly concerned with the feelings
and deeper workings of the mind ; whereas Darwin
maintained that poetry ought chiefly to confine itself
to the word-painting of visible objects. He remarks
(*Loves of the Plants,* Interlude between Cantos I.
and II.) that poetry should consist of words which

express ideas originally received by the organ of
sight; 'and as our ideas derived from visible objects
are more distinct than those derived from the objects
of our other senses, the words expressive of these
ideas belonging to vision make up the principal part
of poetic language.   That is, the poet writes principally for the eye; the prose writer uses more abstracted terms." (P. 95, *Erasmus Darwin*, by E.
Krause, translated by W. S. Dallas.)   A quotation
from Addison's first essay on the pleasures of the
imagination will show how exactly Darwin's theory
of poetry was in harmony with Addison's opinion.
" There are few words in the English language which
are employed in a more loose and uncircumscribed
sense than those of the Fancy and Imagination.   I
therefore thought it necessary to fix and determine
the notion of these two words, as I intend to make
use of them in the thread of my following speculation, that the reader may rightly conceive what is
the subject which I proceed upon.   I must therefore
desire him to remember that by the pleasures of the
imagination, I mean only such pleasures as arise
originally from sight, and that I divide these pleasures into two kinds : my design being, first of all,
to discourse of those primary pleasures of the imagination which entirely proceed from such objects as
are before our eyes ; and, in the next place, to speak

of those secondary pleasures of the imagination which
flow from the ideas of visible objects, when the
objects are not actually before the eye, but are called
up into our memories, or formed into agreeable
visions of things that are either absent or fictitious."
Addison's definition is, as he hardly attempts to
conceal, arbitrary. These secondary pleasures which
he describes are, as words are commonly used, alone
pleasures of the imagination, and the pleasures which
" proceed entirely from such objects as are before
our eyes," are not so called. The essays are inci-
dentally on the imagination, but his definition makes
them on the faculty of vision. Nevertheless, such a
definition was almost satisfactory till the time came
when the art of music acquired importance. The
only way in which Addison's theory could be extended so as to make it take in music, was Alison's
method as above described. It could not be said
that composer, executant, or auditor, saw the sounds
either actually or in imagination, but it was just
possible to pretend that intelligibility is the highest
excellence. Of course this satisfied no one ; and
thus with the advance of music the world was reminded that the poet is not simply a word-painter,
but is an utterer of feeling. The change of opinion
rapidly gathered strength, and the classical Greek
theory reappeared as nearly as modern habits of

thought permit. Lord Tennyson has described the
poet as one who would fain utter the thoughts which
arise in him. He is thus once more the *vates sacer*
who obeys an overpowering impulse, but wrestles
with a sense of impotency. This theory had never
entirely perished, but had remained in obscurity.
Inspiration and madness were in Greece, as they still
are in Oriental nations, almost one, and the poet was
not dishonoured when called a maniac. Modern
Europe could not help seeing a connexion, but could
not allude to it without conveying a sneer. Dryden
says in apologetic, and, at the same time, satirical
words,

> " Great wits to madness sure are near allied,
>   And thin partitions do their bounds divide."

So far as form was concerned, the difficulty could
be evaded by a loose use of the word " paint." Pope
winds up his story of the loves of Abelard and
Heloise with

> " He best can paint them who shall feel them most."

Strictly speaking, he can best paint who sees most
clearly, not he who feels most strongly, and the
logical result appears in Lord Tennyson's language
when the poet is an utterer of thoughts, not a
painter. Thus the void which the Romans filled up
by the invention of genius has again appeared, and

the more advanced rationalism of the present age is as ill-satisfied with genius by way of explanation, as the Romans were with inspiration. The realistic theory offers an apparent solution suitable to the sentiments of the age. This theory puts on as many disguises as Proteus, but is everywhere based on rationalism. It is the expression of a desire to deny or conceal the scholastic saying, *omnia exeunt in mysterium.* Genius becomes intelligible when described as a love of truth. Every one knows that there is or may be such a thing as a love of truth, and that it is an excellent quality. Moreover Carlyle had the happy thought of introducing the word "veracity." Arguments which will not bear a close examination seem more plausible when uncommon and pedantic words are put in the place of ordinary words. It was rather easier for Carlyle to persuade his readers that his military heroes were unusually veracious than that they were unusually desirous of the truth, and thus their unusual veracity served to connect them with other great men. But the realistic theory does not appear in its fully-developed shape in Carlyle's writings. He assumes that the true historian has a kind of intuition, and that this intuition is the result of an unusually intense love of truth. Dryasdust is supposed to be deficient in respect of this sentiment, and consequently cannot discern the truth. But intuitions cannot be assumed in argumentative criticism, and the doctrine that genius is veracity brings with it the doctrine that artists must offer evidence. Poetry is thus turned into history or science. The veracity of the poet must be proved by the veracity of his description, and this can only be established by an appeal to evidence. Mr. Gladstone has applied the theory in this way in his volumes on Homer. He compares the description of the Infernal Regions in the *Æneid* with the description in the *Odyssey*, and, affirming the superiority of the latter, cites historical evidence to prove that Homer was more truthful than Virgil. Every one, he says, of the period which Virgil describes, believed in the existence of the Infernal Region, and many of Virgil's contemporaries believed ; but Virgil displays a manifest incredulity, and his description is for this reason inferior to Homer's, who conveys an impression of good faith. Mr. Gladstone speaks as if this showed a higher degree of moral truthfulness in Homer, but his own statement contradicts him. Virgil's fault was, as thus stated, an untimely honesty. He was sceptical, and he let it be seen that he was sceptical. If the atheist is necessarily dishonest, doubtless Virgil was dishonest, but, this denied, historical evidence can only prove that Homer's description

has more historical value than Virgil's. It may be
quite true, as a matter of fact, that the description
in the *Odyssey* has a higher poetical value, but this
can be proved only by the effect on the reader's
feelings, and the historical evidence does not touch
the question. This theory has, however, left literature comparatively untroubled in this country and
confined its attacks to pictorial art. It floats in the
air, and dramatic authors seem to be more seriously
vexed when accused of historical inaccuracy than
when taxed with dulness; but Shakespeare's plays
remain an insuperable obstacle to a complete
triumph. In France the conditions are reversed.
The Académie des Beaux Arts and a well-organised
system of instruction have partly protected painting, while Corneille, Racine, and Molière combined, have not been equal to Shakespeare. The
quality of veracity has there been found very convenient. Paul de Kock is far too trivial for a
scientific age, and it is indeed quite evident that his
thirst for the veracities was not great. But when
the ghost of Paul de Kock consents to put on the
masquerade of a philosopher, and comes forward as
a student of psychology, every honour is paid him.
The novelist who describes the details of an amorous
intrigue can always find some friendly critic to
commend the incomparable zeal for truth which has

produced so admirable a result. No one is deceived by this pretence, but appearances are saved, and the dignity of the author is intact when he can reply that truth is sacred.

The most uncompromising advocates of veracity in painting are obliged to admit that a line must be drawn somewhere. None now deny, as an abstract proposition, though some critics imply a denial in their arguments, that what the French call *trompe l'œil* is illegitimate. The example of *trompe l'œil* usually given is a fly so perfectly imitated that the spectator takes it for a real fly. An imitation of the texture of substances, chiefly manufactured substances, such as satin, velvet, or canvas, when extraordinarily perfect is also so called. It is not meant that the spectator is actually deceived, but that he is almost led to think that such substances are stretched on the surface of the picture. Quasi-deceptions of this kind should be, if the realistic theory were quite sound, the perfection of art. The painter who is representing a bunch of flowers or basket of fruit is bound by the obligation of veracity to represent a fly, if one happens to settle on the flowers or fruit, and is also bound to represent with the utmost fidelity in his power whatever he undertakes to represent. But the artistic opinion has prevailed, and it is generally recognised that *trompe*

l'œil is unlawful.   Pliny did not know this principle.
He tells a foolish story of some grapes painted by
Zeuxis and a curtain by Parrhasius which deceived
the spectator, and thinks apparently that he is pay-
ing these artists a compliment.   His story is un-
questionably a myth, embodying an ignorant
conception of art.   No painter ever succeeded in
painting grapes or drapery with such perfection, nor
is it in the least likely that any artist of repute
would have desired to accomplish such a *tour de
force*.   If Pliny could have consulted the shade of
Zeuxis, he would have been told that these were
" the dregs of art."   It is therefore worth while to
ascertain the nature of *trompe l'œil* and of the objection to it.   A moment's reflection shows that it
consists of a suggestion of depth or the third dimension.   The real fly stands out ; the painted fly is
flat.   A perfectly smooth surface is length and
breadth ; texture is produced by interstices of different forms and magnitudes.   The prohibition of
trompe l'œil is the prohibition of a perfect imitation
of the relations of light and dark where these suggest
the third dimension.   The rule does not apply
where the magnitudes are great.   The modelling of
the countenance or figure cannot become faulty by
excess of perfection, nor can the planes of distance
in a landscape be too faithfully rendered.   The

difference between the two cases is that in the latter
the process of binocular vision interferes to prevent
any ambiguity.   Experience has taught the eye
that where the third dimension is absent, two
identical images are formed in the eyes, and where
it is present, two different images, which unite to
form one in consciousness.   But when the visible
object is very minute, as in the case of a fly, or a
globule of water, or each inequality in a piece of
canvas, the difference between the two images
formed in the two eyes is so exceedingly small that
it is practically worthless, unless the eye is brought
very near.   Consequently the eye, in such cases, finding the relations of light and dark which ordinarily
would be produced by a projection or depression
of the surface, and not finding the instinctive warning
which binocular vision affords when the projection
or depression is greater, infers that there is here a
projection or depression.   This is *trompe l'œil.*   The
fly or the drop of water seem to stand out, though
no amount of skill can make a larger object stand
out in a similar way.   In the debased kind of art,
which the realistic theory is forming, artists are trying by every trick of art to overcome this, and it is
now thought, as Pliny would have thought, that a
picture in which one figure seems to be detached
from the rest is a triumph of art.   If the phrase

trompe l'œil were strictly accurate, the objection which is felt to it might be taken to confirm the realistic principle that veracity is the highest quality of art, but it is in fact an exaggeration and a metaphor. A momentary mistake may occur in the instance of the fly or the drop of water, but in most cases no one is really taken in, nor do artists desire or hope to take any one in. There is really no question of deceitfulness. Such a feat as Pliny ascribes to Parrhasius has never been attempted and could not succeed. The objection to this kind of imitation is that it arrests the attention, and by fixing it on one point, destroys temporarily for consciousness the rest of the work of art. Things which have three dimensions are realities, and as realities cannot be created, painting ceases to be creative or poetic art when a thing in three dimensions intrudes. Many unsatisfactory attempts have been made to define a *reality*, because it has been treated as if it were a word with an absolute meaning, whereas it has a relative meaning only. That which is real in one relation is unreal in another. Land is real property in relation to gold, but gold is real property in relation to imaginary property. The epithet "real" is usually connected, in the explanations which are given of it, with the idea of permanence, and it is clear that there is a connexion.

Land is more permanent than coin, and is therefore more real than coin. But though, in the contrast which we so frequently find between "the real" and "the imaginary," it is easy to select instances which satisfy the test of permanency, it is not difficult to find others to which this test cannot be applied. The image which is seen in a mirror is not a reality, as words are commonly used, and the explanation that it is not permanent applies. When the beholder changes his position the image changes, and disappears altogether if the position is greatly changed. But the image which is seen in a picture is also, as words are used, not a reality. The real Philip the Fourth of Spain died long ago : the Philip who meets the eyes of the spectator in our National Gallery is unreal. Yet he is more permanent than the real Philip in two ways. His forms and colours remain unchanged, whether beheld from the right hand or from the left, though a real person's appearance is different from different points of view, and he remains unaltered by time, though a real man is ever undergoing change. It is said that an aged monk once pointed to the figures in Titian's " Last Supper " in the Escurial and said that he was sometimes tempted to suppose that those were realities, and that he and his companions were unrealities, for that he had grown old and most of the friends of his youth were gone, while those figures remained unchanged. But he was only tempted to think this, and he knew that this permanency was not the true test. Nor can there be any doubt what test he would have suggested if one had been required. "Handle me and feel me," would have been his answer, "and you will find that I am a reality : handle and feel them, and you will find that they are not realities." The decisive test of reality in ordinary language is, therefore, tactual sensation, and the too-perfectly painted fly in the picture is a fault because it brings to mind a sensation of this kind. The idea of permanency is, however, indissolubly connected with tactual sensation. A creature, whether on land or in water or in the air, is supported by a resistant substance, and while consciousness lasts there are always tactual sensations. Other sensations come and go. Light is only a generic name for colour, and colours have no existence in total darkness. But though tactual sensation and the idea of permanency are linked together by experience, and that which is tactually knowable is real in popular philosophy, an examination of the logical history of the word real shows that the idea of permanency is not the essential idea. "Res" (a thing) is first the name of every possible object of thought. One who thinks must think about some *thing* (*de re aliquâ*).   Things, then, subdivide themselves into persons and things.   This is the origin of the legal distinction between real and personal property.   In this contrast a thing is inferior to a person.   A slave is a thing, not a person.   But things being thus separated from and contrasted with persons, again subdivide themselves (except in law) into things *par excellence* (*res reales*) and things relatively not-things (*res non-reales*).   The latter class are unrealities.   Although in this distinction the question of permanency is important, inasmuch as a permanent thing is usually more valuable than a thing which passes away, this is only an incidental point.   The essential point is that things which cause tactual sensations cause pleasure and pain : things which do not come into contact with the nerves cannot cause pain or pleasure. There is no real exception to this, though there are apparent exceptions.   The physical sensation of taste is excited by the contact of material particles with the nerves of the tongue ; and the pleasures which are attached to the senses of seeing and hearing are formed by an association.   When light becomes so intense as to cause a distinct pain, the sensation is localised in the eye, and has become a tactual sensation.   In the same way a sound, when so loud or harsh as to cause a physical feeling of discomfort, causes a tactual sensation in the ear. The sensations of temperature are tactual, because they are local and directly or physically pleasant or unpleasant. A reality is that which is relatively important. It is a thing which is pre-eminently a thing, and as the things which can be felt by touch are the important things, these are the realities in popular philosophy. The metaphysician who holds that matter does not cause feeling, but that feeling creates a belief in matter, holds that feelings are more real than matter. But as matter is important or real only as a cause of tactual feeling, the canvas or panel of wood on which a picture is painted, with the coating of pigment, is a reality, as causing a tactual sensation—the figures represented in the picture are unrealities, as undiscernible by touch. A prolonged experience has, however, taught every one that, although many things are visible which cause no tactual sensation, a tactual sensation may arise if a voluntary movement takes place. Every one knows by experience that although he sees, and does not feel, the chair on the other side of the room, he may feel it if he gets up and walks up to it and puts his hand on it. Hence has arisen the popular doctrine that there is one common substance, called matter, in which both tactual and visible qualities inhere. This doctrine is formed by inference, though the inference is implicitly drawn, and is not explicitly stated, except by metaphysicians. A further doctrine is, however, popularly formed which philosophers refuse to recognise. As the invariable presence of tactual sensation compels the belief in an ever-present material world formed of resistant substance, so there arises a tendency to think that, besides the material substance which is known to touch, there is another substance in which visual qualities inhere. It is in this manner that ghosts and apparitions are conceived. Philosophers vainly argue that it is absurd to believe in ghosts, inasmuch as a truly spiritual substance cannot be visible and a material substance must be resistant : these arguments are ineffectual because an implicit belief in another kind of substance, which is neither spiritual nor material, naturally forms itself. Apparitions are, accordingly, unreal even to those who believe in them. Macbeth addresses Banquo's ghost as "unreal mockery." The thing had the appearance of Banquo, and Macbeth knew that something was there, but was persuaded that the substance of which it was composed was non-resistant, and it was to him unreal. He drew the inference that it might not be permanent, and ordered it "Hence!" but the fundamental point was that it did not consist of the substance which is known to the sense of touch.

The imagination, in Addison's sense of the word, operates by utilising this unphilosophical tendency to believe in a third substance which is neither strictly spiritual nor strictly material, and the alliance between the imagination and the faculty of sight, which is the theme of his essays on the pleasures of the imagination, is formed in this manner. Hence arises the necessity of excluding *trompe l'œil* from pictures. The knowledge that there is no such substance as imagination postulates is always ready to assert itself, and any suggestion of the third dimension brings it to mind. The end of the painter is to create a phantom world ; but a phantom which can be touched is not a phantom. We have here the explanation of that precept of Sir Joshua Reynolds which aroused the anger of Mr. Ruskin,—that the forms of vegetation should be generalised. When the image which the painter presents corresponds to the pre-existing image in the mind of the spectator, the attention is not arrested and the phantom-substance is not destroyed. But mankind (with the exception, perhaps, of a few botanists) come to the picture with general images in their minds of vegetable forms, and the play of the imagination would be interrupted if corresponding forms were not found in the picture. For a like reason the forms of animals cannot be generalised.

Distinct and definite images pre-exist of human beings, cows, horses, sheep, etc. ; and a generalised animal would catch the eye as certainly as a minutely-particularised plant does. This is the radical difference between Sir Joshua Reynolds' and Mr. Ruskin's theory. In the opinion of the former landscape painting is an art which, like poetry, affords a pleasure of the imagination, and all considerations should be subordinated to this end ; in the opinion of the latter it is an art of which the end is to instruct the spectator in botany and geology, though, as it is, I presume, almost superfluous to add, Mr. Ruskin does not keep to his theory.

Distance is said to lend enchantment. It does this by making objects less distinct. Most terms which are used in mental philosophy are metaphors taken from the senses. To distinguish is etymologically to know by touch, and a distinct object is one which suggests the thought of tactual knowledge. In pictures art lends this enchantment, which distance lends to natural objects, in a more perfect degree by the contradiction to experience which it offers. The relations of light and dark, which projections and depressions cause, are found in pictures, but there comes with them a perfect conviction that they are not caused as they are in natural objects. When a natural scene is sur-

veyed, the mind of the spectator fluctuates between
two opposite modes of thought, which may be called
observation and contemplation. The former is the
mode which the sense of touch has formed, the
latter is derived from the sense of sight. Mr.
Herbert Spencer has described the latter mode in
the following terms :—" A like explanation may be
given of emotions which leave the subject of them
comparatively passive, as, for instance, that produced by scenery. By compounding groups of
sensations and ideas there are at length formed
those vast aggregations which a grand landscape
excites and suggests. An infant taken into the
midst of mountains is totally unaffected, but is
delighted with the small group of attributes and
relations presented in a toy. Children can appreciate
and be pleased with the more complicated relations
of household objects and localities—of the garden,
the field, and the street. But it is only in youth
and mature age, when individual things and small
assemblages of them have become familiar and
automatically cognisable, that those immense assemblages which landscapes present can be adequately
grasped, and the highly integrated states of consciousness produced by them experienced. Then,
however, the various minor groups of states that
have been in earlier days severally produced by

trees and flowers, by fields and moors and rocky wastes, by streams, by cascades, by ravines and precipices, by blue skies and clouds and storms, are aroused together. Along with the immediate sensations there are partially excited the myriads of sensations that have been in times past received from objects such as those presented ; further, there are partially excited the multitudinous incidental feelings that were experienced on these many past occasions, and there are also excited certain deeper but now vague combinations of states which were organised in the race during barbarous times, when its pleasurable activities were chiefly among the woods and waters. And out of all these excitations, some of them actual, but most of them nascent, is composed the emotion which a fine landscape produces in us." (*Principles of Psychology*, vol. i., p. 485, ed. 1870.)

This admirable description of the feeling which a fine landscape produces contains the true theory of painting. The subject, it is said, is comparatively passive, and this state is found when "individual things and small assemblages of them have become automatically cognisable." Hence, the foreground foliage of a landscape must, in a picture, be the counterpart of the image which pre-exists in the spectator's mind. Otherwise, he is led to observe

the forms (they being no longer automatically
cognisable), and thus mentally comparing them with
plants which he has seen, he ceases to be passive.
It may be observed here that the word *æsthetic*
may be used to designate complicated groups of
feeling, such as are described in this passage, without any philosophical inaccuracy. It is purely a
verbal question whether it is or not proper in this
sense, and the practice of writers who cannot be
suspected of an irrational preference for learned
words seems to show that it or some similar term
is required. The assumption made by Baumgarten,
and those who believe in the *science* of æsthetic, is
quite another thing, and although undoubtedly the
word was first introduced by way of supporting
the fictitious science, it does not follow that it is
illegitimate, if necessary, in a different sense. The
peculiarity of the state of mind which Mr. H.
Spencer describes is that it is made up of a mixture of different sensations and ideas. But such
combinations can only exist where all are feebly
felt ; any one sensation or idea vividly present
destroys for the moment all others. This is known
to be true even of physical pain. A sensation which
is extremely acute, when no other sensation rivals it,
vanishes when one more acute comes into competition with it. The same law holds good of mental

S

activity.   A concentration of the attention in one
direction implies a temporary elimination of all
other thought.   If, therefore, we please to adopt
the term *æsthetic emotion*, it is clearly superfluous
to assume that there must be a something called
Beauty which creates this emotion.   The simpler
explanation is that an emotion which, in some cases,
is so strongly felt that it monopolises the attention,
is, in others, so faintly felt as to permit an intermixture of other emotions which arise as the imagination plays.   But the surest way to prevent an
emotion from obtaining an exclusive supremacy is
to keep distinctly present to the   mind of the
spectator or auditor the fact that the artist has
forged an " airy nothing," or called up an " unreal
phantom."   So long as this conviction is present,
whether the work of art is a poem, a picture, or a
statue, it cannot arouse a feeling of pity, anger,
hate, or approbation so intense as to paralyse the
imagination and destroy the æsthetic (*i.e.* mixed)
emotion.   The painter accomplishes this by not
allowing the spectator to forget that the things
which he creates are phantoms.   It is impossible to
be seriously angry with a phantom or to pity it
sincerely.   No one really pities the ghost who is
supposed to escape for a time from torment, and
then to return to it.   The idea of pain is united by

experience with flesh, and it is absolutely impossible to think that the ghost, who is fleshless, can feel pain. The theologians who insist on the doctrine of the resurrection of the body are right in connexion with their view. The unsubstantial phantom evoked by the painter cannot excite any sympathy except an æsthetic sympathy. Thus the tender-hearted philanthropist, who would shrink with horror from the thought of an innocent young man tied to a tree and pierced all over with arrows, can gaze with perfect equanimity on the picture of St. Sebastian. The idea of pain cannot connect itself with a fleshless image or a thing of two dimensions, and taste finds an instinctive gratification in the forms and colours, which the corresponding reality could not provide, though the same forms and colours might be present in it. Art has not added anything to the reality—at any rate, has not necessarily added anything. It has abstracted something, to wit, solidity, and with it the idea of pain. If, therefore, Mr. H. Spencer has well analysed the pleasure of imagination which a fine landscape affords, and Sir Joshua Reynolds rightly held that the art of painting, like poetry, is addressed to the imagination, the realistic theory of the importance of historical accuracy is in direct opposition to the true theory of painting. The end sought by the realistic artist is, by every means in his power, to divert the attention from the present unreality to the absent reality.   In his historical subjects he laboriously investigates the details which interest the antiquarian : paints these with an obtrusive exactness, and, lest they should even then fail to catch the eye, advertises the fact that a scrupulous fidelity has been observed.   This is called veracious art.   It is, in fact, the only unveracious art.   An ostentatious historical accuracy in details and accessories is an implied assertion that the representation, as a whole, has a historical value, whereas in most historical subjects the figures which are introduced are purely imaginary.   It is a ludicrous inversion of legitimate interest to make the chief figure, or all the figures, in pictures of a historical kind, mere pegs on which to hang antiquarian illustrations. The climax of absurdity is reached when a picture of the Saviour is commended as a great work of art on the score that the carpenter's tools are correctly designed.

Artistic representation is effected in two ways : 1. By signs ; 2. By a partial presentation of attributes.   All literary representation is effected by signs.   Words are signs of thoughts, and visible signs are presented when the poem is read ; audible, when it is recited.   But painters and sculptors

present a part of the attributes of the things which
they represent, and their representations are not
presentations, because they do not present all the
attributes. The painter represents man by presenting the colours without the three dimensions ;
the sculptor by presenting the three dimensions
without the natural colour. The fundamental distinction between the arts of the two latter and the
art of the poet arises from this, and not from the
difference between successive and simultaneous
presentation into which Lessing vainly attempts to
resolve it. The importance of this distinction is
due to the law of psychology that newly-formed
impressions are more vivid and have a greater
effect on feeling than those which are preserved in
memory and are half-effaced by time. When a
wrong is experienced, or an act of injustice witnessed,
the feeling of indignation which is at first acute
becomes fainter as time passes, though all the
circumstances may be perfectly remembered, and
the nature of the wrong or injustice as clearly understood as it was in the first instance. This applies
to everything, and as the painter presents colours
which the poet cannot present, colour quality has a
degree of value in a picture which it cannot have
in a poem. The science of beauty, accordingly,
attempting to frame laws which can be applied to

poetry and painting, is fighting against nature and the constitution of the mind. It is therefore absolutely impossible for those who believe in this science to cling to their own doctrine. They start with the assumption that in all objects which are called beautiful there must be one common beauty, an assumption which belongs to an obsolete kind of theory, and base their science on this. When they proceed to apply this fiction, they are obliged to affirm that there are two kinds of beauty—a higher and a lower—and they contend that if the arts of sense were duly purified and refined, the lower or sensuous beauty would cease to exercise an attraction. But this cannot be, because a present quality which forms a new impression has relatively a greater influence than an absent quality which is imagined. Since in a picture forms and colours are present without any other attributes of the things represented, these are in a picture more important. No theory can get over this. No conviction, for instance, that it is better to be wise and virtuous than to be comely can prevent comeliness of appearance from being the most important attribute in pictures of human beings. In poetry, where this and all attributes are represented by words or signs, it falls into the background, and the character, or moral and intellectual characteristics are the more important. In

the drama, which is composed of the two modes
of representation, signs, and presentations, a rule is
derived from this, which Horace stated, but did not
explain rightly. He said that Medea must not
murder her infants on the stage, and he put this as
if it were an exception to the principle which he had
previously laid down that sights (*quæ sunt oculis
subjecta fidelibus*) have a greater effect on feeling
than sounds (*demissa per aurem*). It is an example
of, not an exception to, his rule. He says that if
the spectacle is presented to him he is disgusted
because he is incredulous, *incredulus odi*. This is
absurd. The disgust would manifestly be greater if
he were credulous, and took the make-believe murder
for a real murder. The true reason why a mother
should not murder her infants on the stage is that a
presentation produces a vivid impression in spite of
an intellectual conviction of the fictitious nature of
the act. The feeling of horror is too strong for the
occasion. But his principle is not correctly worded
and is true only if taken in connexion with the
context. The sounds which produce less effect
(*segnius irritant animos*) are those which are signs
of thoughts and conceptions ; those which are expressions of feeling produce an effect as great as,
or perhaps greater than, sights. Now, when realism
is triumphant, actors occasionally try experiments

which are justified by the theory but fail in practice.
Not many years ago an actress who played the part
of the Traviata, influenced by the theory that art
should be veracious, introduced a cough as a
symptom of illness. This *demissum per aurem* was
found intolerable, though the visible signs of illness
are tolerated on the stage. So too, if when Medea
is supposed to be murdering her infants behind the
scenes, their shrieks and lamentations were heard,
this would probably be more intolerable than the
spectacle. Perhaps this experiment has been tried.
It is at any rate worthy of the predominant theory.
Horace in this passage was dragging in the realistic
principle, and it is a very good test of its value, for
the logical result is that which he here implies, that
the play of *Medea* would be more agreeable if the
spectator were persuaded that a murder is committed.
But Aristotle in the Poetic Art, though he did not
give the whole reason, gave at least a part of it, and
in doing so protested by anticipation against realism.
The drama was to most of the Greeks what miracle
plays have been in more recent European history.
It was rather a reproduction of history than a
" play " which diverted the fancy. But it is discussed by Aristotle as pure art, *i.e.* poetic or creative
art. It shows, he said, a poverty of resource and is
inartistic to complete the representation by showing

things to the eyes (διὰ τῆς ὄψεως). This practice which he condemns is the favourite device of realism. The actor's part is shorn of its just proportions by costly and elaborate studies of dress and decoration, and the scene-painter either relieves him of his task or enters into successful competition with him. Fortunately for great actors, Shakespeare held with Aristotle that acting is creative art, and they escape from realistic fetters when they fly to his sympathetic genius. He did not think that the end of acting is to teach history and geography, and though the unveracity of an author who assigned a seashore to Bohemia is disgraceful in the accepted theory, the sin is forgotten when Shakespeare is the criminal. When acting is regarded as creative art, the theatrical adjuncts serve to remind the spectator that the veracities have been dismissed for a time, and that all which he witnesses is an organised fiction ; that the treacherous host who murders his guest in *Macbeth*, and the jealous husband who murders his wife in *Othello*, are but unreal phantoms which will lose their existence when he turns his eyes away. A theatrical style of elocution, differing from that of ordinary life, serves the same purpose. These adjuncts are in the drama what the absence of the third dimension is in the art of painting. They keep the imagination of the spectator in the realm of unrealities which alone belongs to it. An act of creation is strictly inconceivable, and is a miracle for this reason. But the idea of creation is faintly suggested when an effect is produced which has apparently no cause. It is thus that painting is creative art. It produces visible effects which in every other known case are produced by solid substances, and as only two dimensions are present in the picture, the artist seems to be a creator. Imitation of marble and wood is condemned by taste in architectural decoration, and the false explanation is commonly given that imitation of this kind is displeasing because it is a kind of deceit. Any one who chooses to consult his common sense will see that this is not the true explanation. The moral sense is not in the least shocked by such imitations, nor does any one feel that the decorator who employs them is dishonest or a liar. But they do not belong to Fine Art, because there is not in this instance that elimination of the third dimension which gives painting its creative quality, and they are a purposeless concealment of the natural substance. As the painted fly in the picture is condemned because it suggests the third dimension too perfectly, so these are condemned because they give no suggestion of it. In like manner, the actor is a creator, because there are found in him all the signs

of love, of hate, of anger, and other passions, while
it is manifest that there is no cause for these
emotions.   In both arts there is a contradiction.
Results are found which must have a cause ; yet the
only known causes are not there.   Fine Art is thus
distinguished from mechanical art.   The condition
of the former is that the artist must fail in what he
attempts, and it is for this reason creative.   The
painter does his utmost to persuade the spectator
that he presents solid objects, but must not succeed
in persuading him.   The actor does his utmost to
convince his auditors that he is influenced by passion,
but the stage must be so arranged as to make his
failure certain.   On these conditions alone can the
æsthetic, or mixed, emotion arise.

There is a distinction which is practically important in the art of painting between painting from
nature and from imagination or memory.   This is,
however, a distinction of degree rather than of kind.
Every artist in every instance paints from imagination,
for at each moment when a touch or a line is added
the eyes must be fixed on the canvas or paper, and
if no image were mentally present when the eyes
are turned away from the natural object, painting
would be impossible.   The difference is that in the
one case the impression is constantly renewed by
a fresh inspection, in the other a store of impressions,

half-obliterated by time, alone are present. But different images are found in different persons, in accordance with differences of interest or ways of looking at things, and the practice of drawing tends to produce a difference between artists and others, with respect to form. Experience, summed up in the precepts of the drawing-school, teaches that the more general relations of lines to each other must be secured before any attention is paid to details, and that error will find a way in if this precaution is neglected. There is formed in this manner an habitual and instinctive tendency to observe the more general forms, and in the mental image which results the artistic whole is in logical terms more extensive and less comprehensive than the non-artistic whole. There results from this the peculiarity which is known as breadth of style. As in all similar cases a taste or instinctive preference for a broad style arises ultimately. This taste is unintelligible to non-artistic critics, and is set down to academic prejudice. The " conscientious " artist who entirely repudiates this prejudice or convention is highly esteemed by the non-artistic critic. But though breadth of style is a natural result of artistic practice, it is a necessary characteristic also of imaginative or poetic art. The logical law that comprehension and extension exist in inverse ratios

is as true of images as of conceptions.   Mr. H.
Spencer shows that the pleasure of imagination
which scenery produces requires an automatic recognition of minor groups ; that is, these minor
groups do not occupy the attention.   The image
formed in the spectator's mind is, like the artistic
mental image of a particular object, of a general
kind.   All which the artist presents attracts attention,
and he must eliminate the minutiæ which oppose the
extension of the imagined whole ; in other words,
his imagination does for the spectator of a picture
what the spectator's imagination does for itself when
a natural scene is present.   Art lends to the artificial scene the enchantment which distance lends to
the natural scene.   But as "use doth breed a habit
in a man," and those who have not cultivated a taste
for natural scenery do not readily fall into the
passive state of contemplation which is required for
the enjoyment of it, but busy themselves with the
observation of details and minutiæ, so the positive
passion for works of art demands a habit of passive
passion which use alone breeds.   The natural or
uncultivated tendency is to observe rather than to
contemplate, to inquire into rather than acquiesce in
a novelty.   The difference between lovers of art
and their antagonists resolves itself into the question
whether pictures are made to be looked at or to be

criticised.   Goldsmith, who held that the fashionable taste for painting was ridiculous, was pleased to see Sir Joshua Reynolds shift his trumpet and take snuff, when they talked of Raphaels, Coreggios, and stuff. He interpreted this gesture as an endorsal of his own opinion.   But he was mistaken.   Sir Joshua did not identify the art of Coreggio with " stuff." The stuff, in his opinion, was the eloquence of the voluble critic who thought that pictures were painted to be talked about rather than to be looked at.

CHAPTER VII.

STATUARY—ARCHITECTURE—MUSIC.

IF Burke's theory that there is a pleasure in the perception of resemblance, or the realistic principle that completeness of representation is the test of excellence, were sound, a coloured figure of wax-work should be a more perfect work of art than either a picture or a statue. The resemblance is greater, and the representation more perfect, in the waxwork imitation, which unites natural colour with natural form, than in pictures or statues, where either the third dimension or the natural colours are omitted. None of the "speculatists" have dared to face this question, and if they have touched it, have avoided the objection by some metaphor, as, for instance, by saying that sculpture "disdains" colour. The realistic theory has, however, endeavoured to gain its ends indirectly, and though its friends have never explained why modern sculptors do not colour their statues, they have declared that the great

sculptors of ancient Greece did this ; and a French
author has beguiled some scholars and some artists
into a belief that Phidias set up at Olympia a
monstrous painted doll, like a figure taken from
Madame Tussaud's gallery greatly magnified, and
that all Greece gazed on this figure with enthusiastic
admiration.   Though Lessing's theory that the
Greeks had fully formed the notion of " art for art's
sake," and that their statues were to them what the
statues in the Vatican are to the modern tourist, is
assuredly false, it would be as certainly false to
contend that the idea of art did not exist for the
artists themselves and some of the Greeks.   Were it
possible to prove that the statues of Greece were
coloured in imitation of nature in the classical
period, the authority of Greece could not be disregarded, and the theory that the essential quality
of mimetic Fine Art is a contradiction of experience,
effected by an omission of attributes, would be
refuted.   A historical digression is, therefore, necessary in order to show that the bubble which
Quatremère de Quincy blew, and which still floats,
collapses as soon as it is grasped.   One point, however, must be taken apart from the historical question, lest a misconception should cause a prejudice.
Gibson, in the latter part of his life, coloured his
statues in imitation of nature, and it may naturally

be supposed that it is possible to cite his authority in behalf of this practice. There is conclusive evidence that Gibson was not guided by his own taste, but adopted this practice in deference to the authority of Greece, misled by the confident assertions of some of his friends that the Greek statues were painted. It is true that after he had begun to colour his own works he vehemently insisted that his taste was satisfied, and that the colour pleased him ; but he coupled this with an incessant reiteration of the cry that the Greeks could not have erred. The conclusive proof that he at first set his own instincts at defiance in submission to a supposed obligation is found in the Autobiography edited by Lady Eastlake. He seriously thought that he had seen a supernatural vision and received a divine mandate. " Gibson was fully persuaded that the little God appeared bodily to him on this occasion, and has left a description of the interview, which draws too much upon the marvellous for insertion here. The gist of their conversation, however, was that the God of Love directed the sculptor to colour his statue." (*Life of John Gibson*, p. 76.) This clearly shows how great the mental struggle was. Gibson was like the patriotic assassin who cannot overcome the instinctive pleadings of his conscience till fancy forges a supernatural messenger.

T

Quatremère de Quincy was the inventor of the doctrine that the Greek statues were painted, and though I cannot speak confidently, I do not think that any German scholar has fallen into the trap which he prepared. But Frenchmen, Englishmen, and Italians have ; and, as often happens, the disciples have gone beyond their master. He was content to affirm that the fact was certain, but admitted that it might show a want of taste. His followers unite in declaring that this addition of colour was a consummate excellence. Monsieur Eugène Véron writes :

" D'ailleurs la statuaire du moyen âge, comme celle de l'Inde, de l'Egypte, et de la Grèce, est toujours peinte ; ce qui équivaut à dire que les civilisations qui ont réellement eu des écoles de statuaire ont pensé que cet art ne pouvait se passer de la peinture." (*Esthétique : Sculpture*, p. 245.) Sir G. J. Wilkinson, who has devoted a large part of a chapter to this question in his volume on Colour, speaks in an equally confident tone. Only one point in the argument of the latter need be noticed, for there is no substantial addition to the French argument. But he adds some instances in which there is evidence that *basso* or *alto rilievo* was coloured, begging the question that this proves the colouring of statues. The questions are distinct. Sculptured reliefs are a part of architectural decoration, and colour is a part of architectural decoration. The question is not whether colour of a decorative kind was introduced in architecture, but whether imitative colour was added to the statue proper for the purpose of augmenting the resemblance, or completing the representation. The latter is the contention of Quatremère de Quincy, which Sir G. Wilkinson sought to confirm. " J'entends ici par peindre une statue, employer les couleurs à donner aux differentes parties du visage et du corps le ton qu'elles ont dans la nature. L'emploi habituel de cette pratique me semble très positivement prouvé par un passage de Platon." (*Le Jupiter Olympien, ou l'art de la sculpture antique considéré sous un nouveau point de vue*, p. 29.) The passage in Plato to which reference is here made is the stronghold of all who adopt this opinion, and they rely for the rest of their case on later authors, such as Pliny. Sir G. Wilkinson has employed the testimony of Pliny in a way so original and felicitous as to deserve commemoration. Pliny said : " Cæpimus et lapidem pingere. Hoc Claudii principatu inventum." "We have begun to paint even marble. This was invented when Claudius was emperor." Sir G. Wilkinson quotes the first half of this, " Cæpimus et lapidem pingere," and observes that this is satisfactory evidence that the Greeks always painted their statues, inasmuch as the Romans would not have adopted this practice if they had not found that it was usual in Greece.

The misinterpretation of Plato's words arises from a misunderstanding of a Greek word which Plato uses. I am conscious that it must seem audacious to challenge an interpretation which the whole world of scholars has accepted, but will, nevertheless venture to argue that the word *andricelum* (ἀνδρέικελον) was never used by Plato, or any other Greek author, in the sense which has been found for it, viz. a flesh-coloured pigment. Every passage in which it occurs obtains a better meaning when it is taken to mean an image, coloured as Quatremère de Quincy thought the ἀνδριάντες or statues were coloured, and every probability is satisfied when it is so translated. The presumptions must be first stated. As regards the etymological presumption I cannot imagine a dispute possible, or that it would be denied that the word *andricelum* must mean rather *a thing which is like a man* than *a thing which is in colour like a man's flesh.* It is at any rate certain that it bore the former meaning in later Greek. The following lines are part of an epigram attributed to Theætetus :—

χιονέην με λίθον παλιναυξέος ἐκ περιωπῆς
λαοτύπος τμήξας πετροτόμοις ἀκίσι

Μηδὸς ἐποντοπόρευσεν ὅπως ἀνδρείκελα τεύξῃ
τῆς κατ᾽ Ἀθηναίων σύμβολα καμμονίης.

It is beyond all question that *andricelum* means in
these lines a statue (*i.e.* a thing which resembles a
man). The point of the whole epigram is that a
block of marble cut in Asia Minor and transferred
to Greece would, when made into a statue, represent,
according to the point of view, either Victory or
Nemesis. Nevertheless it is said that this same word
in classical authors means a flesh-coloured pigment.
Not only are the etymological presumptions set at
defiance when it is so interpreted, but a presumption
of an artistic kind is violated which scholars have
not observed. Although it is true that if etymology
is disregarded the Greeks might have known some
pigment, or combination of pigments, by the name
of *andricelum*, " flesh-colour," just as there are now
some colours called salmon-colour, olive-colour, or
rose-colour, this cannot have been true in the sense
which is required for the interpretation of these
passages. The assumption which is made is not
simply that a certain tint was known as flesh-colour
—there would be no improbability in this—but that
this preparation was so-called because it was used
by artists to imitate flesh. Now flesh cannot be
imitated by a prepared homogeneous mixture.
When cosmetics are applied to the natural counte-

nance, every care is taken to preserve, so far as is possible, that infinite variety of tones which is found wherever the colours have been laid on by the sweet and cunning hand of nature. A little white is added in one place, a little red in another, but an opaque coating is not applied, and if this precaution is neglected, a hideous effect is produced as if a skin had been stretched on the face. The artist must imitate nature, and can only do this by a skilful intermixture of a thousand different nuances. If *andricelum* was employed by Greek artists in the manner which is supposed, they must have been satisfied with the vilest kind of signboard art. This interpretation of the word is derived from the Platonic Glossary of Timæus. Ruhnken confirmed it, and it has since passed unchallenged. The probabilities of the case must be weighed against this authority, and the question decided by an examination of the passages in which it is found.

The following is in the *Œconomicus* of Xenophon (cap. x.):—ἢ εἴ σοι μίλτῳ ἀλειφόμενος καὶ τοὺς ὀφθαλμοὺς ὑπαλειφόμενος ἀνδρεικέλῳ ἐπιδεικνύοιμί τε ἐμαυτὸν καὶ συνείην ἐξαπατῶν σε καὶ παρέχων ὁρᾶν καὶ ἅπτεσθαι μίλτου ἀντὶ τοῦ ἐμαυτοῦ χρωτός; ἐγὼ μέν, ἔφη ἐκείνη, οὔτ᾽ ἂν μίλτου ἁπτοίμην ἥδιον ἢ σοῦ, οὔτ᾽ ἂν ἀνδρεικέλου χρῶμα ὁρῴην ἥδιον ἢ τὸ σόν, οὔτ᾽ ἂν τοὺς ὀφθαλμοὺς ὑπαληλιμμένους ἥδιον ὁρῴην

τοὺς σοὺς ἢ ὑγιαίνοντας. A husband is in this passage explaining to his wife that she ought not to employ cosmetics, and he asks her whether she would like him the better if his natural complexion were disguised with a coating of paint. Commentators take the word andricelum to mean flesh-coloured paint. But when it is so construed the passage is downright nonsense. Becker points this out in the notes to his *Charicles* (vol. ii., p. 235). He observes with perfect justice that when the eyes are stained, a dark colouring matter is added, and that it is wholly impossible that they can ever have been coated with flesh-coloured pigment. Nevertheless, he was so prepossessed with the notion that andricelum must be some kind of paint, as to miss the requisite emendation. He suggests a sweeping emendation of a purely conjectural kind which, after all, does not greatly improve the sense. But the rules of critical emendation allow us to insert the word εἴκελον after the word ἀνδρεικέλῳ in the first sentence. When this emendation is made, the whole paragraph may be translated as follows:—
"'Or if I, rouged and with my eyes stained, were to exhibit myself to you like a barber's block, and were to consort with you, deceiving you and offering to your sight and touch rouge instead of my own skin?' 'I,' she answered, 'should not so willingly

embrace rouge as you, or gaze with such pleasure
on the colour of a barber's block as on your colour,
or on your eyes stained as on your eyes with the
natural appearance of health.' " This emendation
gives a satisfactory meaning, though Becker's does
not, and is of a kind which is justifiable, for it is
well known that when two words almost identical
occur together, one of them is sometimes dropped in
transcription.   I have translated the word andricelum, "a barber's block," because there is reason to
suppose that the andricela were, like barber's blocks,
usually made of coloured wax.   The Greeks were
familiar with the use of wax in conjunction with
colour.   It is said that the evidence which there is
of this induced Sir Joshua Reynolds to try the
disastrous experiment of compounding his colours
with wax.   It may be that there is proof that they
used wax in painting.   Archæologists seem to agree
in thinking that it is certain ; but some of the passages in which wax is named may refer to the
manufacture of wax images or andricela.   There is
a point with regard to this which has not been
observed.   Theophrastus, in a catalogue which he
gives of different pigments with the localities in
which they are found, says of *miltus* or red, μίλτον
δὲ παντοδαπὴν ὥστε εἰς τὰ ἀνδρείκελα χρῆσθαι τοὺς
γραφεῖς (περὶ λίθων, sect. 51).   "Red is found in

all shapes (*i.e.* this particular red called miltus), so that painters use it for their andricela." Now why, if an andricelum is a flesh-coloured pigment, should red alone be named? Red and white do not produce flesh-colour. A large quantity of yellow must be added to produce anything like the requisite tone. But in the sentence which precedes the words quoted yellow had just been named, and nothing said about the use of this for andricela. There is great uncertainty about the meaning of the Greek names for the different pigments, but apparently cinnabar was the usual name for vermilion, miltus both for red lead and red oxide of iron. Even vermilion mixed with white does not make flesh-colour, but it comes rather nearer than red lead and white. But the words of Theophrastus, though incomprehensible if the andricela are taken to be flesh-colours, are what might be expected if they were wax figures or busts. When a translucent substance, such as unclarified wax, of a yellowish colour, is compounded with a small quantity of red, the result is a fair imitation of the colour of flesh. The question then is why the Greeks made these andricela, and why the word is so uncommon. There is not much difficulty in answering this. The andricela were the same as the " pictæ imagines " or " expressi cerâ vultus " of the Romans : they were portraits ; and thus, though the word seldom found its way into literature, it was a familiar and household term.   It is evident that Plato, Xenophon, and Theophrastus knew well what it meant, and took for granted that their readers would be equally well-informed ; but it is more likely that every one would know the common name for a portrait than that all should know a technical term employed by artists for a certain mixture of colour. Two points must be remembered in estimating the probability of this explanation.   1. There is no artistic criticism in Greek literature, and there were in Greece no disputes about copyright in engraving, and there was no art of photographing.   If every mention of portraits which occurs in these con-nexions were expunged from modern literature, an enormous mass of writings might be explored with-out the discovery of anything about portrait-painting. 2. The waxen *imagines* of the Romans were more important to them than portraits were to the Greeks, because family history was more important, and these busts were the family pedigree.   But as the use of wax was certainly known to the Greeks, it would be strange if it had not occurred to them to use it as the Romans used it ; and there is a passage in Pliny which, if his testimony may be trusted, proves that Greece had forestalled Italy in this.

He says : " Hominis autem imaginem gypso e facie ipsâ primus omnium expressit, cerâque in eam formam gypsi infusâ emendare instituit Lysistratus Sicyonius, frater Lysippi de quo diximus.   Hic et similitudinem reddere instituit : ante eum quam pul-cherrimas facere studebant."   (*Pliny* xxxv. cap. 44.)

Pliny does not literally say that the first portraits were made in this way, but he connects the use of wax with this invention.   The passage seems to me to mean : " Lysistratus of Sicyon, brother of the Lysippus previously mentioned, was the first who took a cast of the face, and he introduced the practice of removing defects by means of melted wax poured into the plaster mould.   He, too, was the first who thought of taking likenesses ; before his time the object was simply to make beautiful faces."   The addition of colour was an obvious improvement— was, indeed, plainly necessary, for nothing could be more ghastly than a face of wax uncoloured, and thus would arise the need for some word which distin- guished these imagines from the ἀνδριάντες and ἀγάλματα—the statues of gods, demi-gods, and men. It appears that for some reason miltus was required by the Athenians in large quantities, for they inserted a clause in a treaty with the inhabitants of the island Ceos which gave them a monopoly of it (*vide* Newton's *Essays on Art and Archæology*, p. 117).   The miltus

named in this treaty is taken by Professor Newton
to be vermilion.   He is probably right in this.   It
is not likely that such a stipulation would be made
about the commoner colour red lead, which the
Athenians could prepare for themselves, and though
miltus is usually translated red lead, vermilion was
probably always used for the andricela.   It may
have been required for other purposes as well, but
was chiefly needed for these portraits.   It is noteworthy that the chief addition to the Fine Arts which
the Romans made in literature as well as in painting
was portrait painting.   The satire of Greece, such as
there is in the plays of Aristophanes, was personal.
Horace, Juvenal, and Persius painted pictures of
society, and these descriptions were the chief contri-
bution of Rome to general literature.   In like manner
many archæologists have observed that the Greeks
did not practise portrait painting, and have been
puzzled to explain the fact.   In Italy the art of
painting was greatly neglected, as is proved by the
epigrams of Martial.   These epigrams contain the
most complete description of Roman life under the
Empire which we have, and though some arts, such
as the art of embossing silver, are frequently named,
there is hardly an allusion to painting.   But the few
which there are are almost entirely about portrait
painting.   Though during the best period of Greek

art the andricela were distinct from the statues by
virtue of their colour, this distinction was afterwards
lost.   In the epigram of Theætetus andricelum is a
generic name for a statue.   Pliny, perhaps, was too
precise when he restricted the invention of painted
marble to the time of Claudius, and it is more likely
that the change was gradual.   This, however, is a
question of historical interest alone.   The theory can
only be affected by the practice of the sculptors of
the earlier period, whose works have made Greece
illustrious as the parent of the arts.   It is most
unfortunate for those who maintain this view that
besides the celebrated passage in the *Republic* of
Plato, one in which Pliny speaks of the *circumlitio* of
statues should be the chief piece of evidence.   Much
has been written about the various meanings which
this word may bear, which it is superfluous to repeat
here.   So far as the point now before us is concerned,
a more direct and simpler answer may be given.
Pliny says that Praxiteles set a higher value on those
of his own works to which one Nicias gave a
"circumlitio" than any others, and the conjecture is
that Nicias coloured them.   Unfortunately for this
argument there are no two facts better established
in the history of Greek statuary than that the
Cnidian Venus was the masterpiece of Praxiteles, and
that this was not coloured.   It is described by

Lucian, or some imitator, in the dialogue called
Ἔρωτες, and an anecdote is there introduced of which
the point is that the spectator's eye was caught by
one dark stain which contrasted with the dazzling
purity of the marble.   It is quite certain that if this
statue were coloured it could not have been described
in the terms which are there used, and there is
besides in the essay or dialogue called " Icŏnes " a
reference to it which would alone be sufficient to
prove that the marble was in its natural condition.

The word andricelum does not occur in the
passage in Plato's *Republic*, which Quatremère de
Quincy cited as proof positive that the Greek statues
were coloured ; but it is used elsewhere by him, and
it is convenient to take these other passages first.
The following is one of them :—οὐκοῦν μετὰ ταῦτα
οἴει ὑπογράψασθαι ἂν τὸ σχῆμα τῆς πολιτείας ; τί
μήν ; ἔπειτα οἶμαι ἀπεργαζόμενοι πυκνὰ ἂν ἑκατέρωσ᾽
ἀποβλέποιεν πρός τε τὸ φύσει δίκαιον καὶ καλὸν καὶ
σῶφρον καὶ πάντα τὰ τοιαῦτα, καὶ πρὸς ἐκεῖνο αὖ τὸ
ἐν τοῖς ἀνθρώποις ἐμποιοῖεν ζυμμιγνύντες τε καὶ
κεραννύντες ἐκ τῶν ἐπιτηδευμάτων τὸ ἀνδρείκελον, ἀπ᾽
ἐκείνου τεκμαιρόμενοι ὃ δὴ καὶ Ὅμηρος ἐκάλεσεν ἐν
τοῖς ἀνθρώποις ἐγγιγνόμενον θεοειδές τε καὶ θεοείκελον.
Ὀρθῶς ἔφη.   Καὶ τὸ μὲν ἂν, οἶμαι, ἐξαλείφοιεν, τὸ δὲ
πάλιν ἐγγράφοιεν, ἕως ἂν ὅτι μάλιστα ἀνθρώπεια ἤθη
εἰς ὅσον ἐνδέχεται θεοφιλῆ ποιήσειαν.   Καλλίστη

γοῦν ἂν ἔφη ἡ γραφὴ γένοιτο. (Πολιτεια, p. 501, Stephens.)

There is in Greek the idiom which we have in English. We speak of "mixing a dose," meaning thereby to mix the ingredients which make a dose. Plato in this passage speaks of "mixing the andricelum of the ingredients," meaning, "mixing the ingredients which make the andricelum." The question is whether the mixture is a mixture of melted wax with colour which produces a wax figure, or a mixture of colours which produces a new colour. The whole sense of the passage requires the former interpretation. The ἀνδρείκελον corresponds to the θεοείκελον. The former is the combination of physical attributes which make up the visible image of man ; the latter the combination of moral attributes which make up the conception of God. The definite article is joined to ἀνδρείκελον. Why should Plato speak of *the* andricelum if andricelum means flesh-colour? But the definite article is required if the word means the likeness of man. The andricelum is that which results when all the elements are present, but flesh-colour is only one of various elements. On this hypothesis it is intelligible that Plato should use the singular, ἀνδρείκελον, though Theophrastus spoke of ἀνδρείκελα in the plural. Plato in his argument passes insensibly from the

concrete to the abstract, from the particular andricelum which was made of wax to the general meaning, the likeness of man, though Theophrastus referred
to the literal or wax images alone.   As it is plain
in this passage that andricelum is not a flesh-coloured
pigment, a third meaning has been invented.   The
word is said to be sometimes the true complexion of
a man.   But surely it must be the true appearance
of a man, not simply his complexion.   This mysterious word makes its appearance in the *Cratylus* in
the following passage :—Ταῦτα πάντα καλῶς διαθεα-
σαμένους ἐπίστασθαι ἐπιφέρειν ἕκαστον κατὰ τὴν
ὁμοιότητα, ἐάν τε ἐν ἑνὶ δέῃ ἐπιφέρειν, ἐάν τε συγκε-
ραννύντα πολλὰ ἑνί, ὥσπερ οἱ ζωγράφοι βουλόμενοι
ἀφομοιοῦν ἐνίοτε μὲν ὄστρεον μόνον ἐπήνεγκαν, ἐνίοτε
δὲ ὁτιοῦν ἄλλο τῶν φαρμάκων, ἔστι δ᾽ ὅτε πολλὰ
συγκεράσαντες, οἷον ὅταν ἀνδρείκελον σκευάζωσιν, ἢ
ἄλλο τι τῶν τοιούτων, ὡς ἂν, οἶμαι, δοκῇ ἑκάστη ἡ
εἰκὼν δεῖσθαι ἑκάστου φαρμάκου. οὕτω δὴ καὶ ἡμεῖς
τὰ στοιχεῖα ἐπὶ τὰ πράγματα ἐποίσομεν, καὶ ἓν ἐπὶ
ἕν, οὗ ἂν δοκῇ δεῖν, καὶ σύμπολλα, ποιοῦντες ὃ δὴ
συλλαβὰς καλοῦσι, καὶ συλλαβὰς αὖ συντιθέντες, ἐξ
ὧν τά τε ὀνόματα καὶ τὰ ῥήματα συντίθεται, καὶ πάλιν
ἐκ τῶν ὀνομάτων καὶ ῥημάτων μέγα ἤδη τι καὶ καλὸν
καὶ ὅλον συστήσομεν, ὥσπερ ἐκεῖ τὸ ζῷον τῇ γραφικῇ,
ἐνταῦθα τὸν λόγον τῇ ὀνομαστικῇ ἢ ῥητορικῇ ἢ ἥ τις
ἔστιν ἡ τέχνη. (*Cratylus*, p. 424.)

In this passage the words ὅταν ἀνδρείκελον
σκευάζωσι must be translated either, "when they are
preparing flesh-colour," or "when they are making a
likeness of a man." The argument demands the
latter sense. The andricelum of the first part of the
paragraph is the "something fair and whole" of the
latter part. It is the sum total which results when
the various elements are duly combined. Plato first
puts the case generally of painters wishing to imitate,
and then the particular instance of making an andricelum, i.e. wishing to imitate a man. The colour of
the complexion corresponds to the ὀνόματα or ῥήματα
which must be finally compounded, but are not
individually sufficient.

It is now possible to understand Plato's words in
which he speaks of painting statues without doing
violence to the natural interpretation. Winckelman
was perplexed by the passage and asked whether
ἀνδριάντες might not sometimes mean pictures. This
is certainly not the solution. The sentence ὥσπερ
οὖν ἂν εἰ ἡμᾶς ἀνδριάντας γράφοντας (p. 420,
Stephens), undoubtedly means: "if when we were
painting statues;" but the answer is that the statue
when painted would cease to be an *andrias* and
would have become an *andricelum*. Plato does not
say, "if the sculptor or artist were painting a statue,"
as he would have done in conformity with his usual

U

practice, if he had intended his example for an instance of the artistic practice, but puts the case, " if we were painting one." It is an illustration which would naturally occur to any one who had often seen the artists finishing the solid portraits of wax, and perhaps the andricela were sometimes made in this way of marble. But it would be a great mistake to suppose that because Plato thought that to paint a statue was a natural and obvious proceeding, the sculptors would have agreed with him. He was a great literary artist, but had not a spark of feeling for the other arts. Goethe's life shows how different the two tastes or capacities are. Goethe's first ambition was to become a painter, and it was not until repeated failures had convinced him of his incapacity that he took to literary art, in which he was destined to hold so high a place. Plato held the realistic theory of all the arts except poetry. They were in his eyes simply so many means of representation, and consistently with this view he never called them Fine Arts. The illustration which Plato gave in this passage in the *Republic* was repeated by Lucian in more elaborate form in the dialogue called " Icŏnes " (*Portraits or Representations*), and the mode in which the latter put it removes all possibility of doubt. The plot is as follows :—Two friends meet, one of them in a state of great excitement.

The latter explains that he has just seen a woman of almost incredible beauty, and the question arises how he can convey a notion of her charms.   He hits on the following device: he bids his friend think of all the most beautiful female statues which are known, and conjure up a mental image in which all their several beauties are united.   The friend presently observes that he has done this, but that he finds a fatal defect in his mental picture, for that it is quite colourless.   He is then bid to think of a number of pictures and add in imagination the necessary colours.   This is conclusive evidence that the statues were uncoloured ; but the point to which I desire to call attention is that which appears in the end of the dialogue.   Lucian forgets in the course of his argument that he had imagined a painted statue, and ends with a comment on the ephemeral nature of wood and wax.   The usual interpretation of this allusion would undoubtedly be that he was thinking of a picture painted on a panel of wood   It may be, however, that he meant an andricelum constructed on a wooden skeleton or frame.   Pausanias tells us that the chryselephantine statues were constructed in this way, and the idea may have been borrowed from the construction of andricela.   In spite of the evidence which there is in this dialogue that the statues were not coloured, some writers have been so fascinated by

Quatremère de Quincy's theory as to maintain that
at least some of the statues were coloured. This is
asserted in the article on Painting in Smith's *Dictionary of Antiquities.* But those who say this have not
sufficiently weighed the testimony of Pausanias.
They attach too much importance to a remark of
Plutarch, and neglect a surer authority. Even
Plutarch does not say that the ἀγάλματα were
coloured in imitation of nature, and if he had said
this, the *Descriptio* of Pausanias would be enough to
convict him of error. In this long and elaborate
catalogue of the statues of Greece the kind of marble
of which each was made is almost always specified,
and it is unintelligible that Pausanias could have
known which each was if they were coloured. But
it is still more unintelligible that if some were
coloured and others uncoloured no comment should
be made on this difference. It is certain that it
would have seemed to him a grave question from
the religious point of view, and that he could not
have passed it over in silence. If, moreover, time
or accident had effaced the colours, both he and most
of the Greeks would have thought that it was a serious
question whether the Deity would be pleased by a
restoration, or whether it were fitter that the statue
should remain as it was. There is not a hint of the
kind to be found in his narrative from beginning to

end. Though it is rash to speak quite positively, I
am tolerably confident that the only places in which
there is any mention of artificial colouring in connexion with the statues are the following :—In Book
II., cap. ii., there is a description of gilded wooden
statues of Artemis and Dionysus, of which the coun-
tenances were coated with red paint, ἀλοιφῇ ἐρυθρᾷ
κεκόσμηται. This word ἀλοιφῇ shows that the colour
was an example of the archaic practice, and was
not imitative colour. There are in Greek two
expressions for painting. To paint mechanically or
coat with colour is ἀλείφειν ; to paint artificially, or
imitate, is γράφειν or γραφῇ μιμεῖσθαι. Pausanias
always observes this distinction. In Book VII., cap.
xxvi., is described a statue of Athene, of which the
face, hands, and feet were of ivory, the rest of wood
ornamented with gold and colours. In the same
chapter a statue of Dionysus is named which was
scarlet. In Book VIII., cap. xxxix., another Dionysus
coloured in the same way. These were relics of the
period when red was the divine colour. Lastly we
find an instance of a plaster figure of Dionysus which
was ἐπικεκοσμημένον γραφῇ. This is the exception
which proves the rule. It is described, or rather
named, in Book IX., cap. xxxii., and does not strictly
count as a statue, because it was made of plaster.
It was in a private house,—ἐν ἰδιώτου ἀνδρὸς,—and

this is an indication that popular sentiment disapproved of it. It is characteristic of the devout caution of Pausanias that he does not express any open disapprobation. He has in another place described the statue of Antinous, and accorded to it the name ἄγαλμα, *i.e.* divine statue, abstaining from all dispute of the right of Antinous to divine honour. This reticence contrasts signally with the torrent of pious vituperation which Clemens Alexandrinus poured forth on this question, and it is impossible to doubt that Pausanias must have felt secretly sceptical.

I will return now to the theory of statuary. The art of painting exhausts the contradiction which forms a Fine Art of the sense of sight. We must assume that a similar art of the sense of touch is required and consider the ways in which touch may be made to contradict itself. There are two ways in which this may be effected. One is by changing the degree of resistance which natural objects cause ; another is by changing the degree of temperature. Both these lead to the result that statuary must be confined to the human body. The fluids, air and water, do not satisfy the conditions by reason of their fluidity. They do not retain any fixed forms, and are unsuitable for the art of the three dimensions. Nor among any natural objects

is there an invariable alliance between forms of a
given kind and a known degree of resistance except
in the flesh or muscles of animals, which are undis-
guised in human beings alone.   A blind person
could obtain a contradiction—not, indeed, so perfect
as there is in pictures—but still adequate, by rendering the forms of flesh in a hard material.   In like
manner living warm-blooded animals alone are distinguishable by a certain fixed temperature.   But in
man alone, where a coating of fur, hair, or feathers
does not interfere, the peculiar temperature is immediately discernible to touch.   Consequently, here
too, if the contradiction is effected by the use of a
cold material, man is the proper subject for the
sculptor's art.   There is a further reason why, on
the hypothesis that statuary is the Fine Art of the
sense of touch, human beings should be selected.
The theory of painting is that all which the eyes
(the instrument of vision) can observe without a
movement of the head resolves itself into one image
which is projected in a plane.   The theory of
statuary must be, on a similar hypothesis, that all
which a continuous tactual observation, made by the
hands (the instrument of touch), without a change
of place, can ascertain, is projected in a three-
dimensioned image.   But an image of this kind is
necessarily of limited dimensions, and must be of

some natural object which is in itself interesting, inasmuch as that variety of interest which a picture affords cannot be present. Human beings with their physical and mental feelings alone fulfil this condition. It is not a mere conjecture that statuary is the art of the sense of touch, for there is a French sculptor, known to fame, Monsieur Vidal, who is blind. But though it is in theory the art of the blind, practically the eyes are used by every one who can use them, and practically sculpture must be reckoned among the arts of sight. The value of this theory must therefore be tested by the history of Greek statuary, on the hypothesis that the Greek statues were first implements of devotion, and that as the artistic sentiment formed itself a tendency would be manifested to prefer the naked human body, and to represent this in such material as would most perfectly contradict the natural quality of flesh, whether for the eyes or for the hands, but especially for the former. It is obvious that the most perfect contradiction which could be obtained would be by the employment of white marble, both as a hard and brittle substance and as white, and this is one of the great changes which occurred as the art was developed. Moreover, the desire to abolish drapery, wherever religious sentiment allowed this, is found. Pausanias observes that the Charites were always clad in the older statues, but that in his time they were always deprived of their clothing. He seems to be scandalised at this want of reverence, and says that he cannot account for the change. (*Vide* Book IX., cap. xxxv.)

As in the first period red was the sacred colour, so wood was the sacred material. Pausanias mentions a number of archaic statues which were of wood and apparently uncoloured, and there seems to have been a reluctance to abandon the use of this material altogether in the early period. This was perhaps a very remote tradition. Though we do not know with certainty how the first idols were made, it is exceedingly likely that there may be some truth in the account of this invention which we find in the *Wisdom of Solomon*. It is said there that when all the uses which could be made of timber, both for construction and firewood, had been exhausted, there were left some hard and knotty pieces which the primitive artist carved in his idle moments into idols. The writer of this does not attempt to disguise that his object is to make idol-worship ridiculous, but his perfect candour with regard to this does not deprive his words of significance. He does not write in the style of one who is inventing, and it is not likely that he would have affirmed this if nothing supported it. The knots which are found

in timber have often a fantastic likeness to man or
some other animal, and it may be that the first
images which were carved were suggested by these.
The custom once introduced, it was an obvious
resource in a rude age to select pieces of wood in
which the task of the image-maker was already half-
accomplished for him by nature, just as the maker
of cameos has frequently utilised the accidental
stains which are found in pebbles or shells. Religious tradition is always conservative, and the
disuse of wood in Greece took place gradually. As
civilisation advanced a new sentiment was formed
which conflicted with the tradition, and which, if the
artists had not been masters of the situation, would
perhaps not have been allowed. The sacred image
was, from the religious point of view, a mysterious
stationary animal endowed with magical properties.
From the purely artistic point of view, it was an
"unreal mockery," or toy for the imagination. But
the latter view arose only by slow degrees, and the
first step was a compromise. Wood was the
material employed for the drapery which concealed
all the form with the exception of the countenance,
the hands, and the feet, and the artist was allowed
to gratify his fancy by rendering these in white
marble. Some examples of this singular combination were left when Pausanias explored the

cities of Greece, and have been described by him.
In Book VII., cap. xxi., an Apollo and an Aphro-
dite ; in Book VIII., cap. xxv., an Erinnys, and
the same goddess with another title, are named.
But as marble was in Greece an ordinary material,
not distinguished in speech from common stone, the
devotional sentiment demanded for the more venerable divinities a more costly substance, and ivory
was employed in place of it in the composite statue
of Athene, which is described in Book VII.   This
sentiment produced subsequently the chryselephantine statues, of which the most celebrated were
the Here of Polyclitus, described in Book II., cap.
xvii. of Pausanias, and the Athene and Zeus of
Phidias.   This invention has been described as an
artistic movement.   It was in truth a sacrifice of
art to devotion, and it is said that Phidias expressed
a preference for white marble, but yielded in deference to Athenian sentiment.   But neither religion
nor art would have desired an imitation of natural
colour in the figure.   The red of the archaic period
was a uniform coating of colour applied sometimes
to the drapery as well as the figure, and was
dropped for the purpose of obtaining a more perfect
contrast instead of increasing the resemblance to
natural man.   There was no objection to the introduction of ornamental colour in the drapery, pro-

vided this colour was the unchangeable colour of natural materials, not the fugitive colour of paint. The garment of the Olympian Jove was thus inlaid with precious stones. In the Life of Phidias, in Smith's *Dictionary of Greek and Roman Mythology and Biography*, it is said that "on the robe were represented (whether by painting or chasing Pausanias does not say, but the former is by far the more probable) various animals and flowers, especially lilies." This is inaccurate, though Quatremère de Quincy is to blame. Pausanias says that these figures were ἐμπεποιημένα. No Greek writer—least of all Pausanias—would use the word ἐμποιεῖν if he meant to paint. In the passage which immediately follows both the usual terms are employed. On the throne there were artistic paintings, γραφῇ μεμιμημένα; the barrier which surrounded it was mechanically painted, ἀλήλιπται. But this is an instance of the way in which Quatremère de Quincy supported his theory. The author of the article on Painting in the *Dictionary of Antiquities* says, with reference to the statues of Praxiteles : "In the circumlitio of Nicias the naked form was most probably merely varnished, the colouring being applied only to the eyes, eyebrows, lips, and hair, to the draperies, and the various ornaments of dress ; and there can be no doubt that fine statues, especially of females, when tastefully and carefully coloured in this way, must have been extremely beautiful : the encaustic varnish upon the white marble must have had very much the effect of a pale transparent flesh." It is futile to dispute about taste, but as Gibson's practice is nearly described in this passage, and as his example has not been followed, it is certainly possible to doubt that marble statues would be improved by this addition, and there is at any rate good evidence that the sculptors of Greece held a different opinion.

Snow is, in the language of religious writers, the emblem of moral purity, because moral impurity is associated with the red colour of the blood and the warm temperature of the blood. The whiteness of white marble in like manner suggests the idea of coldness, though it is not really colder than other substances. As it is also hard no fitter material can be discovered for the representation of flesh. But though the artistic instinct is perfectly satisfied when the forms of the muscles are represented in this substance, it is attracted by the folds of flowing drapery also, which, when executed in unyielding material, afford a very perfect contradiction to experience. The sculptors of Greece indulged this instinct, and the rigid lines of the earlier draperies assumed the charms of the " flowing line " as art progressed. When the drapery as well as the figure became in this manner the property of the artist, and the whole statue was a creature of the imagination, bronze was a material as suitable as marble, for the contradiction now was in the idea of resistance alone, and a metal is perhaps even better suited to give this idea than marble, These two materials were so greatly superior to wood by reason of their manifestly greater hardness that the latter substance fell into disuse, though not before the word ξόανον, which is etymologically a scraped or polished thing, and thence a wooden thing, had acquired the meaning "an idol." Too many of the ancient bronzes have found their way into the melting-pot, but enough remain to prove that this substance can rival marble for the sculptor's purposes. The artists of Greece seem to have preferred it for the representation of transitory or momentary attitudes. There is in our museum a marble copy of a bronze discobolus by Myron in an attitude of this kind. Lessing affirms that artists must reject all momentary attitudes. " Erhält dieser einzige Augenblick durch die Kunst eine unveränderliche Dauer : so muss er nichts ausdrücken was sich nicht anders als transitorisch denken lässt." (*Sämmtliche Werke*, Carlsruhe, 1824, vol. iii., chap. iii., p. 33.) This, however, was only one of the mistakes into which his theory led him. The realistic theory weighs heavily on the modern sculptor in this matter of drapery.   It taxes him with unveracity if he dares to ignore the stiff style of modern costume, and demonstrates triumphantly that at the present day loose and flowing robes are out of fashion.   Fortunately for him, collegiate gowns and robes of office are still sometimes worn on state occasions, and he can explain to his tyrant that he has seen these dresses with his own eyes and is not utterly unveracious.   Nevertheless, the realistic arbiter of taste detects the academic prejudice, and reserves his full commendation for the artist who does not condescend to this subterfuge.

Lessing's theory of the Laocoon is that the sculptor desired to represent a beautiful form in pain. "Der Meister arbeitete auf die höchste Schönheit unter den angenommenen Umständen des körperlichen Schmerzes" (chap. ii., p. 28).   Winckelman had said that the countenance of Laocoon is calm, because the Greeks thought that it was unworthy of a great man to lose self-possession and cry like a child.   Lessing appeals to the drama to refute this, and declares that the artist desired to embody the idea of pain, and represent the expression of it with the utmost fidelity ; but that he abstained from giving full expression to it in the countenance, solely because the lines of the face in repose are more beautiful than they are when distorted.   The theory is, therefore, the realistic theory that perfection of representation is the test of excellence, but it is practically limited in its application by the consideration of " The Beautiful." But Lessing does not explain why the artist should have desired to embody the idea of pain in a beautiful form. Physical beauty is, in his theory, a kind of moral virtue. He is, as regards this, more Greek than the Greeks themselves. Why should he or any one be pleased to find an unusually virtuous person in great distress and suffering? His reference to the play of Philoctetes is foreign to the point. This peculiar moral virtue, physical beauty, is not in the play presented to the spectator ; and the thoughts of the reader or spectator are greatly occupied with the plot and characters and incidents. If it were true that it is delightful to behold a beautiful form in physical pain, and that the delight is justifiable, a gladiatorial combat, if the gladiators were well chosen, would be much superior to the Laocoon. Alison passed over the same question in his argument about music. The " higher beauty," he said, is called into existence when the idea of revenge is vividly expressed. Why should the higher beauty be pleased by this ? Juvenal said that revenge is the pleasure of a small, narrow, and feeble mind, and Christianity agrees with him about this. Why should the higher beauty find this contemptible passion so attractive? The indiscreet admirers of the higher beauty do her injustice.   She is free from these unamiable propensities.   The great poets of all ages and countries have been her architects, and have built her many fair mansions from which she has no desire to escape.   When Alison wrote thus about music he was thinking of Dryden's lines—

" Revenge, revenge, Timotheus cries," etc.—

and was fabricating an explanation of the fact that Handel's music is more attractive than the words of Dryden.   But his explanation is the exact contradictory of the truth.   Such ideas as revenge fade from the mind when music asserts her sway, and some profounder feeling, too vague for analysis, steals over the wrapt mind of the listener.   In like manner the idea of pain is banished in the presence of the Laocoon.   The thing is hard, is cold, is brittle.   Such things cannot feel.   Were it tinted and coloured, as the realistic theorists think it should be, and made to resemble a pathological illustration in a surgical museum, undoubtedly we should find this excellence which Lessing claims for it.   It would then be a beautiful form in pain, and would be repulsive.   As it is, it is a beautiful form in a fantastic attitude, at which imagination can

X

smile, because imagination knows that it is its own creature.

Architecture is the art of touch and sight acting together. The works which it creates are not images corresponding to a series of visual observations as in painting, or a series of tactual observations as in statuary, but are inventions. The composer and executant are distinct, and the invention is the union of colours and forms which are not found in natural objects. These inventions belong to Fine Art only when they suggest and contradict at the same time an idea. The idea which architecture thus suggests and contradicts is that of organic growth, derived from animal organism. The idea of a subordination of parts to a whole, which is itself given by animal organism, is the essential idea. A row of houses which adjoin each other does not constitute an architectural whole, nor does a single room. A work of architecture is one in which parts are varied, but are so arranged as to produce a unit. This is the definition of Vitruvius. " Architectura constat ex ordinatione, quæ Græce τάξις dicitur, et ex dispositione—ordinatio est modica membrorum operis commoditas separatim, universæque proportionis ad symmetriam comparatio" (Cap. ii.) He also derives the idea from the forms of the human body. "Namque non potest ædes ulla sine sym-

metriâ atque proportione rationem habere composi-
tionis, nisi uti ad hominis bene figurati membrorum
habuerit exactam rationem " (Book III., cap. i.)
Perhaps he goes too far when he insists that the
proportions of a building must answer exactly to the
proportions of the body ; but the idea of proportion
has probably this origin.   There is no apparent reason
why a square room should be less pleasing than an
oblong room unless it is that the latter is more like
the form of the body.   As the idea of architecture is
thus an organic whole, the requisite forms are those
which Plato described as eternally beautiful.   These
are not found in natural organisms, and supply the
necessary contradiction.   As the religion of Greece
was anthropomorphic, the architecture of Greece was
of this kind, consisting of oblong rectilinear buildings, and the circular form which was more conspicuous in the architecture of Rome was also, in
all probability, connected with the religious creed of
the Romans.   Though the Romans had statues and
images, their great God was the ever-burning fire of
Vesta ; and Vesta was not represented by an image.
It cannot be reasonably doubted that the sacred fire
of Vesta represented the sun ; and that her temple
was round because the orb of the sun is round, cannot be an extravagant conjecture.   The same form
reappears on a grander scale in the Pantheon, and

later ecclesiastical architecture was developed out of the basilicas with semi-circular apses in which the two forms, circular and rectilinear, were united. Ovid's confession that at one time he had supposed that Vesta had a statue shows how little importance the Romans attached to image worship, and how different they were from the Greeks in this respect—

> " Esse diu stultus Vestæ simulacra putavi :
> Mox didici curvo nulla subesse tholo :
> Ignis inextinctus templo servatur in illo :
> Effigiem nullam Vesta nec ignis habet."

Perilous as it is to write *a priori* history, this mode must be adopted in writing the history of sentiments, and if religious sentiments can have a natural origin, there is a strong presumption that primitive creeds must be either some form of sun-worship, or of ancestor-worship, or of both combined. As regards the sun there is abundant testimony that both in the new and the old world it has been an object of reverence, and the fact that it was deified is not disputed. But the presumption that ancestors must be deified in primitive races is at least as strong. Children regard their parents as beings of a different order to themselves, and possessed of infinite knowledge, wisdom, and strength. As this sentiment has been felt from the first dawn of intelligence during countless generations at the time of life when the sentiments are formed, there must have resulted in adults a tendency to believe in a generation superior to themselves, whose protecting power might still be experienced, and whose favour could be won by obedience and submission. There are united, accordingly, in primitive creeds, two distinct sentiments : one, a reverence for the sun as the manifest daily cause of good ; the other, an instinctive belief in, and reverence for, a higher kind of human being. The architecture of Rome was guided chiefly by the former, of Greece by the latter, sentiment. The latter might, moreover, having given the form of the temples, have added the cruciform character of Christian churches, even though the cross were not a sacred symbol in Christianity. Crosses have been discovered in America which were sacred, though it is certain that they were in no way connected with Christianity. Dr. Réville's theory is that these crosses were sacred to the winds, and represented the four points of the compass. If they had been placed horizontally so as to point with their arms to north, south, east, and west, this would be a probable explanation, but as they were vertical, and only pointed in two directions, it is doubtful. Religious writers are too apt to forget that the cross was invented to suit the forms of the human body, and may have been a

symbol of humanity in heathen religions. A discovery which was made last century at Palenque,
a ruined city of Mexico, strongly supports the conjecture that this was the true origin of these crosses
which have caused so much speculation. A sculptured slab was found, on which was represented an
elaborately decorated cross surmounted by a strange
bird, and a priest in the act of making an offering
to this compound idol. As this was a relic of the
kind of religious creed known as Totemism, it is
more probable that the cross and bird represented
the mythical man-bird which the race revered, than
that it was connected with the worship of the winds.
The slab was broken up and the fragments taken to
different places, but a woodcut of it, restored, is given
in the *Travels in Mexico*, by F. A. Ober (Boston,
1884). Undoubtedly, as a matter of fact, the cruciform shape of churches is chiefly due to the influence
of Christianity, but, if Vitruvius is right in his theory,
may be a genuine architectural form apart from this
association. In like manner the greater attention
which the ancestors of the Romans paid to the orb
of the sun may have given the first idea of the arch
as a means of construction. Familiar as we now are
with this form, the history of Greece shows that art
and civilisation may make great progress without a
discovery of it.

Shakespeare has embodied the idea which under-
lies music in the character of the melancholy Jaques.
It is lawless law, or discord in the spheres. Jaques
throughout the play incessantly cries out for music,
yet his friend is astonished that he, compact of jars,
should turn musical.   Music and architecture are
the two scientific arts.   In the latter the contradiction is the substitution of mechanical for organic
laws in an organic whole.   In the former mathematical law contradicts itself.   The harmonies are
not perfect harmonies; the symmetry is unsym-
metrical; the repetitions are not exact repetitions.
Impulse is lawless, and the art of uttering feeling
cannot be trammelled by the mathematical precision
to which architecture submits.   When the science
or art of composition had reached a certain stage,
a marked tendency appeared to reject the formal
obligations which confined the earlier styles.   Wagner's theory is based on the assumption that this
tendency has no limits; that the forms of earlier
compositions have been derived from dance music,
and that the respect which has been paid to them is
what in the art of painting is called an academic
prejudice.   This theory evidently is needed to support the realistic doctrine that music is an art of
representation, unless it can be maintained that the
thing which music represents is, like an architectural

unit, a symmetrical whole. In cruder and earlier
speculations the latter view found favour, and music
was said to represent the perfect arrangement of the
universe. Hence the often quoted phrase, the music
of the spheres. But this theory could not suit
Wagner, who added the doctrine that academical
prejudice must be overcome, and the dance-music
propensity driven out. Music must in his theory
represent something, but that something could not
be an organic unit. He fell back, accordingly, on
the doctrine that music represents the Cosmic Will,
—a doctrine which cannot be conclusively refuted,
owing to the difficulty of ascertaining with certainty
the nature of the Cosmic Will. Between Alison's
definite and intelligible statement of the realistic
theory, and Wagner's, or rather Schopenhauer's, incomprehensible doctrine, an infinite number of intermediate forms are found of which it is superfluous
to quote examples. All spring from the desire to
prove that music is in some way an art of representation, and therefore an aid to the understanding ;
but as each writer in turn tries to improve on his
predecessor's mode of stating the argument, and as
those who know most of music adopt the most
indefinite modes of statement, the inference may be
fairly drawn that the theory is untenable. It is
equally certain that the classical theory is unten-

able, and that the analogy is false between the
harmony of music and the harmony or adjustment
of the spheres.   Not only is a discordant element a
necessary part of harmony in music, but the recur-
rence or repetition of musical phrases occurs with a
difference.   Mozart, in most of his sonatas, obtained
the requisite variety by a simple artifice which has
not satisfied more recent composers.   He introduced
a melody, dropped it for a time, then took it up
again in a new key, and repeated it from beginning
to end without the change of a single note.   This
artifice of a recurrent phrase is a favourite one of
Wagner's.   He would not have admitted that his
and Mozart's practice were based on a similar sentiment.   His, he would have said, represents the
Cosmic Will, Mozart's was an academic prejudice.
It is more likely that, as Hogarth forgot the flowing
line when he painted, Wagner forgot the Cosmic
Will when busy with musical composition.   But the
realistic movement is always of a retrograde kind,
and as in Alison's speculation the Pre-Handelian
theory was defended, so a still more primitive theory
is declared in the music of the future.   The nightingale is an admirable songster, and he has a fine
taste for some musical effects, among others the
beauty of a *crescendo*.   But his compositions lack
artistic finish because there is no obvious reason why

he should leave off when he does, unless it is that he is fatigued for the moment. This is a characteristic of the more advanced school of music. Musical composition has hitherto conformed to the law which the other arts obey, that each work of art should be of such magnitude as forms an imaginary unit. An epic poem or a play is defective as a work of art if the beginning, the middle, and the end are uncon- nected, or cannot be thought of as forming a whole. When the eyes are turned away from a picture, a statue, or a building, there remains in the mind an image which includes all the parts of each. But that which cannot be remembered cannot be im- agined. When music meanders on from day to day no memory can retain the earlier parts and conse- quently no imagination can represent them. Music is sacrificed on the realistic altar when united to dramatic trilogies. The incidents of the plot can be remembered, because these produce definite feelings ; but the indefinite emotion, which the presentation of musical sound causes, cannot be remembered with equal fidelity, and the musical memory derives no aid from the artificial connexion with dramatic in- cident. In Wagner's theory music is like the song of the nightingale. Each part as it comes may charm the listener, but no artistic whole is formed which imagination can retain, and an essential quality of Fine Art is absent. The notion that the forms of music have been derived from dancing is a pure fancy which no presumption and no evidence supports. It is suggested by the fact that certain kinds of music stimulate physical action, so far as it is not a mere guess. Some kinds of music have this effect, and music has been an instrument of war for this reason. But other kinds have the opposite effect. They induce a solemn calm, and transport the auditor in imagination to some distant and unknown place or time. These are the kinds which are dear to religion. The third kind is festive music, which has doubtless more of the dance characteristic, though it would be an exaggeration to derive even this entirely from this source, for music without dancing was an accompaniment of Jewish banquets. The methodical and symmetrical quality of music was not invented to suit the dancer, but is a contrast to the natural utterance, and thus serves to give the composition its artistic character, inasmuch as an impulsive utterance is naturally irregular and wanting in form.

All the four arts of the senses are thus based on a contradiction. Painting is the art of unsubstantial substance, statuary of inanimate animation or insentient feeling, architecture of inorganic organism, music of passionless passion or unimpulsive impulse.

CHAPTER VIII.

ART AND NATURE.

BACON'S description of nature has a world-wide celebrity, and has been quoted and approved, both by authors whose general views of philosophy resemble his, and others who reject all his teaching except in this one respect. In speculation, as in politics, strange alliances are sometimes formed to attack a common foe, but when the victory is won, and the spoil is to be divided, the victors turn their arms against themselves. The general character of Bacon's philosophic creed is well known. The following extract from the *Essay on Atheism* declares it :—" It is true that a little philosophy inclineth man's mind to atheism, but depth in philosophy bringeth men's minds about to religion, for while the mind of man looketh upon second causes scattered, it may sometimes rest in them and go no farther, but when it beholdeth the chain of them confederate and linked together, it must needs fly to Providence and Deity."

It would not be readily supposed that the writer of
this had found a warm and able advocate in John
Stuart Mill, but it is the fact that Mill's posthumous
Essay on Nature, repeats and confirms, with a certain modification, Bacon's account of the difference
between art and nature. The latter described the
task which he had undertaken in his philosophical
writings as follows :—" Conficimus historiam non
solum Naturæ liberæ ac solutæ (cum scilicet ea
sponte fluit et opus suum peragit) qualis est historia
cælestium, meteorum, terræ et maris, mineralium,
plantarum, animalium, sed multo magis naturæ con-
strictæ et vexatæ, nempe cum per artem et minis-
terium humanum de statu suo detruditur atque pre-
mitur et fingitur." This is Bacon's first definition of
art. The artificial is that which has been thrust
from its *status* by man's intervention, and is pressed
and fashioned, and is in this shape *natura constricta
et vexata.* The second definition is given near the
end of the *Destributio Operis*, and is the following :—
" Homo enim naturæ minister et interpretr tantum
facit et intelligit quantum de naturæ ordine opere
val mente observaverit : nec amplius scit aut potest.
Neque enim ullæ vires causarum catenam solvere
aut perfringere possint, neque natura aliter quam
parendo vincitur. Itaque intentiones geminæ illæ,
humanæ scilicet scientiæ et potentiæ, vere in idem

coincidunt, et frustratio operum maxime fit ex
ignoratione causarum." This is translated as follows
in Stebbing's edition of *Bacon*, in the General Preface
to the *Philosophical Works* by Ellis :—" For we can
command nature only by obeying her, nor can art
avail anything except as nature's handmaid. We
can affect the conditions under which nature works ;
but things artificial, as well as things natural, are in
reality produced not by art but by nature. Our
power is merely based upon our knowledge of the
procedure which nature follows. She is never really
thwarted or controlled by our operation, though she
may be induced to depart from her usual course,
and under new and artificial conditions to produce
new phenomena and new substances." This is not
meant for a literal translation, but it fairly represents
the sense of Bacon's words. Now, supposing it to
be true, as is said in this passage, that " our power
is merely based upon our knowledge of the procedure which nature follows," or as Bacon puts it,
knowledge and power are the same, what is the
explanation of the fact that a human being is deprived of his knowledge when a rope is tightly bound
round his arms and legs ? It is quite certain that
a man who can move a chair across his room, when
not so tied, is unable to do it when he is fastened
and bound in this way. If those two intentions,

knowledge and power, *vere in idem coincidunt*, knowledge must have been taken away when the rope
was tied.   Further, how comes it that nature can be
thrust from her *status*, vexed, pressed, and fashioned,
as is said in the first definition, if, as is said in the
second, the only way to conquer nature is to obey
her?   Vexing, thrusting, pressing, and fashioning, is
not the kind of obedience which usually pleases
high-spirited persons, such as nature is depicted in
the second passage.   Mill, however, has adopted
both these descriptions of nature, with such modification as suited his purpose, though that, as it is
superfluous to say, was not to prove that man must
needs fly to Providence and Deity.   Bacon had in
his mind two different things when he gave these
two accounts.   When he wrote the first passage, he
was thinking of *natura naturata*, the sum total of
the phenomena which he proposed to investigate,
and he was obliged to admit that man is, at least in
part, the cause of these phenomena.   When he wrote
the second, he was thinking of *natura naturans*, the
cause of all phenomena, and as *natura naturans* was
in his philosophy only another name for God, he
was unwilling to admit that man could overrule the
latter.   Mill had a different end in view.   He was
haunted by that spectre, the nature of the will, and
feared lest, if he allowed that man could turn nature

from her course, the theologian would reply that, if
man, surely God can do this.   They agreed in their
desire to minimise, if they could not quite suppress,
the difference between art and nature ; but the one
proposed to draw the inference that there is only
one first cause, the other that there is no first cause
known.   Bacon, however, either did not understand,
or was reluctant to state clearly, the theistic view.
It has been given by Bossuet, who knew his own
mind and had no hesitation, in his treatise on *Free
Will.*   " Mais tel qu'il (Dieu) est à l'égard de toute la
matière, et de tout son mouvement, tel a-t-il voulu que
je fusse à l'égard de cette petite partie de la matière
et du mouvement, qu'il a mis dans la dependance
de ma volonté."   This is the view which Bacon's
philosophy requires.   One small part of material
substance (*i.e.* the voluntary muscles) has been sub-
jected to the authority of man, or, as it should rather
be, of animals.   The term nature being substituted
for God, it is also the view which Mill's philosophy
requires, though he had not discovered this when he
composed the *Essay on Nature.*   What is meant
when it is said that " we " can move things ?   Is the
body a part of the " we " or not ?   If it is not, the
integrity of the " we " cannot be impaired by a
paralysis of the muscles.   But any one who could
move the smallest object in the slightest degree, in

spite of a total paralysis of the muscles, would have wrought a miracle. If, on the other hand, the body is a part of the "we," our power cannot be "based merely on our knowledge of the procedure which nature follows," for the most irrational animals share it. The fish who swims against the stream possesses it, but he knows nothing of the procedure which nature follows. Mill in his *Logic* has cited Bacon as an instance of the danger of using metaphor and rhetoric in philosophy. He should have taken warning, and mistrusted a description of nature which could not be given without metaphors. A definition which brings in phrases about obedience and handmaids is self-convicted of error. It cannot be true that nature can be vexed and pressed and fashioned, and at the same time only overcome by obedience, and Bacon only says this because his theological opinions, which he professes to forget in his philosophical speculations, would not permit themselves to be forgotten. Nor could Mill forget his, though he subsequently saw that he could not bear arms by the side of Bacon. It is said in the Preface to the *Essays on Religion* that Mill was well satisfied with this *Essay on Nature*, though he did not publish it. A comparison of it with the later essays on Theism will show that this must be a mistake.

Y

The following is Mill's version of the Baconian description :—" Nature, then, in its simplest acceptation is a collective name for all facts, actual and possible ; or, to speak more accurately, a name for the mode, partly known to us, and partly unknown, in which all things take place. For the word suggests not so much the multitudinous details of the phenomena, as the conception which might be formed of their manner of existence as a mental whole by a mind possessing a complete knowledge of them ; to which conception it is the aim of science to raise itself by successive steps of generalisation from experience. Such, then, is a correct definition of the word Nature. But this definition corresponds only to one of the senses of that ambiguous term. It is evidently inapplicable to some of the modes in which the word is familiarly employed. For example, it entirely conflicts with the common forms of speech by which Nature is opposed to Art, and natural to artificial. For in the sense of the word Nature which has just been defined, and which is the true scientific sense, Art is as much Nature as anything else, and everything which is artificial is natural. Art has no independent powers of its own ; Art is but the employment of the powers of Nature for an end." It is not surprising that Mill never published this ; the wonder is that, having written it, he left it standing

The concluding words of the paragraph, " Art has no independent powers of its own ; Art is but the employment of the powers of Nature for an end," is as much as to say, " Art has no independent powers except its own independent powers," and, in the words which precede, there is the classical and mediæval superstition that words have some sacred value, and are not simply the implements of thought. No one was usually more quick than Mill to point out that the true scientific use of words cannot be one which "entirely conflicts with the common forms of speech," and no one would usually have been more prompt to ask how it can happen that men of all ages and countries have drawn a distinction between art and nature, if "Art is as much Nature as anything else." He subsequently repeats and sums up this definition in the following terms :—" It thus appears that we must recognise at least two principal meanings in the word Nature. In one sense it means all the powers existing in either the inner or the outer world, and everything which takes place by means of those powers. In another sense, it means not everything which happens, but only what takes place without the agency or without the voluntary and intentional agency of man " (p. 8). It is true that there is this double use of the word " nature," which Mill describes, but he omits an all-important *item*.

There is in popular opinion and ordinary speech a
double contrast.   The natural is set in opposition to
(1) The supernatural ; (2) The artificial.   Mill entirely
ignores the former contrast, and by omitting it so
defines the word nature as to give it the meaning of
The Absolute.   He treats it as a collective name for
every possible object of thought.   This kind of error
is not uncommon.   Controversialists who desire to
prove that some opinion is wrong, begin by denying
that such opinion exists.   It is strange that Mill
should have made such a mistake, but he certainly
has in this essay.   In all the earlier part of it he
entirely keeps out of sight the fact that mankind do
believe in the supernatural, though his chief purpose
is to convince them that they ought not to do so.
The result of this is, that as it is quite impossible to
investigate The Absolute, the second meaning of the
word nature, in which it is contrasted with art, is
surreptitiously introduced in all the earlier part of
the essay which treats professedly of nature in " the
true scientific sense."   Nature must be distinguished
from something for the purpose of discussion, and, as
he refuses to distinguish the natural from the supernatural, he is obliged to distinguish it from the artificial.   In this dilemma he attempts, as Bacon did,
in his second definition, to prove that if human
intervention has some effect on nature, it is, at any

rate, insignificant. The style is different, but the
end in view is the same. It is to reduce to a mini-
mum the operations of art. The following passage
is a sample :—" In these and all other artificial
operations the office of man is, as has been often
remarked, a very limited one. It consists in moving
things into certain places." Mill cannot have been
satisfied with this, and his later essays prove that he
was not. Is the " office " of man, when he moves
things, the same as the " office " of the running
stream, or the gale of wind which moves things ?
If it is, the statement is false, because man has not
even a limited office as opposed to nature. Is it a
different " office," and one which inanimate nature
does not discharge ? If it is, it is not a limited
office, for it is one to which there is, as Mill afterwards saw, only one parallel, viz. the power of God
to work miracles. In the *Essay on Revelation* he
wrote as follows :—" Those who argue thus are
mostly believers in Free Will, and maintain that
every human volition originates a new chain of causation, of which it is itself a commencing link, not
connected by invariable sequence with any anterior
fact. Even, therefore, if a divine interposition did
constitute a breaking-in upon the connected chain of
events by the introduction of a new originating cause
without root in the past, this would be no reason for

discrediting it, since every human act of volition does precisely the same.   If the one is a breach of law, so are the others.   In fact the reign of law does not extend to the origination of volition." (*Three Essays on Religion*, Longmans and Co., 1874, p. 227.) This is the position which Mill was obliged to take when he proceeded to argue about miracles : that the reign of law does not extend to the origination of volition.   He had fought on the other side his whole life through, and he finally laid down his arms. When he wrote the *Essay on Nature*, he still clung to the doctrine that the wind which carries a feather is a cause of motion in the same sense in which a bird which carries a feather in its bill is a cause.   The former kind of cause belongs to what he and most others call the reign of law, and he would not allow that any motion of any kind was outside this kingdom.   But, finding it impossible to assert this consistently, he adopted the device which appears in the sentence quoted above, where the office of man is said to be limited, and motion is described as an insignificant phenomenon.   It is, in fact, the one grand phenomenon of the universe, and if man, by the aid of the voluntary muscles, can move one thing from one place to another, he can do (though on a narrower scale) all which theologians affirm that God can do without the intervention of muscles.   If

the vital principle is a thing, when the dead are
restored to life, the miracle has consisted in putting
that thing back into a position which it had quitted ;
if it is not a thing, the miracle has consisted in putting the atoms which compose organic substances
into the place from which they had departed in the
process of disease and decay.   In various passages
in the *Essay on Revelation* Mill seems to have seen
for a moment that the real question about the possibility of miracles is simply the question whether
what is called volition can cause a movement in any
substance except the voluntary muscles; but he never
completely grasped the truth, because he clung to
the last to the belief that volition is something quite
different in kind from a wish.

In the *Essay on Revelation,* which contains his
last words on this subject, he says, " In the first case
(human action) all the physical phenomena except
the first bodily movement are produced in strict
conformity to physical causation ; while that first
movement is traced by positive observation to the
cause (volition) which produced it " (p. 228).   Now
it is quite evident that if it is possible to trace a
bodily movement by observation to volition, it must
be possible to observe volition.   If no such country
as America could be observed, it would be impossible
to trace the origin of the potato to America.   It is

equally obvious that volition cannot be observed by
the physical senses.   We cannot handle, smell, taste,
see, or hear it.   If, therefore, it can be observed, the
observation must be a mental introspection, and it
must be observable as the feelings of anger or hunger
are.   Let us, therefore, take an example of a voluntary act, and inquire what can be observed.   Let us
suppose an indolent person lying in his bed, thinking
that it would be wise to get up, and wishing to get up,
but still lying on.   At last the voluntary act comes.
He gets up.   What can be observed in consciousness ?
Absolutely nothing except a sense of effort.   If, therefore, volition is not the same as wish, it is a name
for effort.   Then occurs the difficulty.   The sense of
effort does not precede the act, and cannot be conceived otherwise than as caused by an act.   Volition
therefore is both cause and effect.   The case would
be clear enough, were it not that there is a distinction
between mental and bodily efforts.   A mental effort
may precede a bodily effort, and mental efforts are
frequently unconnected with bodily efforts.   It may
be that if physiology were capable of discovering the
whole truth, it would be found that mental efforts
are muscular efforts.   It is certain that they exhaust
the physical powers like bodily efforts, and that illness or want of food, which .destroys the capacity for
the one kind of effort, weakens also the capacity for

the other kind. But whether this is so or not, it still remains true that volition taken as a name for effort is at once cause and effect. As a feeling it can be observed ; as a cause it is a fiction of logic which accounts for the feeling. But it is usually discussed as if there could be no doubt about the meaning of the word, and the difficulty is treated as if it were a metaphysical one about the intercommunion of body and mind, instead of a logical one about cause and effect. Professor Clifford made this mistake in his essay called *Body and Mind.* He put the case as follows :—" Again, if anybody says that the will influences matter, the statement is not untrue, but it is nonsense. The will is not a material thing ; it is not a mode of material motion. Such an assertion belongs to the crude materialism of the savage. The only thing which influences matter is the position of surrounding matter, or the motion of surrounding matter. It may be conceived that at the same time with every exercise of volition there is a disturbance of physical laws ; but this disturbance being perceptible to me, would be a physical fact accompanying the volition, and could not be the volition itself, which is not perceptible to me." It may be well to explain, first, that Professor Clifford's remark about the crude materialism of the savage has reference to an argument which preceded this

passage.   He had borrowed Mr. H. Spencer's account
of the way in which savages acquire a belief in
ghostly personages, and he treats a belief in ghosts
as if it were a belief in a material will.   It is almost
superfluous to observe that no one could rightly be
called a savage who was capable of forming and expressing an opinion about the nature of the will.   In
the argument there are two contradictory views.   He
begins by saying, that if any one says that the will
influences matter, this statement is not untrue, but is
nonsense.   Having affirmed this, he immediately
shifts to the other point of view ; and assuming that
the statement has some meaning, proceeds to demonstrate that it is untrue.   He then loses himself
in a labyrinth of self-contradiction.   He declares
that it may be conceived that there is a disturbance
of physical law, though the whole object of the essay
is to demonstrate that this is inconceivable, and
speaks as if in his philosophy it were denied, or
could be denied, that feeling affects matter, and matter
feeling.   There have been philosophers who have
denied this, but he is not one of them.   Anger and
fear are immaterial, yet they affect the circulation of
the blood and cause tremor.   The feelings of colour
and of sound, and all the physical feelings, are immaterial as well as the mental feelings, yet an irritation of the material nerves causes them.   This is not

denied in the philosophy of Professor Clifford, and
he is not really troubled by the metaphysical difficulty which he introduces. But he is obliged to
argue the question in this way, because he cannot
shake off the belief that the word volition has some
meaning for him. It cannot be conceived that there
is a violation of physical law, for the all-sufficient
reason that a violation of physical law is a contradiction in terms. A physical law is an invariable
sequence, and though it is easily conceivable that a
supposed law may be disproved, no one can conceive
that a sequence is both variable and invariable. It is
equally impossible, if his account is taken, to conceive
an exercise of volition. He says that volition is not
perceptible to him. If it is not, the word must be a
name for nothing ; but it is no more possible to conceive an exercise of nothing than it is to conceive
that a given proposition is both universally true, and
not universally true. In the latter part of the essay,
where miracles are discussed, there is a metamorphosis
of opinion like Mill's, and all which is denied in this
paragraph is treated as an elementary and obvious
truth. Theological complications have everywhere
involved the question in an artificial obscurity. It
is connected with the mystery of personality and
responsibility, and all who write about it are secretly
attacking or supporting a thesis which they do not

avow. It would not have found a place in Professor Clifford's writings if he had adhered to his own principles. His philosophy is of the kind which is known commonly by the ill-chosen name "positive." He insists that the true philosopher should observe facts with an unprejudiced mind, and remember that the question which should guide his studies is the question "what," not the question "why." An attempt to answer the latter will, he says, only bewilder the inquirer, and prudence requires that he should keep to the former, which is not beyond his powers. Perhaps philosophy will decline to be limited in this way ; but a sound philosophy cannot deny that it is desirable to settle the "what" of things before the "why" is investigated. If the question what a particular word means is answered differently by different controversialists who use it, and differently by the same writer in different places, the controversy must be both fruitless and endless. But little care has been taken to ascertain what volition means. A very large part of the innumerable dissertations on this question are about the nature of wishes or desires. These can be discussed, because they can be observed, and are not fictions of logic. But the word volition or will is allowed to wander, and take from time to time other meanings, and Mill seems never to have made up his mind what he meant by it. In his *Logic* he says, " A habit of willing is commonly called a purpose; and among the causes of our volitions, and of the actions which spring from them, must be reckoned not only likings and aversions, but also purposes" (vol. ii., p. 489). In the *Essay on Nature*, he says, " Even the volition which designs, the intelligence which contrives, and the muscular force which executes these movements are themselves powers of Nature." In the former of these definitions purposes are said to form a part of the cause of volition ; in the second, it is said that volition designs, *i.e.* is a cause of purposes, unless there is a difference between design and purpose. If there is a distinction, it is very subtle. If one man said that he designed to build a house, and another that he purposed to do so, it would not be easy to distinguish between the two mental states. The habit of willing, of which Mill speaks, can, in fact, be resolved into a habit of imagining some feeling which is not felt at the time. The indolent person in bed imagines the discomfort which will ultimately be felt if he does not get up ; imagines at the same time the sense of effort which the act of getting up will cause ; imagines that the former discomfort will be greater than the latter, and does get up. Imagination creates a desire to get up, which would not come into existence without its intervention.

This particular kind of wish or desire, which can only be gratified by an act which is accompanied by a sense of effort is called volition ; but if it differs from other wishes, differs only in the fact that without intelligence, or the faculty of imagining and comparing things, it would not come into existence. If, therefore, the principles of " positive " philosophy are granted, it must be allowed that man is a first cause in the only sense in which a first cause is conceivable, inasmuch as a movement can be traced to intelligence. We cannot get beyond intelligence, or the faculty of comparing, but can trace the history downwards. It creates an artificial desire ; this desire directs the nervous energy into a channel which otherwise it would not take, and man, as a compound of muscles, intelligence, and desires, of which the nerves are the connecting link, is a first cause. The . nervous energy, " determined" in this way, overcomes some resistance, and sense of effort is felt as this *vis inertiæ* is overpowered.

Theologians and atheistical philosophers are alike unwilling to admit that man can be a first cause : the former, because they will not allow that there is any first cause except God ; the latter, lest they should be found fighting in the theological ranks if they admit the possibility of a first cause. But the theologians are inconsistent when man is in question,

for it is a part of their creed that God made man in
His own image, and their antagonists are inconsistent
with regard to animals generally, for it is a part of
their creed that like causes produce like effects, and
they can only defend their position, as Mill did, by
denying that there is a difference between art and
nature.   But Mill, in his *Essay on Nature*, relying on
the false statement with which he began that there
are in common use two contradictory meanings of
the word nature, emphasises in the latter part of his
argument the contrast between art and nature which
he denied in the earlier part.   He discusses in the
latter part *natura naturans*, attributing to it for the
moment the meaning which it had in Bacon's writings, and caricatures it as follows :—" Such are
Nature's dealings with life.   Even when she does
not intend to kill she inflicts the same tortures in
apparent wantonness.   In the clumsy provision which
she has made for that perpetual renewal of animal
life, rendered necessary by the prompt termination
she puts to it in every individual instance, no human
being ever comes into the world but another human
being is literally stretched on the rack for hours and
days, not unfrequently issuing in death.   Next to
taking life, equal to it (according to a high authority)
is taking the means by which we live, and nature
does this too on the largest scale and with the

most callous indifference" (p. 30). "The course of
natural phenomena being replete with everything
which, when committed by human beings, is most
worthy of abhorrence, any one who endeavoured in
his actions to imitate the natural course of things
would be universally seen and acknowledged to be
the wickedest of men" (p. 65). In these passages
Mill is attacking the so-called Law of Nature. The
following words show what was in his mind :—" But
even though unable to believe that Nature, as a
whole, is a realisation of the designs of perfect
wisdom and benevolence, men do not willingly
renounce the idea that some part of Nature, at
least, must be intended as an exemplar or type ;
that on some portion or other of the Creator's works
the image of the moral qualities which we are
accustomed to ascribe to him must be impressed ;
that, if not all which is, yet something which is,
must not only be a faultless model of what ought
to be, but must be intended to be our guide and
standard in rectifying the rest" (p. 41). If the
theologicum odium had not taken possession of Mill
when he wrote these and other passages like them,
he could hardly have failed to be struck by the fact
that the wickedest men, or even moderately wicked
men, might greatly improve their conduct if they
would strictly imitate the actions of nature. Wicked

men are in the habit of taking things which they did
not give in the first instance. But if nature takes
life it is only fair to remember that nature first
gave life, and if nature inflicts pain, nature sometimes
affords pleasure. Wicked men do not imitate her in
this respect, and their imitation is very one-sided.
When Mill afterwards composed the essays on
Theism, he found that a philosopher who desired to
deny the existence of a beneficent Deity could not
affirm the existence of a Devil, even though it might
be called Nature. Life would have come to an end,
if it ever came into being, if there were at work a
potent malignant influence which was not counter-
balanced by a beneficent influence. In the earlier
essay nature is said to use art and kill or torture
with malice aforethought. This is a fit sequel to
the doctrine that there is no difference between art
and nature. But in the *Essay on Attributes* there is
the following very different account :—" Along with
the preserving agencies there are destroying agencies,
which we might be tempted to ascribe to the will of
a different Creator ; but there are rarely appearances
of the recondite contrivance of means of destruction,
except when the destruction of one creature is the
means of preservation to others. Nor can it be
supposed that the preserving agencies are wielded
by one Being, the destroying by another. The de-

Z

stroying agencies are a necessary part of the preserving agencies; the chemical compositions by which
life is carried on could not take place without a
parallel series of decompositions. The great agent
of decay in both organic and inorganic substances is
oxydation, and it is only by oxydation that life is
continued for even the length of a minute. The
imperfections in the attainment of the purposes which
the appearances indicate have not the air of having
been designed. They are like the unintended results
of accidents insufficiently guarded against, or a little
excess or deficiency in the quantity of some of the
agencies by which the good purpose is carried on,
or else they are consequences of the wearing out of
a machinery not made to last for ever; they point
either to shortcomings in the workmanship as regards
its purpose, or to external forces not under the
control of the workman, but which forces bear no
mark of being wielded and aimed at by any other
and rival intelligence" (p. 185). What a difference between Mill the philosopher and Mill the
theologian !

The wild bird shut up in a cage batters its wings
against the wires in a vain attempt to escape, but
is not supposed to possess a will as distinct from a
wish, because intelligence does not direct its efforts.
The prisoner who, immured in a cell, labours to

remove a stone, is said to will as well as to wish to escape, because his understanding shows him how he can gratify his desire, and turns his energies into a definite course. The terms "wish" and "will" may therefore be employed as the point of view of the speaker determines. The prisoner wishes to escape, and therefore it is his will that the stone should be removed, or it is his will to escape, and he therefore wishes to remove the stone. When it is said that he will escape, his imagination is supposed to be concentrated on the general result, and the task of removing the stone is like the action of the bird ; when it is said that he will remove the stone, his attention is supposed to be concentrated on this operation, and his desire to escape is like the bird's. Will or volition is, accordingly, a name for wishes which are derived from intelligence, and as the intelligence of animals exists in every possible degree, a wish cannot be absolutely distinguished from volition, but passes into it imperceptibly. A given act is caused by the will or a wish in accordance with the idea of a co-operation of the understanding. The general wish of a prisoner to escape changes into a special wish to remove a stone, when his intelligence tells him that he can satisfy his general wish in this way, and it is then his will that the stone should be removed. Again his intelligence shows him that he can gratify this wish if he can obtain a knife or a nail, and this in turn becomes his will. His thoughts are directed to the means by which he can obtain them, and if he can think of a way, it is his " intention " to do so, *i.e.* the imagined act is constantly present to his mind, and forms a fresh set of special wishes. When the knife or nail is obtained, a new wish to find a crevice into which he may insert one of them becomes his will and causes a new set of actions. If the discussion is confined to that which can be observed the sequence is plain enough. Impulse is replaced by desires which can be traced to memory, intelligence, and imagination. The necessity of postulating a thing called " volition " has arisen, as Mr. H. Spencer has observed, from the prior fabrication of an entity called the *ego.* It is not surprising that a logical fiction attached to a logical fiction should have bred an interminable controversy. But whatever the metaphysical and theological truth may be, the *ego,* as a cause of motion, has no existence except when it includes the physical frame. Magicians claim for themselves an *ego* of a different kind, but claim at the same time a supernatural power. The will is, therefore, distinguishable from a wish only as species to genus, and this distinction is only relative. The efforts of the bird in a cage are, relatively to the

efforts of a prisoner in a cell, the results of wish and
impulse ; but are, perhaps, relatively to the actions of
some lower animals, the results of wish and intelligence.   The bird may have a faint knowledge that
it can sometimes overcome obstacles by flying against
them, and may imagine that it can break the wires.
Those who think this might say that its efforts are
caused by the will ; those who think otherwise would
deny the operation of volition.   But every definite
and positive idea is attended by an indefinite negative
contradictory.   It is impossible to think definitely of
a phenomenon or set of phenomena as caused by
volition without, at the same time, recognising in-
definitely other phenomena as not caused by volition.
A name is therefore required for unintentional as
well as for intentional phenomena.   As the phenomenon which attracts most attention, and is at the
same time most inexplicable, is the birth and evolution of organic substances, the word nature has
become in all languages the name of the non-
intentional.   The natural is either that which is not
caused by the Divine Will or that which is not
caused by the will of man.   One person, looking at
a phenomenon, and thinking of it in connexion
with its cause, may exclude it from the natural ; to
another it may be present in thought only as a fact
of consciousness which need not for the moment

be explained, and be classified with the natural. Philosophy, however, surveys all phenomena in turn and seeks to explain them, and the philosopher has four courses to choose from.   He may either, like Bacon, admit a *natura naturans* identifying it with God ; or he may, with Plato in the Laws, protest that it is impious to speak of nature as if it could be a cause ; or he may, with many philosophers both ancient and modern, abstract the idea of force or energy from the compound impression of intelligence, desire, and muscular power, and postulate this abstraction as the universal cause.   If he declines all these three courses he must say, as Professor Clifford says in his *Essay on the Physical Forces*, that a sound philosophy discards the question "why" and keeps to the question "what," for each day adds to the proof that ideas have, like tastes and sentiments, a natural origin, and are not derived from inspiration, and cannot be created.

The phenomena which attract attention, and for which, consequently, imagination demands a cause, are the unusual ones.   The changes of the seasons, the alternation of day and night, and the ordinary fluctuations of the weather, seem to most to be natural, or not caused by intention, because they are constant and familiar phenomena.   But a shower of falling stars, an eclipse, an earthquake, an unusual period of

drought or rain, startle the beholder or excite his
interest by the mischief which they cause, and they
are regarded as warnings or penalties.   Most or all
of those who hold such opinions would, if compelled
to examine their own creed, say, as Plato said, that
it is impious to treat any phenomena as caused by
nature, and that ordinary as well as extraordinary
phenomena are all part of the divine scheme.   But
practically the distinction is drawn, and those who
in theory deny nature and chance, do not scruple to
use such phrases as "it happened to be fine," or "it
is natural that all should die."   As the natural is
thus the constant or familiar, inasmuch as the constant or familiar is that which need not be explained,
the natural is further contrasted with the unnatural
as good with evil.   Both the theory of evolution, in
which it is supposed that a process of adaptation
goes on, and the theological theory that all things
are pre-ordained by a beneficent Providence, lead
up to the result that the constant is the good.   The
natural man is corrupt in the theological theory, only
because in that theory a temporary disturbance of
the divine scheme has been permitted.   But the
intentional acts of animals, or those which can be
traced to their intelligence and desires, pass at
both ends of the scale by a continuous transition
into natural acts, or acts which cannot be traced to

this origin.   At the one end such a feeling as the
craving for food becomes gradually a conscious desire
of food as a pleasure or necessity, and intelligence
joins hands with instinct in the means adopted to
gratify it ; at the other, the acts which are at first
intentional become automatic and form a second
nature when they have been often repeated.   Art is
therefore the mistress, not only of inanimate nature,
but of man's nature, or of those attributes which are
constantly present in man.   It is natural for the
savage to live in caves, but it is equally natural for
civilised man to live in houses, because repeated acts
form habits, and the attributes of civilised man are
the product of a natural or unintentional transmission
of habits.   But the fittest survive, and the second
nature must be an improvement on the first nature.
So soon, therefore, as art, or intention, begins to
qualify nature a conflict arises.   On the one hand, as
the fittest survive, the nature of man is ever adapting
itself to the conditions in which he is placed ; on the
other, the conditions are ever being changed, and
the fittest is never fit.   The fittest to survive when
society was ill-organised and war was the chief
interest is not the fittest now, and the fittest in the
backwoods of America is not the fittest in London.
The second nature being a temporary and changing
nature is not a true nature, and the Golden Age is

not all a dream. But it was a Golden Age of a
negative kind, such as the brutes enjoy, untroubled
by an artificial nature imperfectly adapted to the
artificial nature of surrounding conditions. The
true or original nature, however, cannot be entirely
destroyed, for it is deeply seated, and art has not
changed all the phenomena which formed it. In
the midst of the pursuits with which the second
nature is occupied there remain the instincts and
sentiments which were implanted, in the manner
described by Mr. H. Spencer, during remote periods
of time. The true or original nature reveals itself
in a desire to fly in imagination from the sordid
cares and petty troubles of artificial life, and to
live once more in a Golden Age untroubled by artificial interests. The Fine Arts gratify this instinct.
Modern society is natural and yet unnatural, good
and yet evil. Its customs, its passions, its opinions,
and etiquette, are inevitable, yet it is sweet to forget
them. The poet and the artist lend their aid.
They transport the reader or the auditor or spectator
to an unknown realm where the realities of the second
nature do not trouble him, and where The Beautiful,
as it is called, is supreme. The Beautiful, in this
wider sense, is only the name of a thousand feelings
so vague that they cannot be defined, and so faint
that one does not destroy another. These are called

into existence by a magic wand which the poet
and the artist hold, and the name of this wand is
genius.

In the *Esthétique* of M. Eugène Véron a definition of the Fine Arts is given which is practically a
denial of genius, and is for that reason an assertion
of the realistic theory, which he nominally rejects.
The peculiarity of the Fine Arts is, he says, that the
genius and skill of the author are admired in his
work.   This definition destroys the distinction
between skill and genius.   It has been repeatedly
said that Homer has genius and Virgil skill, and the
proof which is adduced is that the latter does not
permit the reader to forget him, while Homer, the
author, is forgotten when the reader takes up the
Iliad.   But it is impossible to think at the same
time of two different things, and to admire an
author when the author is forgotten.   The proof of
Homer's genius being that his poem monopolises
the attention, it cannot be true that Homer's genius
is admired when the poem is read.   Virgil's skill is
admired and Virgil is not forgotten.   M. E. Véron,
however, says that this holds good of all the Fine
Arts, and cites, by way of proof, the fact that a
representation of a disagreeable reality is sometimes
pleasing, observing that this is a proof that something has been added to the representation which

was not in the reality. This something, he says, must be the genius of the author or artist. His argument contains a fallacy. The superiority of the representation may be due to an omission as well as to an addition. A dish which is flavoured with garlic may be distasteful, though the same dish may please the taste when the garlic is omitted. It is more certain that in the art of painting, to which he refers, something has been omitted, than that anything has been added, for there can be no doubt that the third dimension has been left out. If, on the other hand, something has been added, whence can this something have come? Skill is the adaptation of means to an end, and comes from the author's intention; but if there is genius also in the work, and if genius differs from skill, it must have a different origin. Cousin's answer is that ideality is derived from the infinite, and that the Fine Arts form a bridge which connects the finite with the infinite. But he has also said that we are separated from the infinite by a chasm which cannot be traversed, and know nothing whatever of it. The word genius is in fact the name of a hypothetical cause of an effect which is felt, but for which there is no adequate explanation. It is like the word nature in etymology, and resembles it in meaning. Nature is the hypothetical cause of phenomena which are not explained ; genius is the hypothetical cause of artistic excellence which is inexplicable. The grace beyond the reach of art which is found in some poems, statues, pictures, buildings, and musical compositions, fascinates the listener or spectator, and banishes for the time the actualities of existence. Some name is required for this magical excellence, and it is called genius.   But it is an afterthought, and is not like skill present to consciousness at the time.   The reader who is walking by the side of Dante and Virgil, and contemplating the horrors of hell, cannot be admiring the genius of the author ; and the lover of music who has been carried by Beethoven to an unknown land where nothing but sound is real, cannot be thinking of Beethoven's powers.   It is, therefore, futile to tie down by a strict definition the meaning of the word.   An inexplicable excellence may be of various kinds. Automatic acts are more perfectly performed than intentional acts.   The hand cannot be lifted to ward off a blow with such quickness and precision as the eyelid is dropped to protect the eye, and the author or artist who selects his means automatically or naturally makes a better and surer choice than he who uses art.   Style is therefore a part of genius. The bird displays genius in the construction of its nest, and the cat when it catches its prey.   The

poet or the artist to whose assistance nature has
come, as it does to the bird or the cat, and who has
an instinctive facility, may be rightly described as a
genius.   But the skill of irrational animals, which is
frequently so perfect that it would be called genius,
if found in a like degree in man, is the accumulated
product of innumerable acts which have been continued through many generations.   The second
nature has been very perfectly formed, because
such intelligence as these creatures possess has
been concentrated on these operations.   In the
human race the individual can form his new nature
more completely than the brutes can, because his
intelligence is higher, and the sum which, in the one
case requires many ages, can be added up more
quickly in the other.   But the store of vital energy
is limited, and a derivation of it in one direction
implies a deficiency in others.   Men of genius are
noted for a neglect of much which others think
important, and for eccentricities which seem to be
allied to madness.   They are monomaniacs, and
"great wits to madness sure are near allied."
Others have drawn a very different inference, and
have said that genius is only a name for unusual
painstaking.   This explanation is, however, one
which has seemed satisfactory rather to those
mighty men whom posterity have agreed to praise

than to their disciples and admirers. The former
have been conscious of their own labour ; others
have perceived that intentional effort cannot lift all
to so high a level. There is, perhaps, in scientific
genius a process which has been called automatic thought or unconscious cerebration. A long
period of mental incubation has usually preceded all
great discoveries. Newton's life presents the most
famous example. Though discoverers like Newton
have observed nothing in themselves except unflag-
ging industry, nature may have lent a helping hand,
which they did not feel, and mechanical thought
may have joined with conscious thought to form an
intuition. Helvetius, however, in the *Discours de
l'Esprit*, gravely argued that genius and painstaking
are one, adding the doctrine that, as a love of fame
is the most potent of stimulants, genius is ultimately
excessive vanity. If this theory were true, a renaissance of the Golden Age might be expected,
and the millennium must be at hand. Warlike
pursuits no longer absorb the faculties, and the
deformed thief fashion patronises the arts and
sciences. Unfortunately for the future the logic of
facts refutes the theory, and it does not seem likely
that Raphael or Shakespeare will be cast into the
shade. Vanity is the most fatal of obstacles to that
concentration of interest whence springs the true

labour of genius. The advance of civilisation may
augment, but does not diminish, the distractions of
life, and Milton allows that ambition is an infirmity
of noble mind, though its last infirmity. The true
man of genius stands in the battlefield of life, as
Socrates stood at Potidæa, heedless of the tumult
which surrounds him, or, if he cannot stop his ears,
cries out with Milton for some high lonely tower
where he may no longer hear it. But high lonely
towers are odious to the vain man, and the deformed
thief ever knocks at the door and summons him to
come forth.

All great discoverers and all great artists have
displayed the bent of their genius in early youth,
and have either returned to their first love after a
brief infidelity, or have remained constant throughout life. Darwin's great law, to which his attention
was chiefly turned, and which his learning established, was that accidental variations occur from
time to time and that the fittest of these survive.
Ultra-Darwinians have turned this truth into nonsense by affirming that circumstances cannot form
character, which would prove, if it were established,
that all hope of reclaiming the criminal classes by
education is vain. Lewes has propounded this paradox in his *Life of Goethe*. He draws, indeed, a
distinction between the modification and the develop-

ment of character ; but it is an empty distinction, and
all the facts which he adduces refute his contention.
He fell into a similar error in his *History of Philosophy.* Erasmus Darwin in the *Zoonomia,* first
offered a philosophical explanation of the charms of
" the flowing line." He traced it to the feelings of
an infant at its mother's breast. There is, perhaps,
some truth in this, though, as I have already
observed, the secret is to be found rather in the
passions of adults. When Darwin's theory was
published, Sheridan made the following retort :—" I
suppose that the child brought up by hand would
feel all those emotions at the sight of a wooden
spoon." This was very well for Sheridan, who did
not call himself a *savant,* and who wrote when it
was not understood that tastes may be retained and
accumulated in successive generations. It was,
moreover, as against Darwin, a valid answer, for the
latter had divined a truth which could not then be
theoretically defended. But this smart answer is
now an anachronism, yet is quoted by Lewes as a
happy example of the way in which ridicule may
sometimes be a test of truth. (*History of Philosophy,*
vol. ii., p. 364.) Lewes leaves himself only one of
two alternatives ; either that tastes and characters
are self-created in the first instance, or that they
have a non-natural origin. The reasonable doctrine

is that they have all a natural origin, and that the tastes and characteristics of races and families are formed by the scarcely perceptible increments of individuals. Reason and observation unite to prove that tastes or preferences may be in part formed in early life by circumstances, and that the virgin cask will long retain the flavour which it first receives. They prove no less that hereditation is a factor, and that one kind of wood may be more thoroughly imbued than another. It is not always easy to decide how much must be attributed to the one, and how much to the other cause. In the various instances which Mr. Galton has collected of heredi- tary capacity and taste, it is impossible to avoid a suspicion that traditions of ancestral eminence may have given a turn to character in early life, and that the traits which reappear are not purely natural. Still the presumption is strong that families (in the narrower sense of the word) have peculiar character- istics as well as races, and that genius, whatever it may be, runs in them. The most striking case on record is where we might look to find it ; in the history of music. The musical genius of the Bach family is a unique phenomenon in the history of mankind. As it cannot be doubted that there was in this family an inherited taste and capacity for music, we may infer that if musical taste first arose

2 A

in the way which Darwin described, the disappear-
ance of the original source does not imply that
musical tastes will be extinguished as time progresses. As, moreover, J. Sebastian Bach, though
less popular than many other composers, has had
greater influence on style than any other, his genius
connects Mr. H. Spencer's theory of music with
Darwin's.   The tendency which culminates in
Wagner's music so to combine concord with discord
that the orchestra seems almost to utter the cry of
a passionate animal, was first pronounced in the
style of Sebastian Bach.   Expression of feeling
became the prominent quality, as the modern cause
of musical taste triumphed over the ancestral cause.
How far this tendency may extend, and whether or
not it has reached its utmost limits, I must leave to
more competent critics to decide ; but Wagner has
composed much which suffices to prove that music
can stand alone, and need not lean on poetry as a
crutch.   As there has been no change in the nature
of the causation in pictorial tastes, there is no reason
to suppose that style can advance in this art as in
music.   Nor is there any evidence that it has
advanced since the seventeenth century.   The judgment of the multitude is safer, broader, and juster,
than the verdict of either artists or connoisseurs
when it is once formed.   This is inevitable, for there

is no appeal from the test *ubique et omnibus.* The fallacy is to argue that the ignorant are the best judges in the first instance, on the ground that the majority are always ignorant. The true public opinion is that which remains when the momentary conflict is over and the fittest has survived. It is the opinion which has been cleared of the crotchets of the hour, and has become natural or constant. But this supreme arbiter which has decided that music advances, as all the sciences advance, and has refused to listen for ever to the antagonists of Handel and of Schumann and of Wagner, has not yet pronounced its verdict in the case of pictorial art. It was at one time almost convinced that a new epoch had arrived in landscape painting, and that Canaletto, who satisfied an earlier generation, is "a little and a bad painter." It now listens once more to the mute eloquence of works such as hang in our National Gallery, and suspects that this decision was hasty. The last word is not yet spoken, and public opinion hesitates between the views that pictures are painted for the spectator, as music is performed for the auditor, or that their proper function is to supply a theme for the critic. But as fashion is a cyclone and not a steady wind, its gales will pass away and artistic opinion will prevail. The realistic furor which carried all before it twenty or thirty years ago, when it was thought that pictures which seemed to be elaborated with the point of a pin were the most perfect samples of style, was succeeded by an opposite exaggeration which has been called impressionism. This also has been sometimes called realism, and perhaps rightly, for it was a reaction which naturally followed the earlier movement. Impressionist art is the artistic theory formulated and exaggerated, as the rules of the academy were formalised last century by the connoisseur. The artistic theory is that the painter copies confidently the image which is formed in his mind. The impressionist artist deduces from the fact that this image contains less than may be observed in nature, a rule that the most perfect work of art is that which contains fewest of the details which are observed. The true artist ignores rules, but submits first to academic practice which forms a second nature. It is pleasant for the *amateur* to think that he has capacities which need no training, and he listens willingly to the flattering clique which assures him that academic rules would only cramp his genius. But the theory that academies exist in order to inculcate rules is an invention of the connoisseur, and their true end is to form artistic facility, leaving taste to form itself. It forms itself as all other tastes do, and when the

artificial nature joins hands with the inherited nature
it rises to the rank of genius.   Nature enters at both
ends, and, though it is never true that "art is as
much nature as anything else," it is true that in the
Fine Arts the two are blended together.   The Fine
Arts owe their mysterious charms to this union.
They are the wedding of the formed and the
inherited nature.   Shakespeare has written many
lines which may be applied in various ways, and the
following are an apt description of the nature of
the Fine Arts :—

> "One touch of nature makes the whole world kin,
>   That all with one consent praise new-born gawds,
>   Though they are made and moulded of things past."

Works of art are new-born gawds, and gratify that
love of novelty which is part of the artificial nature
formed by the ever-changing conditions of civilised
life, though they are made and moulded of things
past.   But it would be a subversion of all known
principles if the artistic tastes were false.   The
nature of the Fine Arts is an artificial nature, and
the nature which works of art form must be most in
harmony with it.   If the artistic tastes are evil ; if
Alison was right when he affirmed that artists have
the strongest propensity and the greatest interest in
corrupting the arts, or Mr. Ruskin when he said

that a study of pictures engenders a depravity in
the human mind, what apology can be offered for a
Government which supports a national collection,
and spends money on buying pictures? The least
it could do would be to appoint an inspector, chosen
from "the many who have never handled the
pencil," to purge our galleries of the rubbish which
they contain. Such an inspector would easily
accomplish his task. Artists often hesitate, balanc-
ing one thing against another, and are so prejudiced
that they would probably find something to admire
in every picture which our National Gallery contains.
But the connoisseur is free from this foible. He
can discriminate at a glance between the utterly bad
and the entirely noble, and could summarily decide
which works ought to be consigned to the lumber-
room. The Salvator Rosas, the Poussins, the
Claude Lorrains, the Canaletti, and all which might
strike him as conventional, or unveracious, or
classical, or ignoble, swept away, he might turn
his attention to the Royal Academicians and inspect
their studios. A salutary rebuke administered in
time might deter them from an excessive attention
to the meaner beauty, and stem the torrent of corruption. But the truth should be told. It should
be allowed that the inspector was sent by the
connoisseur, and it should not be said that his

warrant was signed by Aristotle and Sir Joshua
Reynolds. Artistic casuistry is, like moral casuistry,
an attempt to frame a set of rules which may super-
sede instinct or feeling, and is, like it, worthless or
pernicious. The true relation of science to the art
of painting is that which it holds in the Lectures
of Professor Helmholtz, who treats the practice of
illustrious artists as a phenomenon to be explained,
but does not arrogate to himself the title of censor.
The science of taste has flourished hitherto, as some
insects are said to live, by imitating the forms of
better protected species. Looked at from a distance,
it seems to be a science, and as the sciences are
sacred, every one fears to attack it lest he should
commit sacrilege. But it has no right to the name
of science. It is a compound of dogmas, moral
principles, and scientific truths, which may be mixed
up together, but out of which no science can be
constructed. It has invaded the venerable home of
the Liberal Arts, but it remains to be seen whether
it will prove itself fit to survive.

THE END.

Printed by R. & R. CLARK, *Edinburgh.*

7
26
27

www.ingramcontent.com/pod-product-compliance
Lightning Source LLC
Chambersburg PA
CBHW030908270326
41929CB00008B/612